When God Speaks through Worship

Stories Congregations Live By

Craig A. Satterlee

THE
ALBAN
INSTITUTE

Herndon, Virginia
www.alban.org

The Alban Institute
2121 Cooperative Way, Suite 100
Herndon, VA 20171

Unless otherwise noted, all Scripture quotations are from the New Revised Standard Version of the Bible, © 1989, Division of Christian Education of the National Council of Churches of Christ in the United States of America, and are used by permission.

Cover design by Tobias Becker, Bird Box Design.

Library of Congress Cataloging-in-Publication Data

Satterlee, Craig Alan, 1959–
  When God speaks through worship : stories congregations live by / Craig A. Satterlee.
       p. cm.
  Includes bibliographical references (p.157).
  ISBN 978-1-56699-383-8
  1. Public worship. 2. Public worship—Lutheran Church—Case studies. I. Title.

  BV10.3.S27 2009
  264'.041—dc22
                                              2008049477

    09   10   11   12   13   VP   5   4   3   2   1

For the people of
St. Timothy's Lutheran Church
Sturgis, Michigan
(1961–2000)
Together, we learned to expect
God to speak through worship.

Contents

Foreword

The novelist Reynolds Price has said that for human beings, the "need to tell and hear stories is essential . . . second in necessity apparently after nourishment and before love and shelter."[1] This assessment of the profound significance of story flies in the face of common conceptions that stories are simply add-ons, or mere illustrations, or primarily for entertainment, or mostly for children. We often think that stories have a moral lesson and that if we get the lesson then we do not need the story. However, when we reflect on stories, even briefly, we realize that they are constitutive of what it means to be human. The sense that we are living in a connected narrative is the only way we make sense of anything. It is the way we tell about our day. It is the means by which we reflect on the past and plan for the future. It is the means by which we relate to others and to the world around us. It is, in fact, the definition of sanity.

Each of us conceives of our life as a story, and we are in the middle of it. We have our version of how we have gotten to where we are now and how we hope our life will turn out. Often we are several stories—the story of our career, the story of our loved ones, the story of our triumphs and tragedies. Sometimes these stories are in conflict with each other. Or our story is in conflict with those with whom we share our lives, and we have to negotiate our story so that it is a shared story. Often we have imagined our story one way, but it has not turned out that way and we have to reconfigure our story. Sometimes we get trapped inside our story. There is an entire field of narrative therapy designed to help us reframe our core stories and regain a sense of coherent meaning in life.

Further, stories are given to us by our parents and schools and churches and communities. We swim in cultural narratives like fish in the sea—the American stories, the stories of our ethnic groups, the expectations of our peers, the narratives of our heroes and models. All these shape our understanding of our lives, often without our being aware of it. Sometimes we resist these cultural stories and seek to write our own stories differently. We may shift our allegiances from one group to another and take on the narratives of the new community.

Most profoundly, we understand our purpose in the world in terms of story—what our life is all about and how we fit into our understanding of the world's story. We have a sense of where the world is going (or ought to be going)—whether it be in terms of the story of prosperity, or the story of peace and justice, or toward a developing care for creation. This is where our story connects with God's story. What is God's story for the world? What is God doing in the world? And in what ways does our story cohere with God's narrative. God's story is about how God created the world and about how the Son of God seeks to redeem creation and about how the Spirit sustains and guides the world. Sometimes our relationship with God's story grows with us from childhood. It matures as we mature. Sometimes we are converted to God's story and change our deepest sense of ourselves and our reasons for living.

Often, in relation to God, we plan our own story and then ask God to bless it. As Christians, however, we are called rather to seek what God is doing in the world and then ask how we can give ourselves to further that work of God. Orienting our story to God's story is often a fundamental reorientation that enables us to give ourselves to something much larger than ourselves, to a "universe story" being woven by our creator and redeemer.

Craig Satterlee speaks to this story in this provocative book. He is seeking to show how we can grasp what God is doing in the world by asking how God reveals God's story to us in and through worship. Craig's focus throughout is not on what we do in worship but on how God is acting in worship to redeem our lives—and how, through our lives, God's mission flows out into the world. And Craig does this in the most profound way—not by offering doctrinal statements or moral prescriptions but by telling stories.

These are personal stories about the ministry of Craig and the parishioners in various parishes he has served. On the surface they are ordinary stories about problems and obstacles to be addressed, differences among parishioners, and conflicts between pastor and parishioners. But they are much more. They are parables about the ways in which worship is the intersection where God's story and our stories come together. Whether it is a matter of lighting candles, holding services of healing, welcoming children, picking hymns, or celebrating vocation, the focus is not on what we are supposed to do in worship to somehow get it right, but on discovering what God is doing.

What a pleasure it is to read this book. I was moved by the wisdom displayed in the stories that led people to try old things and new things, to change their tunes, to be open to the unexpected, to learn through struggle and triumph. Sometimes people got instruction first and then tried something new. Mostly they just went ahead and tried the new things and then changed their stories as a result of their experiences. As I read these stories, I found myself alternatively laughing out loud with satisfaction, welling up with tears, or making an inward affirmation at the outcome of some episode.

People can change their stories. That's a theme here. And you, too, might change your story as you read this book and reflect on worship in new ways. It will certainly get your creative juices flowing, whether you are a worshiper or a worship planner. And you will come away with the conviction that the author most wishes to convey, namely that "God is transforming the world through worship."

DAVID RHOADS
Professor of New Testament, Lutheran School of Theology
at Chicago

Preface

I have come to deeply respect the power of telling stories. When I wrote *When God Speaks through You: How Faith Convictions Shape Preaching and Mission*, my second book in the Vital Worship, Healthy Congregations Series, the people I enlisted to review the manuscript found the vignettes from the preaching discussion group of the fictional St. Ambrose Church the most compelling part of what I wrote.[1] The stories that I intended to be an introductory device for each chapter became the driving force of the book. While writing *When God Speaks through Worship*, I team taught a course for senior seminarians on the transition from the seminary to the congregation. My teaching partners, a professor of leadership and a retired bishop, and I brought to the class more material than we could possibly cover in a semester. Yet, our students repeatedly told us that they appreciated the stories we told about pastoral ministry and found them more helpful than our providing information, giving direction, and offering advice. Instead of helping our students understand the ideas, theories, and concepts we were presenting, the stories we told assisted students in exploring, clarifying, understanding, and appreciating their experience. The stories we told stimulated conversation, kept things real and concrete, and often resulted in people telling more stories. Theories and concepts became tools for understanding the stories.

When God Speaks through Worship: Stories Congregations Live By is a collection of stories of congregational worship in which, upon reflection, God's ongoing presence, speech, and activity are apparent. On the one hand, they are small, unassuming stories of God's involvement in the weekly worship of congregations where I served as pastor. On the other hand, these are stories those congregations lived by, instances in which they experienced God giving them new life and gathering them to share God's work of bringing new life to the world. The themes of the stories in this book are things Christians do when they worship—preach and pray, baptize and bless, light candles and sing songs, share Holy Communion, commend loved ones to God and the communion of saints. Yet, the stories are not about Christians; they are about God speaking and acting in worship when Christians do these things. The thread that holds these stories together is the connection between God's saving activity in Scripture and God's saving activity in worship. Their purpose is to celebrate the good news that worship is God's work of saving and recreating the world, before it is an activity of the church or the Christian.

I am increasingly concerned that, today, much Christian worship is people centered or us centered rather than God centered or Christ centered. The church stresses what we do in and get out of worship over what God is doing in and through worship. Those who plan and lead worship may construct services that reflect their identities, values, and agendas. Worshipers tend to judge services according to how well they conform to their preferred style and taste or what they get out of the service. Those who teach and study worship, like me, sometimes get so trapped in their understanding of what God is *supposed* to do in worship that they miss what God is actually doing. I believe that when Christians and congregations enter into and reflect on worship, they do well to shift their focus from *their* preferences, *their* needs, and *their* mission to consider instead how *God* is present in worship speaking *God's* promise, bringing Christians and the church new life, and empowering them to share in *God's* work of bringing new life to the world. I find that stories of times when people experienced God speaking and acting in worship are the best tools for helping people look for God's presence, listen to God speaking, and apprehend God's activity in their worship. Stories help people name and claim those experiences for themselves. So I regularly tell such stories, including many in this book, when I speak in congregations and at conferences.

This book makes me uncomfortable for at least four reasons. First, I don't want this to be a book about me. This is a book about God. Yet, the stories in this book are told from my perspective; they are narratives that grow out of my reflection on and conversations about God's involvement in worship services that had a significant impact on worshiping communities of which I was a part. Inasmuch as I was frequently the pastor at these worship services, I play a significant role in the stories. Yet, I certainly do not want to shine a spotlight on myself and leave God in the shadows. Also, since I tell these stories from my perspective, the fact that I am legally blind finds its way into this book more than I anticipated and wanted. Many years ago, my friend Faustino "Tito" Cruz, academic dean and executive vice president of the Franciscan School of Theology in Berkeley, California, told me that he hoped that, in one of my books, I would both identify myself as someone who is legally blind and offer my perspective on Christianity as a person who lives with a disability, because he thought this perspective would be of value to the church. While this was not my aim when I wrote this book, it seems to have happened along the way.

My approach in writing this book is the same as when I lead worship; I try to be transparent. As Paul says: "For we do not proclaim ourselves; we proclaim Jesus Christ as Lord and ourselves as your slaves for Jesus's sake. For it is the God who said, 'Let light shine out of darkness,' who has shone in our hearts to give the light of the knowledge of the glory of God in the face of Jesus Christ. But we have this treasure in clay jars, so that it may be made clear that this extraordinary power belongs to God and does not come from us" (2 Cor. 4:5–7). As you read this book, I encourage you to attend to the treasure, and not the clay jar.

The second reason this book makes me uncomfortable is that I do not want to give the impression that celebrating God as the speaker and actor in worship means anything goes in worship. Worship is not a time to lay out some interesting things for God to play with, sit back, and watch to see what God will do. Like a river, which has a set course as it flows to the sea, worship has a certain movement and direction as God's love and life flow through the worshiping church into the world, carrying all creation into the reign of God. In worship, God uses patterns, words, actions, and songs handed down through the ages to express the church's unity and continuity with Christians of all times and places as the body of Christ serving the world. Some patterns, words, and actions are central and indispensable; others are not. For example, reading Scripture is essential to Christian worship; lighting candles is not. I do not want to give the impression that, since God can speak and act through any part of Christian worship, all parts are equally important.

Apart from God, the most important part of Christian worship is the congregation, the assembly, the people the Spirit gathers in Jesus's name. For, while God is the primary speaker and actor in worship, God does not act alone. God's people, then, are more important than both those who lead the service and what is written in worship books and projected on screens. Moreover, the world is more important than the congregation. God's people are not an end in themselves in worship; God has something more in mind. As God said to Abraham, "I will make of you a great nation, and I will bless you, and make your name great, so that you will be a blessing. . . . And in you all the families of the earth shall be blessed" (Gen. 12:2–3). Since God wants to reconcile and recreate the world, God blesses the church in worship for the sake of the world.

The third reason for my discomfort is that Christians and congregations worship, as well as understand and practice their faith, out of specific theological traditions. Even nondenominational churches have acceptable and established ways of reading Scripture, for example. I do not want the theological frame and presuppositions that I bring to this subject to prevent readers from exploring, experiencing, and reflecting on worship as God speaking and acting. I am a Lutheran Christian, pastor, and teacher. The Lutheran theological tradition frames how I experience, understand, and reflect upon worship. I have been very aware of my Lutheran "bias" as I have written this book. So that you can be equally aware, I will briefly describe my Lutheran theological frame or bias.[2] I understand Lutheranism as a way of being Christian and participating in the life of the church. For Lutheran Christians, the Christian church is first and foremost a worshiping community. It is "the assembly of all believers among whom the Gospel is preached in its purity and the holy sacraments are administered according to the Gospel."[3] For Lutheran Christians, the gospel is the good news that all people—all creation—are saved by the grace of God alone, not by anything we do. We only need to trust that God forgives our sins for the sake of Christ, who died to redeem us. God gives even this trust as an outgrowth of the relationship with God that God has established through baptism. Lutheran Christians identify two sacraments as God-given means for penetrating the lives of people with grace—baptism and the Lord's Supper. Although they are not the only means of God's self-revelation, baptism and communion are visible acts of God's love. In baptism, God freely offers God's grace and lovingly establishes a new community. In baptism people become members of the church. That baptism is God's gift is most obvious when infants are baptized, since infants cannot do anything except receive God's grace. In the Lord's Supper, those who come to the table receive in bread and wine the body and blood of their Lord. This gift is itself the real presence of Jesus Christ, who gives God's forgiveness and mercy, nourishes believers in union with Christ and with each other, and empowers the church to serve the world. The church exists solely to proclaim the living Word of Christ, administer the sacraments, and give itself away to the world in deeds of service and love. Lutheran Christians consider the Bible to be the only true standard by which teachings and doctrines are judged.

Lutheran Christians believe that the church includes all who have received Christ as the Son of God and Savior of the world in baptism. The church is the fellowship of those who have been restored to God by Christ. Lutheran Christians, therefore, understand themselves as belonging to a community of faith that began with the gift of the Holy Spirit on Pentecost, continues through the ages, and includes a fellowship of churches beyond Lutheranism. Many Lutheran Christians still consider themselves as a reforming movement within the church catholic (universal), rather than a separate denomination. These are among the theological assumptions that shape how I both tell and reflect upon the stories in this book. I invite you to identify and use your own theological frame as you read these stories and reflect upon what God is speaking and doing in worship.

The fourth reason I am somewhat uncomfortable is that the stories in this book are about Christians and congregations that I served as pastor and that I continue to honor and love. I do not want to say anything that will embarrass or hurt them. In these pages, I share times when the light of Christ shone through them and times when they revealed their very human selves. In writing this book, I sought always to lift up their faithfulness, commitment to the church, openness to the Spirit, and willingness to serve. I do not include anything that was not public information. I changed many names to protect identities. I encouraged those who reviewed drafts of this book to tell me if I was being insensitive or hurtful. I trust that those who find themselves in these pages will also find my genuine respect and affection.

So why did I write a book that makes me feel so uncomfortable? I am convinced that it will spark a graceful and joyous conversation about times when God speaks through *your* worship. Over the years, I have found the best part of telling the stories in this book is that people tell me their own stories about God speaking through and acting in worship, reconciling the world to Godself, and bringing new life. I pray that the stories in this book inspire you to enter worship expecting God to be present and active, to attend to what God is saying and doing, to share your experience with others, and to participate in God's saving work in worship and as the river of God's love and life carries you from worship into the world.

Acknowledgments

This book was inspired at a meeting of the North American Academy of Liturgy. Well, not exactly. This book was inspired by one of those later-in-the-evening conversations among old friends, which are often the best part of academic meetings. After spending a satisfying day discussing worship as an academic discipline, my friends Kent Burreson, who teaches liturgical and systematic theology at Concordia Seminary in St. Louis; Paul Galbreath, professor of preaching and worship at Union Theological Seminary in Richmond, Virginia; and I were talking about worship in congregations, particularly the ones where we had served as pastors. I began telling stories about St. Timothy's Lutheran Church, the tiny congregation where I served as interim pastor for the five years I was in graduate school. After I told a few stories, Kent interrupted, "You really need to write these down," he said. Paul agreed. "They make clear that God is the actor in worship, that worship is about God and not about us." "Do you think anyone would read a book of stories about worship?" I wondered aloud. "If the stories are about God *speaking through worship*," my friends responded, making a playful jab at the two books I had written for the Alban Institute, people will read it. I am most grateful that Kent and Paul encouraged me to write this book and that the Alban Institute, in partnership with the Calvin Institute of Christian Worship, agrees with them that it is a worthwhile project.

Writing for the Alban Institute has become a communal enterprise. A book project is an opportunity to get the gang together. While I once thought of writing as sitting alone at the computer in my study, I now regard writing as conversing. Each member of the team reads drafts of chapters in turn and talks with me about them. My writing conversation begins with me, as I clarify what I think. When I am satisfied with a chapter, I converse with my student assistant; for this book, the conversation started with Jordan Miller and finished with Emily Carson. Both wise and intelligent younger women helped me to consider worship from vantage points other than my own and handled administrative tasks so that I was free to write. Chapters then go to Gretchen Freese, my pastoral colleague, former student, and dear friend; Gretchen brings expertise in systematic theology and years of experience of leading worship with me. Gretchen encouraged me to think of this book as a collection of parables rather than systematic theology and reminded me that this is what Jesus did. Next, with just a few words, Beth Gaede, Alban's editor and my friend, manages to cheer and question so that the book becomes more than it was. Finally, Andrea Lee, who copyedited this book, served, in essence, as the first reader of the finished work and offered that perspective. As the conversation unfolds, what I have written is questioned, corrected, clarified, challenged, improved, and, I am humbled to say, genuinely celebrated. The conversation and the process work because they are based on trust and affection. In a sense, the cast of characters keeps me writing. I thank them for their partnership.

The other two people who keep me writing are my wife, Cathy, and daughter, Chelsey. While some authors thank their families for tolerating the hours they spend away writing, my family sends me to my study when I spend too much time attending to them. They recognize that writing brings me joy and celebrate that joy with me. Cathy and Chelsey regularly help in quiet ways when I lead worship; they were part of many of the worship services that I tell you about in this book. Their memories inform how I tell the stories in this book, and I thank them for sharing those experiences with me.

My original conversation partners for this book are the congregations where I served as pastor and regularly led worship. I served as pastoral intern at Trinity Lutheran Church in Midland, Michigan, assistant pastor of Bethlehem Lutheran Church in Fairport, New York, and pastor of Holy Nativity Lutheran Church in Endicott, New York. I currently serve as consulting pastor of St. Andrew Lutheran Church, Glenwood, Illinois. I am also privileged to serve as dean of Augustana Chapel at the Lutheran School of Theology at Chicago, where I teach, and to work with students and colleagues who expect God to speak and act in worship in powerful ways. I gratefully thank these communities for inviting me to preach and lead worship and to consider with them what God is saying and doing through worship. Yet, with nothing else to hang on to, the people of St. Timothy's Lutheran Church, Sturgis, Michigan, and I learned that, when God speaks through worship, a congregation has stories to live by; that is, ways of participating in the life of Christ. I dedicate this book to those saints.

Introduction

Disappointing Advice

My mandate was clear when they called me to be their pastor: "Help our church to grow." Looking back, I was very naive. It honestly never occurred to me that the members of a congregation would, on the one hand, say they want to grow, and, on the other, resist the changes that would facilitate growth, such as welcoming people different from themselves and involving newer members in leadership. Yet, that is what that congregation—let's call it Epiphany Lutheran Church—did. In fact, many of the members of Epiphany Church seemed to do whatever they could to preserve the congregation's self-identity as a "small church" and the ways they related to each other and made decisions as "a close-knit family." I failed to recognize these behaviors as the natural—even expected—ways people protect their world of meaning and respond to change and the losses change brings. Instead, I told myself, "These are good people. They want their church to grow. If they understand the things we are trying to do and the reasons we are doing them, they will be supportive. I just need to do a better job of explaining." So, I taught and explained, and we changed some things to attract and integrate new members. For a couple years we experienced modest but steady growth. A few more people came to church on Sunday, and newer members became involved in activities beyond worship.

Then the congregation started to decline, numerically and in terms of participation. The major employer in town transferred a good number of our newer members out of town. Others found their way to a neighboring congregation, where "contemporary worship" had caught their fancy.[1] I was left with the core of long-time members. Many resisted, even resented, the changes we had made to attract new members; some understandably felt ignored, displaced, and disrespected by their pastor and chose to stay away. The decline in church attendance brought a corresponding decline in giving. In response, the leaders of the congregation gave up on outreach and growth and seemed to circle the wagons and settle into a survival mode. Spending on programs all but stopped. Efforts to attract new members were replaced by efforts to get old members back, as the church council decided to contact people on our inactive rolls and ask, "What about Pastor keeps you from coming to church?"

I failed at what I was called to do, "help our church to grow." My denomination had taught me well that faithful, successful pastors grow churches. I learned from seminary professors and denominational higher-ups that pastors are to be *missionaries*, who bring people to faith, and *evangelists*, who grow the church; pastors are not to be *chaplains* who care for church members. Now this congregation was declining. Worse, priorities we set and changes we made angered some members of the congregation, and they were angry with me! I was not doing well as either a missionary or a chaplain. Not knowing what to do, I contacted my bishop. My bishop was an *evangelist*, committed to the church's mission. He would know what I should do next.

The advice my bishop gave me was, in a word, disappointing. In a long letter, he wrote, "Preach the gospel, administer the sacraments, teach the faith, visit the sick, bury the dead, and leave the growth to God." I felt a bit like the man who, running up to Jesus and kneeling before him, asked, "Good Teacher, what must I do to inherit eternal life?" (Mark 10:17). "Preach the gospel, administer the sacraments, teach the faith, visit the sick, bury the dead?" I found myself thinking. "I have done all these since my ordination." And as he did for the man in that Bible story, Jesus, looking at me, loved me, and said, "You lack one thing." No, Jesus was not asking me to go, sell what I own, and give the money to the poor. But Jesus was saying, "Come, follow me" (Mark 10:21). Through my bishop's letter, Jesus was asking me to give away all I thought I knew about successful pastors and growing churches and to trust God to work through the things the church does in worship—preach and teach, baptize and break bread, visit and bless—rather than trust myself, my strategies, and my ability to explain them to my congregation.

Worship Is Mission

I always trusted God to work through the things Christians do when we worship—proclaim the gospel, teach the faith, pray, sing, baptize, bless, share bread and wine in Jesus's name—to bring grace to individuals and to empower them to live as God's people. I also knew that for Christians and congregations to live as God's people and be Christ's body in the world, they need a vision for their mission and a plan for implementing it, as well as participation, commitment, and even a willingness to sacrifice. I understood that, in worship, God inspires and empowers a congregation to do the things it needs to do. But I believed that a congregation certainly has to do something more than worship. A congregation needs to worship God and respond to God in mission. Looking back, I saw worship and mission as related but distinct activities. I had bought into the alleged dichotomy, even competition, between worship and mission, which leads pastors to think they must choose between being a chaplain and a missionary and which in so many congregations fuels a "worship war." In this tug-of-war, congregations and pastors seem to emphasize and even choose either worship or mission. The greater church often discounts congregations that choose or emphasize worship as inward looking *clubs* and their pastors as *chaplains* who only care for members. Congregations that approach worship as the prelude to or a means to carry out the real work of making disciples are praised as *mission outposts* and their pastors hailed as *evangelists* who grow churches. I am now convinced that distinguishing between mission outposts and clubs, evangelists and chaplains, and mission and worship is harmful to leaders, congregations, and the church.

In my second book for the Vital Worship, Healthy Congregations Series, *When God Speaks through You: How Faith Convictions Shape Preaching and Mission*, I describe three ways of understanding the relationship between worship and mission, which I call *mountain, plain,* and *river*.[2] I used to operate out of an understanding of worship as a *mountain*. In worship, we encounter God, receive God's grace, and are spiritually empowered to proclaim the gospel to those who have not heard or received it and to serve the neighbor in acts of justice and love. Worship empowers mission. I learned a different perspective on worship and mission as I watched colleagues endeavor to transform worship from a mountaintop experience for the faithful into a *plain*, into level ground where the church introduces Jesus to the unchurched. Worship is a means of or an occasion for mission. Yet, in both these approaches, worship and mission are distinct; the members of the congregation have to do something in addition to worship for mission to occur, whether go out from worship to proclaim the gospel and love the neighbor or gather the unchurched and bring them into the church building, where the congregation introduces them to Jesus.

I no longer subscribe to the distinction between worship and mission, nor do I think of myself as either a chaplain or an evangelist. Over the years, I have come to understand Christian worship as a *river*, rather than either a mountain or a plain. As my friend Lester Ruth and I wrote in our book *Creative Preaching on the Sacraments*, like a mighty river, "the life and history of Israel, the saving work of Jesus, and the mission of the early church as these events are proclaimed in Scripture [are] connected to one another and to the church's worship . . . as the single, continuing story of God's saving activity in Jesus Christ."[3]

Some people find it more helpful to think of God's single, continuing, saving activity as a *stone dropped in a pond*, rather than a mighty river. If we think of history as a pond, rather than a line that moves from beginning to end, the stone that God drops is the event of Christ's life, death, and resurrection. Like a stone dropped in a pond, Christ sends ripple effects both forward and backward in time. The backward ripple effects are recorded in the Old Testament. This view of history is evident in 1 Corinthians 10:1–4, for example, where Paul calls Israel passing through the sea "baptism" and declares that the rock from which they drank was Christ. The forward ripple effects are the church's worship, where Christ continues to reconcile and save.

Whether we think of this perspective as a *river* or a *stone dropped in a pond*, Christian worship is God's initiative and activity in human history and the world, as well as in our individual lives, before it is an activity of Christians or the church. Worship is a place where God's liberating grace is already present and active in words and actions. God speaks and acts in and through the ritual of Christian worship to save, reconcile, and recreate humanity and all creation. The judgment and mercy of God, proclaimed and enacted in worship, signify God's ultimate judgment and mercy for the world. Orthodox theologian Alexander Schmemann argues that the liturgy of the Eucharist is the church's journey or procession into the presence of Christ and the dimension of the reign of God where we "arrive at a vantage point from which we can see more deeply into the reality of the world."[4] Like a river flowing to the sea, God's work of reconciliation, recorded in Scripture and accomplished in Christ, continues in the church's worship and through worship overflows into the world.

Rather than being the means or the motivation by which the *church* carries out its mission, worship is the location where *God* carries out God's mission. Worship is the way God gathers people to witness to and participate in God's work of reconciling the world to God's own self. In and through worship, individuals and the community encounter, experience, and celebrate the God who is the source and goal of the rest of their lives. The church proclaims God's reconciliation and shares in God's mission by living in the world in ways congruent with what it experiences God doing and enacting in worship. In this way, God's people worshiping in the midst of the world enact and signify God's own mission for the life of the world. Rather than being distinct yet related activities the church engages in, worship and mission are God's single activity of reconciliation. God is the first and primary actor. While Christians and congregations can participate in, be indifferent to, resist, and even undermine God's saving activity in worship, they can neither achieve nor stop it. Like a mighty river, God's work of salvation, accomplished in Christ and continued and enacted in worship, will not be stopped until it reaches its destination, the fullness of the reign of God.

Although theologians gave me language with which to describe this relationship of worship and mission, I did not come to understand worship and mission as God's single activity of reconciling the world to God's own self from either attending idyllic worship services or reading profound theological books. I experienced worship as the river of God's mission in the *Sunday services* of the congregations where I served as pastor, especially after I received my bishop's disappointing advice. Immediately after I received my bishop's letter, preaching the gospel, administering the sacraments, teaching the faith, visiting the sick, burying the dead, and leaving growth and outreach to God seemed to me like giving up on mission and becoming a *chaplain*—the pastor serving the congregation rather than the congregation serving the world. I had this nagging feeling that I should be doing something more. I was wrong. Thankfully, not knowing what more to do and with nothing to lose, I took my bishop's advice, first at Epiphany Church, then in another congregation. I have been following my bishop's disappointing advice ever since in congregations where I serve as an interim, sabbatical, or consulting pastor. I do not approach worship as either an end in itself or a means to an end, but as the saving activity of God to which everything else a congregation does points and from which everything else a congregation does flows.

I did not come to the realization that worship is God's way of reconciling the world to God's own self on my own. People helped me along the way, particularly my parishioners. They seemed to know instinctively that worship is "primary theology," an experience of God rather than the church's reflection on its experience of God.[5] When Epiphany Church started to decline and before I wrote my bishop, I redoubled my efforts to grow the church. I attended an evangelism conference, where we were taught that pastors need to get out of their congregations, which are full of people who go to church, and be visibly active in the community to meet the unchurched. Among other things, we were counseled to spend considerable time each week getting to know the regular patrons in a restaurant or coffee shop near the church. We could learn their concerns and needs and ways the congregation might minister to them. Then, when the opportunity presented itself, we could invite them to church. So I spent time sitting at the counter of the restaurant across the street, sipping coffee, talking with the regulars, and waiting for the moment when the Spirit would nudge me to invite them to church.

After a few weeks of this, some key members of the congregation made their way into my office. "We're here to find out what's wrong," they said. "Your preaching is off. The whole service seems off." I told them I was being an evangelist and explained how I was getting to know the unchurched. The room exploded in conversation. After listening a good while, a soft-spoken man named Ernie raised his hand. The room got quiet. "Pastor," he said, "I understand the importance of evangelism, and I really admire you for taking it so seriously. I also appreciate how hard you're working. How about this? I'll go across the street and drink coffee. I know a lot of the people there, and I promise I'll invite them to church. We need you here studying Scripture, writing your sermon, and planning worship, because that's where we come into God's presence."

The people in another congregation were even clearer about how I should and should not spend my time. While I was in graduate school, I was called to be the part-time pastor of a very small congregation—St. Timothy's Lutheran Church. The congregation had been without a pastor for a long time; when it came to their church, the people were very self-sufficient. At our first meeting together, the members of the church council laid out their expectations of their new pastor. "We only get you for a few hours a week," they said. "You need to do the pastor stuff and stay out of the other stuff." By "pastor stuff," they meant preaching, leading worship, visiting the sick and homebound, providing spiritual care, attending to the dying, teaching the faith, and not much more. They understood the "other stuff" as everything else, which was their responsibility. I quickly learned that the people of St. Tim's took their responsibility to do the "other stuff" very seriously and that the best thing I could do was to stay out of the way and do the "pastor stuff" really well.

The correspondence between the expectations these two congregations had of me as their pastor and the advice I received from my bishop is not lost on me. These congregations were not looking for a chaplain who would only take care of them. They were not inward looking. They experienced God acting powerfully in worship and knew that attempting anything apart from or at the expense of worship was fruitless, futile, foolish, and perhaps even unfaithful. These congregations did not want either a chaplain or an evangelist. They wanted a pastor who takes God's presence and activity in worship seriously and trusts that, when God is present and active in worship, something missional will happen, because that is who God is. When these congregations perceived that I was not treating worship as the place where we encounter God, they let me know.

In an era in which congregations routinely expect pastors to be personnel officers, plant managers, financial analysts, and community organizers, I am often asked how I managed to be blessed with such wise parishioners. I suspect it has something to do with the fact that I am legally blind. Congregations that choose me as their pastor have to be unusually open to God doing something new and uncommon in their midst. I wear thick glasses, walk with a white cane, cannot easily recognize people's faces, and do not drive; I am vulnerable and dependent in many ways. The people I serve cannot pretend their pastor is perfect and can do everything; neither can I. The congregations I served never imagined their pastor would be someone who also manages a disability; yet, when asked to consider this, they saw opportunities where other congregations only saw problems. They were excited by the possibilities even before they had answers to their practical and legitimate questions. Although they did not know all the ways their notions of church and ministry—their own as well as their pastor's—would change, they were aware that their understanding of church and ministry would change, because conventional ways of doing ministry simply were not going to work. Many people in these congregations told me they felt the Spirit doing something new and different as we worshiped together as part of the interview process, and they wanted to be part of whatever God was doing.

It's Not All about Us?

When my editor and friend, Beth Gaede, read the first draft of this book, where I describe worship as God's initiative and activity in human history and the world, as well as in individual lives, before it is an activity of Christians or the church, she responded excitedly, "What an interesting notion!" Like many others, including distinguished Danish theologian Søren Kierkegaard, Beth thought that in worship the members of the congregation are the actors and God is the audience. Even theologically aware worshipers find it novel to think of worship as *God's* activity. In fact today, much Christian worship is people centered rather than Christ centered or God centered. What *we* do in and what *we* get out of worship is stressed over what God is doing in and through worship. We make everything about us. Congregations shape worship according to preference, taste, marketing, liturgical correctness, ideology, or agenda. The goal is worship that reflects the congregation (or individuals or groups within the congregation), the culture, or a predetermined purpose. I believe the church regularly emphasizes people rather than God in worship for several reasons.

First, understanding, analyzing, and explaining worship as something Christians do, rather than as God's activity or mission, is the natural consequence of our individualistic, consumer-oriented culture and, in some instances, church. In both obvious and subtle ways, we are so "me centered" in every other area of our life that it never occurs to us that our perspective and participation may not be the primary lenses through which to consider Christian worship and mission. To suggest that people are not primary, that everyone who gathers for worship is subordinate to the congregation, and that the congregation is subordinate to God is a countercultural, even offensive declaration. It is also a prophetic word we need to hear.

Second, our emphasis on people rather than God is also a reaction to the state of much Christian worship. Every Christian can name worship experiences that fall short of the marvelous claim that God acts in worship to reconcile the world to God's own self and bring new life. We can even name worship patterns and practices that diminish or contradict the gospel. We can all point to ways that an unchanging, supposedly divinely inspired order of worship perpetuates oppressive systems opposed to God's work of reconciliation, including patriarchy, cultural insensitivity, and numerous forms of exclusion. When these things happen in worship, people frequently talk about how the service contradicted the gospel, rather than what God might be doing in—and perhaps in spite of—the service. Conversation shifts to how to change worship and make it better. People forget that all worship except that before the throne of God is imperfect and that God reveals the treasure that is Christ in the clay jars of congregational worship, "so that it may be made clear that this extraordinary power belongs to God and does not come from us" (2 Cor. 4:7). Conversation about God being the primary actor in worship is lost.

Third, in our results-oriented culture and church, permitting God to make the first move in worship makes us nervous, because God may produce something other than what we desire. I am frequently asked whether I have, in fact, "grown a church." The inquirer, usually a pastor, wants to know whether I have produced significant, sustained numerical growth in a congregation or whether I have created a megachurch. I have not, though I am sure I could. When asked for a surefire, quick-fix approach to growing congregations, the program I frequently propose costs $5,200 a year and is guaranteed to produce numerical growth. The church treasurer goes to the bank and gets fifty-two one-hundred-dollar bills; each week, sometime during the sermon, the preacher simply hands one to someone in the congregation. The church will grow numerically. The question, of course, is: What are the hidden costs?

Understanding God as the primary actor in worship led me to reexamine what the phrase "growing churches," which a friend likes to remind me is not found in the Bible, really means. Often, the phrase "growing churches" is used as shorthand for numerical growth. An evangelism consultant once told me that growing churches "decide how they want to grow numerically" and "do whatever it takes to grow." If congregations must do whatever it takes to gain more members, I am not convinced that God intends every congregation to grow numerically. While God intends all congregations to grow in faith, discipleship, and sharing the life of Christ, the growth God intends for some congregations has nothing to do with numbers. As I work with congregations, I find myself both prayerfully pondering and asking others what God is doing in worship and the ways God invites us to participate in it.

God grows some congregations by inviting them to welcome the service and ministry of people whose contributions are not valued anywhere else. St. Timothy's Church, for example, could not do what it would have taken to grow numerically when leaders were advised that growing numerically meant firing the woman who had served God as the church musician for decades so that the congregation could hire someone more professional or more talented whose music would attract more members. Congregations like St. Timothy's might even resist numerical growth if members perceive that more people in worship will cause people to feel anonymous. Other congregations might discern that God has invited them to grow by taking a stand in the public square, fully aware that the stand they take will inhibit numerical growth. For example, in worship, members of a congregation might experience an equality as brothers and sisters in Christ, which leads them to fight for those who are not treated equally in society; the congregation's advocacy may lead people who benefit from social inequality to find a different church. Still other congregations may determine that, rather than growing numerically by benefiting from the struggles of neighboring congregations, God is calling them to grow by partnering with and supporting those struggling congregations. A large congregation cannot include prayers for the well-being of a small, struggling congregation in worship and then achieve numerical growth by "sheep stealing" that congregation's members. In fact, prayer may lead some members of the large congregation to join that neighboring church in order to help it.

In these and many other instances, the growth God intends for a congregation is something other than numerical. Congregations ought not do whatever it takes to grow numerically when what it takes is contrary to what God says and does in worship. Some congregations even *choose* not to grow beyond the number their church can accommodate in a single Sunday worship service. As they see it, the congregation must be together to hear God speak and experience what God is doing in worship; people hearing God speak and experiencing God's activity together at a second worship service are, in effect, a second congregation. While God wants every congregation to grow, to enter more fully into God's purpose, the growth God intends may not be numerical.

When God Speaks in Worship . . .

Yet, as I pastor churches, consult in congregations, and speak with groups of clergy and congregants at conferences, it regularly occurs to me that the primary reason for our people-centered perspective on worship is much simpler than complicity with the culture, worship that undermines God's activity, or the desire for numerical growth. The main cause of our people-centered worship is that we don't know how to talk about what God is saying and doing in worship. While we can describe our involvement and experience in worship personally and concretely, our talk of God's message, activity, and involvement in worship often becomes theoretical and academic. Even those excited to think that God is the primary actor in worship and that worship is God's mission ask how we know and name what God is saying and doing in worship. In response to the models of the relationship of worship and mission, which I discussed earlier in this introduction, a pastor once remarked, "I have been to the mountain; those experiences don't last. I worked hard on the plain and came away empty and exhausted. I want to get wet in the river. How do I get in, and how do I know when I'm there?"

Stated simply, we get into the river by worshiping. Though the extent and intensity of God's transformation of our lives, our congregations, and the world may remind us of a lazy river rather than a rapid stream, God works in worship over time to shape and move us, as surely as flowing water smooths stones and carries them to the sea. Even when the current of God's reconciling love does not knock us over and sweep us away, we can worship with the expectation that God is present, speaking, and acting. Expecting God to speak and act in worship makes us actively engaged worshipers and worship leaders. In addition to remaining attentive, even anticipant, during the service, we prepare ourselves for the service, whether we are worshipers or worship leaders. We might read Scripture and pray during the week. We might center ourselves and become aware of both Christ's presence and the presence of the community as we enter the worship space. We might risk worshiping, whether we are sitting in a pew or leading part of the service, with heart and body as well as with mind and voice.

Expecting God to speak and act in worship changes our attitudes as well as our actions. We listen for God to speak as Scripture is read; we pray and attend to prayer in a manner mindful that we are speaking to God; we preach and listen to sermons trusting that God will speak to us; we sing because God and the world hear; and we come to the table in the awareness that the Lord is the host and the table is God's before it is ours. In all these ways, we remain open to what God is doing in worship, and we strive to be alert because God often works slowly and subtly and seems to sneak up on us, both individually and as a congregation.

We also discover what God is saying and doing in worship by reflecting on our experience of worship with other members of the worshiping community. The issue is not what individuals like and do not like or how worship makes people feel, but what God is saying and doing in and through the congregation's worship. My friend Mary Catherine Hilkert, who teaches theology at the University of Notre Dame, describes the task as "naming grace found in the depths of human experience."[6] As witnesses to Christ, we describe the salvation that has happened in our midst and only then speak of the power of God at work in the world. We know ourselves to be saved by God before we dare to speak to the world on God's behalf. Of course, naming grace inevitably leads to God's invitation to repentance and conversion, and God's promise of power to accept that invitation.

We have a general idea of what God says and does in worship. God saves, reconciles, recreates, gives new life, and gathers people to participate in God's work of reconciliation. The challenge is to get more specific about what God is up to, so that we can concretely name, witness to, and participate in it. Individuals rarely discover God's particular activity on their own or by only talking with people who share their perspective. Paul's reminder that we are the body of Christ and individually members of it and his admonition to pursue love and speak to build up the church are helpful principles for Christians exploring together what God is doing in worship (1 Cor. 12:27; 14:1, 4). Paul also provides helpful guidance for the manner of conversations about worship. This is not the occasion for "lofty words or wisdom." We speak of God's activity in worship "in weakness and in fear and in much trembling" (1 Cor. 2:1–3). In other words, we name what God is saying and doing in worship humbly, reverently, and tentatively.

Just as no Christian can name what God is saying and doing in worship apart from the worshiping community, so no congregation can identify what God is saying and doing in its midst without being in dialogue with the whole church. Our conversations about God's speech and activity in worship include the experiences of both Jewish and Christian ancestors in the faith, in particular the story of Jesus, as these are recorded in Scripture. As part of their conversation about worship, congregations also look to church history and the global church so that they can give voice to the unique ways the church tells Jesus's story, worships, and lives the faith from generation to generation, culture to culture, and place to place. In so doing, the worship life and faith tradition of the church furnish congregations with both a framework for considering their experience of God in worship and language with which to describe it. Hilkert calls this framework "an echo of the gospel."[7] For Hilkert, this gospel echo is the good news that humanity is united with God in Jesus, who invites us to "come and see" and to "go and do likewise," to make Jesus's story our story, and in so doing to experience worship and—from worship—experience all life as graced.

Stories Congregations Live By

I find the best way to help people to understand, enter into, and reflect upon worship as God's mission is through stories of congregational worship in which, upon reflection, God's ongoing presence, speech, and activity are apparent. These are the stories congregations live by, narratives of God coming, speaking God's promise, bringing people new life, and empowering them to live and share that new life in the world. Stories keep conversations about worship real and concrete. Stories also frame the mystery of God's involvement in worship in ways we can understand. Human beings think, dream, and imagine in stories; our hopes and fears reside in stories. We conceive of ourselves and make decisions in stories. We also come to know God in and through stories. Before it is anything else, the Bible is a collection of stories. In Scripture, God reveals Godself in the concrete, historical stories of Israel, Jesus, and the early church.

Telling stories is also increasingly recognized as an effective form of leadership.[8] Stories inspire and motivate in ways no other forms of communication can. Stories get people's attention, create a desire for a different reality or future, and enable people to see possibilities they may have missed. Stories possess great power to effect deep change in people and move them beyond themselves. The best stories are small and unassuming, because they spark a new story in the mind of the listener. This new story, which listeners create for themselves, connects with them emotionally and leads them to act. In fact, this new story becomes a story they live by.

More than anything else, this book—*When God Speaks through Worship: Stories Congregations Live By*—is a collection of small, unassuming stories of God's involvement in the weekly worship of congregations where I served as pastor. The stories that follow are, first and foremost, my stories. While they are not about me, they are told from my perspective; they are narratives that grow out of my reflection on and conversations about God's involvement in worship services that had a significant impact on the worshiping community. Others would undoubtedly recall and relate these stories differently. The stories in this book are also more than my stories. I regularly tell these stories when I speak in congregations and at conferences to help Christians look for God's presence, listen to God speaking, and apprehend God's activity in their worship, and people seem to resonate with them. Like all stories, they have been shaped and simplified as they are told and retold, particularly in ways that respect and protect people's identities.

The themes of the stories in this book are things Christians do when they worship—preach and pray, baptize and bless, light candles and sing songs, share Holy Communion, commend loved ones to God and the communion of saints. Yet, the perspective is not what we do but what God is doing. I am reluctant to label these stories as chapters, both because they do not necessarily build upon or follow from one another and because assigning them numbers implies a determined sequence. I prefer to think of this book as an anthology. If any thread holds these stories together, that thread is the connection between God's saving activity in Scripture and God's saving activity in worship. As a preacher, I am never far from Bible stories, images, allusions, and connections, which surely find their way into the narratives. Also, in keeping with my custom when writing Alban books, I include questions at the conclusion of each story, which I hope stimulates your own reflection and conversation.

John D. Witvliet, who edits Alban's Vital Worship, Healthy Congregations Series, states that this series "is designed to invite congregations to rediscover a common vision for worship, to sense how worship is related to all aspects of congregational life, and to imagine ways of preparing both better 'content' and better 'process' related to the worship life of their own congregations."[9] I offer these stories of actual congregational worship as a means of helping others catch the vision of worship as *God's* activity—to end the old and begin the new, to bring life out of death and speech out of silence, to redeem the world through the church. I hope they will inspire and encourage worship planners and leaders, who are often diminished by opposition and disheartened by the lack of results, to "not grow weary in doing what is right, for we will reap at harvest-time, if we do not give up" (Gal. 6:9).

For Reflection and Conversation

- Do you consider your pastor (or yourself) to be an evangelist or a chaplain? Do you consider your congregation to be a mission post or a club? How is this evident in worship, ministry, and leadership? Are these helpful categories? Why or why not?
- Do you experience God as the primary actor in worship, or is worship something the pastor or congregation does? Why?
- What does growing a congregation mean in your context? Name three ways God may be calling or inviting your congregation to grow.
- Name one story you would tell about a worship service in your congregation. How does this story connect with the larger narrative of God's work in the world?

Chapter 1

Give God the First Word

Sometimes when people experience God speaking and acting in worship, they want to worship more, because they sense God doing something important and want to be part of it. Some people who think of worship as God's activity may speak of that activity as centering, nourishing, teaching, strengthening, empowering, changing perspective, or giving peace. Others might talk about Jesus creating a community and making them part of something bigger than themselves. Still others are certain the Spirit is slowly and surely nudging both them and the congregation in a particular direction, which the Spirit reveals a little at a time as the congregation worships together, a direction that is part of God's work of transforming the world. While people who think of worship as God's activity may have different ways of describing their experience, they are saying that worship is an important way God encounters them, and so they want to worship more often.

Like many Lutheran congregations, Epiphany Church worshiped on Sunday morning and on Wednesday evenings during Advent and Lent—the weeks before Christmas and Easter. Some members asked if we could worship midweek year round. The conversation resulted in a Wednesday morning communion service. It was small and simple. About a half dozen people came to church at 7:30 am. They listened as Scripture was read and I preached a five-minute homily. Then we held hands in a circle and prayed, shared Christ's peace, and gathered around the altar to celebrate the Lord's Supper. The service lasted a half hour, and afterward some of us went across the street for breakfast, to the restaurant where I had tried to be an evangelist.

Jesus compared the kingdom of heaven to yeast a woman took and mixed in with three measures of flour until all of it was leavened (Matt. 13:33; Luke 13:20–21). This Wednesday morning worship service was yeast for the people who attended, and they, in turn, became yeast for the congregation. The Wednesday worshipers told other members of the congregation and friends outside the church how meaningful they found the service and that receiving the Lord's Supper every Wednesday had become especially important to them. Unbeknownst to me, those who worshiped on Wednesday were inviting and bringing their friends to church. Even more to my surprise, we welcomed a visitor or two on Wednesday morning who had no connection to anyone in worship but had heard about the service and decided to check it out—something that no longer happened on Sunday. Our visitors usually came carrying heavy burdens, their own and those of the people they loved, for which they were told we would pray. They had also been told they were welcome at the Lord's Table. After worshiping with us, visitors reported that the service "felt like church" and provided a "back door" through which they could "sneak" into worship. When these visitors finally found their way to worship on Sunday morning, they were surprised and disappointed to discover we were not having communion that day. Before long, a group somewhat larger than the Wednesday worshipers wanted to know why we didn't have Holy Communion every week *on Sunday*. God's yeast was doing its work; the dough had begun to rise.

Moving toward Weekly Communion: Two Approaches

Epiphany Church celebrated the Lord's Supper on the first and third Sundays of the month and on festivals like Christmas and Easter. Explaining to people who asked for weekly communion that they could receive it every Wednesday did not seem to satisfy them. "Why not every Sunday?" they asked. "What about people who come on Sunday and need communion, and we're not having it? Do we say, 'Come back next week'?" Celebrating the Lord's Supper every Sunday is certainly in keeping with the Lutheran theological tradition. True, for decades many congregations in my denomination had celebrated communion only monthly, quarterly, or, I am told, even annually. But by the time I was serving as pastor of Epiphany Church, my denomination had affirmed the weekly celebration of the Lord's Supper, and congregations were increasingly celebrating Holy Communion more frequently, a trend that was initially inspired by the liturgical renewal movement of the 1960s and 1970s and that continues. Including the Lord's Supper as part of the Sunday service is also my personal and pastoral preference. Yet, weekly communion was not the congregation's practice, and most people had not requested a change. So what were we to do about the yeast, which wasn't going away?

As seasoned pastors know well, changing worship practices is perhaps the most difficult challenge congregational leaders can undertake. Conventional wisdom teaches that pastors should enlist congregational leaders, introduce the change slowly, educate prior to the change, and listen to and learn from the congregation before making the change. I sought the counsel of appropriate leaders, including the worship committee and church council, some of whom attended the Wednesday service. They encouraged me to preach and teach on the Lord's Supper. So I preached on Holy Communion whenever the lectionary—that is, the system of Scripture readings appointed for worship on a given day or occasion—made that appropriate. We held classes on Holy Communion. People wrote newsletter articles and had conversations about their experience of Holy Communion. We had pilot programs and trial periods during which we celebrated the Lord's Supper every Sunday for a specified period of time—during the Lent and Easter seasons, for example. We also tried to help people understand that God's gift of Holy Communion is bigger than what we sometimes think. Some Lutherans think of Holy Communion almost exclusively as the forgiveness of sins, leading one member to protest, "We don't need communion every week. We don't sin that much." Rather than focusing exclusively on the forgiveness of sins, we also talked about the Lord's Supper as sustenance to live as God's people, participation in the communion of saints of all times and places, and a foretaste of God's great and promised feast. Most important, we repeatedly emphasized that communion is God's gift and that while individuals do not need to receive communion weekly if they do not desire it, the church offers communion every week for those who desire or need to receive it on any given Sunday.

Education and conversation seemed only to solidify people's previously held positions. Those who desired weekly communion became more enthusiastic; those that did not became more vocal in their opposition. "Martin Luther would be rolling over in his grave if he knew what you were doing," one person said to me. When I shared some quotes from Luther encouraging people to receive communion more often rather than less, she retorted, "Who says we have to listen to him, anyway?" Another member reminded me of her connections with the bishop and assured me that if I stopped stirring up trouble, she could help me find my way to a bigger church. A third explained why we could not have weekly communion this way: "You *say* I don't have to receive communion every Sunday. But if communion is offered and I don't receive it, how will that look? What will people think of me?" People also raised concerns about the cost of additional wine and wafers, the time communion would add to the service, and extra work for the altar guild.

Eventually, the congregation agreed that we needed to make a decision, and we would decide by secret ballot. At the congregational meeting where the election was held, celebrating the Lord's Supper every Sunday passed by a few votes. The win-lose approach to deciding left a bad taste in everyone's mouth, and no one went away from the meeting feeling happy. Education and conversation did not seem to have worked. But we started celebrating the Lord's Supper weekly. Ten years later, I received a letter from a member who had opposed weekly communion. "We finally understand," the letter said. "The Lord's Supper is Jesus's gift of himself for us."

In another congregation, St. Timothy's Lutheran Church, I stumbled on a different approach to moving to more frequent communion. As I indicated in the introduction, shortly after I started graduate school at the University of Notre Dame, the local bishop called and asked me to be the very part-time pastor of a tiny congregation in Michigan, just across the border from South Bend, Indiana. The members of the congregation were very much a family. In our initial meeting, everyone was trying to be formal and impressive, saying things like, "We of St. Timothy Lu-

theran Church are truly honored to have you as our pastor." Like
a mischievous teenager, the congregational president, a guy my
age, took a slightly different approach. "Welcome to *St. Tim's*," he
said, looking around approvingly at the stunned expressions and
raised eyebrows of some older members. Everyone laughed, and
relaxed. The members then described themselves as open and flex-
ible; they had been cared for by supply preachers for so long, often
a different preacher coming every Sunday, that they had become
accustomed to trying new things. The only thing the congregation insisted on was that we sing the hymn of praise, "This is the
feast of victory for our God," every Sunday. They celebrated Holy
Communion once a month. The people of St. Timothy's were very
grateful that the same pastor would be coming every Sunday. The
opportunity was also a blessing for my family and me. Now living
on a student's stipend, the additional income was pure grace. My
wife, Cathy, wisely advised me to preach, lead worship, and devote
all my energy to my studies. In other words, my wife was telling
me not to blow it.

I was excited to bundle doctoral work with parish ministry.
My questions about the relationship of preaching, worship, and
mission led me to study liturgy and homiletics. While I had been
discovering God at work in what many congregations call "traditional worship," other pastors argued that, for the sake of the
church's mission, worship and preaching had to be transformed
from a mountaintop experience for the faithful into a level plain
where the unchurched could meet Christ. Sermons needed to
be simpler, the worship service "user friendly," and sacraments
downplayed, since seekers often experience baptism and the Lord's
Supper as exclusive. These voices spoke urgently, as if the church
was in uncharted territory. My hunch was that, somewhere in its
history, the church dealt with seekers and the unchurched. I was
curious about the relationship of worship and mission in those
chapters of the church's life.

I began my pastoral ministry at St. Timothy's in early September, when the lectionary devotes five Sundays to John 6—Jesus
feeding the multitude and his discourse on the bread of life. Sunday after Sunday we sang, "This is *the feast* of victory for our
God." We listened as Jesus said, "I am the bread of life. Whoever

comes to me will never be hungry, and whoever believes in me will never be thirsty" and "I am the living bread that came down from heaven. Whoever eats of this bread will live forever; and the bread that I will give for the life of the world is my flesh" (John 6:35, 51). I preached on the bread of life. And we did not celebrate the Lord's Supper.

The irony was not lost on me. In fact, by about the fourth week, the irony got the best of me and I sort of lost it. In the middle of my sermon, I spontaneously walked over to the empty altar, stared down at it, looked up at the congregation, and to the tune of their beloved hymn of praise, sang, "*Where* is the feast of victory of our God?" I then launched into an impassioned proclamation of the Lord's Supper as the bread of life, Christ's gift of himself, and declared that we should be eager to receive Christ, the bread of life, each and every Sunday.

At the coffee hour after worship, the members of the church council, about half the congregation, huddled together in a corner, obviously discussing their new pastor. "You couldn't keep your mouth shut for a month," Cathy said as we stood alone, sipping coffee. "You had to rock the boat. You know, we really need this job." After a while, Kelly, the council president, walked over, stood next to me, and stared down at his shoes. So I stared down at my shoes. After a few minutes of silence, Kelly said, "Having Holy Communion every Sunday seems important to you." "Yeah," I said sheepishly. "Can you explain it to me? Can you tell me why?" Kelly asked.

Perhaps it was grace or the Holy Spirit. Maybe my experience of explaining and explaining Holy Communion to the people of Epiphany Church—the congregation voting with a secret ballot to more frequently receive Christ's gift of himself in the Lord's Supper, and communion barely passing—made me hesitant. But I answered Kelly, "I don't think I can explain it. I think we have to experience the Lord's Supper every week for a while before we try to understand it. We have to give God the first word." "But, if we were to have communion every Sunday," Kelly asked, "you'd help us to understand it as we go, right?" "Certainly," I answered, uncertain of what Kelly was asking. "Would it be okay if we start next week?" Kelly asked. "Sure," I said, stunned. Kelly looked up from his shoes and over at the church council. "We're going to start next week," he said. "Pastor will explain it to us as we go."

The next week we started celebrating Holy Communion every Sunday. At the coffee hour after worship, we would talk about it. Rather than my explaining what communion means, people would share, even debrief, their experience of the service, particularly receiving communion. We discovered that, on the same Sunday, communion affected some people profoundly, while others were left flat. Over time, people talked less about how they felt and more about God. They became more aware of God connecting them to each other and sustaining them individually. They also began to make connections between the Lord's Supper and justice. One person quipped, "I was really afraid that taking communion every week would make it less special. It has. Now communion is more essential."

Explanation Follows Participation

For centuries, the church has operated out of the assumption that explanation precedes participation. The assumption has been that people need to intellectually (and correctly) understand Christian worship before they can participate in and appreciate it. In certain instances, such as admission to the Lord's Supper, the church required people to demonstrate proper understanding before they were permitted to participate. For example, people could not receive communion until they understood themselves as sinners. Today, some congregations challenge this way of operating by removing from worship everything that is not readily accessible or requires explanation. They might stop celebrating the Lord's Supper in their primary worship services. In the early centuries of its life, the church did not follow these approaches. Rather than teaching the meaning of worship in advance or eliminating from the service everything that required explanation, the church trusted God to encounter seekers through what the church did.

As late as the fourth century, for example, the church is said to have observed a "discipline of secrecy."[1] From their sermons, we can tell that fourth-century bishops Ambrose of Milan and Cyril

of Jerusalem gave no instruction on the meaning of key elements
of Christian worship, including baptism, the Lord's Supper, and
the Lord's Prayer, until *after* people participated in and experienced these rites for the first time during the worship service at
which they were baptized, namely the Easter Vigil. Another bishop, Theodore of Mopsuestia, taught people the meaning of baptism in the days before they were baptized but withheld instruction on the Eucharist until after people received it at the Easter
Vigil. These leaders then drew upon people's own experience of
Christian worship as the starting point and method of instruction.
They asked, "What did we do?" "What did you see?" "What did
you say?" Then, using biblical, natural, and cultural images, they
moved people from recalling the images, words, and actions they
participated in and observed in worship to understanding, even
experiencing, the significance of these images, words, and actions
for Christian faith and their implications for Christian life.

These examples from the church's early life invite the church
today to reconsider the assumption that understanding precedes
participation and to ask instead what instruction, if any, is necessary and helpful prior to participating in Christian worship. The
practice of the early church invites us to rediscover the value of
"the pedagogy of silence," the recognition that remaining silent
about what worship means is itself a way of teaching that allows
the worship service itself to be the first teacher.[2] In this approach,
God acting in worship gets the first word, before the church talks
about how God acts in worship. Rather than telling people how
they should understand worship and what they are supposed to
experience, the church might alert people that they will experience God at work in worship, tell them the biblical stories of faith
as keys for both understanding their experience and the language
with which to describe it, and encourage them to be open to and
consider the ways God is shaping their lives and the world.

At St. Timothy's, we used this approach in our ongoing conversation about Holy Communion. I also began to use this approach in prebaptismal and first communion instruction. So, for
example, rather than drilling the doctrine of the real presence, a
staple of a Lutheran understanding of the Lord's Supper, into the
heads of fifth graders, we read the biblical accounts of the Last

Supper, and I taught them the mechanics of receiving communion. Then, after they had been receiving communion for a while, we would talk about their experience. I learned, among other things, that communion is like Thanksgiving dinner at Grandma's house. No matter how many people there are, everyone has a place at the table and gets enough to eat, and that is the way Christ's family is supposed to be. Yet, the power of giving God the first word in worship was nowhere more profound than in our Maundy Thursday services.

Maundy Thursday

During the years when they did not have their own pastor, the people of St. Timothy's became ingenious at finding ways to celebrate church holidays. On Good Friday, for example, they participated in the community worship service. Some years, Christmas Eve worship consisted of reading the Christmas story, singing lots of carols, perhaps observing a Christmas pageant, lighting candles, and skipping the sermon. On Maundy Thursday, the congregation held what it called an "agape feast." Loosely based on the Jewish seder meal, the worship service was a church supper that included readings from Scripture by members of the congregation. Toward the end of the meal, a neighboring pastor would arrive, after leading worship at his or her own church, so that the congregation could have Holy Communion. On my first Maundy Thursday in the parish, I wasn't sure the congregation knew what to do with me, other than to ask me to celebrate communion after dessert. I recall that the major question when planning the service was whether to serve corn dogs or pot roast. (We decided on pot roast.) I also recall that we had to interrupt the Scripture readings for a brief intermission to refrigerate the mayonnaise dishes. I went away from the service genuinely amazed; it truly was a love feast.

The second year, as we prepared for Easter, people wondered if the Maundy Thursday service could be a bit more worshipful, without losing the agape feast, and asked if I had any ideas. I explained that the name *Maundy* comes from the Latin word for "commandment" and refers to the new commandment Jesus gave to his followers, to love one another as Jesus loved them (John 13:34). I said that some congregations wash feet on Maundy Thursday as a way of both remembering how Jesus washed his disciples' feet and sharing in Jesus's humble, loving service. "You want us to take off our shoes and socks in church and have our feet washed?" someone asked. "Actually," I said, smiling, "I'd like us to take off our shoes and socks in the fellowship hall and have our feet washed before supper." "Can you help me to understand what this is?" Kelly asked once again. "I don't think I can," I said. "I think we have to try it, and then talk about what God's up to."

We decided to try it. Carol Ann, who headed up the altar guild, brought an antique pitcher and basin and lots of towels. We read the story of Jesus washing his disciples' feet. I explained this would be a symbolic washing rather than a real scrubbing. We decided that those who did not want their feet washed could have their hands washed. People came forward, sat in a chair, and put their feet in the basin. I poured water over their feet, wiped them with my hands, and dried them with the towel. After a while, Barry, a member of the congregation, tapped me on the shoulder and asked if he could take over. Before long people were taking turns.

Over supper we talked about what it felt like to take off our shoes and socks, to have our feet washed, and to wash other people's feet, and we discussed what Jesus might have been trying to show us and teach us. Everyone agreed that they preferred to wash other people's feet. Many did not like having their feet washed because it made them uncomfortable. Taking off their shoes made most people feel vulnerable—one person said naked. They said that having their feet washed and washing feet was an intimate act; we found it hard to think of Jesus touching us that intimately. We identified with Peter, who said, "You will never wash my feet" (John 13:8). "But Jesus did it for the disciples," one person said, "and Jesus touched us that way in baptism." Another person observed that loving one another as Jesus loves us means we are to be that vulnerable and intimate with each other. That made everyone feel uncomfortable. Finally, someone said, "If washing feet makes us that uncomfortable, and generates this much conversation, something important is going on. So we better do it again next year."

So we washed feet the next Maundy Thursday, and the Maundy Thursday after that, and the Maundy Thursday after that. During the year, something happened that I did not expect. Carol Ann started bringing her pitcher and basin to church on those special Sundays we had a baptism, and we used them rather than the finger bowl in the wooden stand that was our baptismal font. Then she brought them on Sundays when we wanted to remember baptism, like Easter and All Saints, and we invited people to dip their fingers in the water and perhaps make the sign of the cross. In my doctoral work, I was studying Ambrose, the fourth-century bishop of Milan, and I was struck by a connection he made. Augustine was concerned not to attach an exaggerated value to footwashing and so described it as a pattern of humility—the meaning the church preserved. Ambrose, on the other hand, recognized the value of washing feet as a lesson in humble service but added a baptismal connection.[3] For Ambrose, in footwashing Christ symbolically gave an extra measure of grace and holiness to help baptized Christians resist the tendency to sin. Interpreting the phrase "and you will strike his heel" in Genesis 3:15 to mean that evil will attack the baptized in the same way the serpent would attack Adam, Ambrose asserted that the feet are washed to protect the baptized from the attack of evil and the poison of sin spreading throughout the body. Though the congregation and I were not as articulate as Ambrose, footwashing became an important reminder of baptism for us. When I left "St. Tim's," the people presented me with my own antique pitcher and basin, to remind me of washing feet and celebrating baptism.

On our fifth Maundy Thursday together, which we knew would be my last Maundy Thursday with the congregation and the congregation's last Maundy Thursday together, our minds were on giving up our church and its furnishings, ending our ministry, and going our separate ways. I suggested that we have communion in church after dinner and then strip the altar in remembrance of Christ being stripped for us. "I know, I know," Kelly responded. "We have to do it to understand it." Carol Ann and I planned the service. We arranged that after communion a member of the congregation would read Psalm 22 aloud from the back of the church. My wife, Cathy, daughter, Chelsey, and Carol Ann were to come forward in turn; I was to hand them the things on the altar, which they would take out of the church through the side door and then come back for something else. When everything was removed from the altar, the women would remove the paraments (cloth coverings) from the pulpit and altar. On Maundy Thursday, when we finished dessert, we made our way from the fellowship hall into the church for communion and the stripping of the altar. "What do we do?" someone asked. "We have everything covered," I said. "Just participate."

When everyone had received communion, the congregation was seated, and the room was quiet, the reader began the psalm, "My God, my God, why have you forsaken me? Why are you so far from helping me, from the words of my groaning?" (Psalm 22:1). Cathy came to the altar and I handed her the communion cup. Chelsey came next, and I handed her the bread plate. Carol Ann came to the altar, and I gave her the leftover bread and wine. The stripping of the altar was deliberately and reverently underway, just as we planned. The three women returned to the altar, received something from my hands, and removed it from the worship space.

"All who see me mock at me; they make mouths at me, they shake their heads" (Psalm 22:7), the reader continued. I was lost in what we were doing. But when I went to hand the altar book, I snapped out of my meditation. The hands waiting to receive the altar book were not Cathy's, Chelsey's, or Carol Ann's. The hands belonged to—a man! After staring at those hands for what seemed an eternity but was probably only a few seconds, I placed the altar book in them and picked up the stand on which it sat. I did not recognize the hands waiting to receive it. Looking up from the altar, I saw the members of the congregation spontaneously getting up from their places and lining up down the center aisle. They were coming to the altar in turn, receiving something, taking it out of the church, then returning to their places to kneel.

I felt tears well up in my eyes and run down my face. Then it occurred to me that I had to have something for everyone who came forward to remove from the altar. So I scrambled to think of things—candlesticks, offering plate, Bible on the pulpit, and eventually my stole and my hymnal. When nothing was left, Carol Ann removed and folded the pulpit and altar cloths. Then she gave them to others, who carried them out of church.

We returned to the fellowship hall in hushed voices. I was among the last to join the group. "We're sorry we ruined the service," someone said to me. "What makes you think you ruined the service?" I asked. "You were crying," someone else answered. I explained that I wasn't upset; I was moved by what the congregation had done. "It's your fault," someone else responded. "You told us to participate."

In our years of ministry together, the people of St. Timothy's and I had grown from needing to understand worship in order to participate in it, to needing to participate in worship in order to understand it. The congregation also determined that participation means being actively involved. We learned this together: God taught us when we entered into Christian worship as a mystery and gave God the first word.

For Reflection and Conversation

- In what ways does God have the first word in your congregation's worship? In what ways does the church speak in worship before God gets the chance?
- Can you name a way you experience God in worship that you cannot explain? In what part of the service does this happen?
- What concerns do you have about trying something new in worship before you understand it? Are there other areas in life where you try things without understanding them?

Chapter 2

Remember Baptism

"Everyone who thirsts, come to the waters" (Isa. 55:1). With these words, the members of the Sacraments Study Group of the Presbyterian Church (U.S.A.), of which I was privileged to be a member, invite the congregations of that church body "on a spiritual journey to explore the deep and joyful waters of baptism,"[1] so that, in the words of Isaiah, "with joy you will draw water from the wells of salvation" (Isa. 12:3). In my own Lutheran parlance, the invitation is to remember baptism. The church has traditionally regarded Jesus's baptism as the model for all baptisms. When Jesus was baptized in the Jordan River, God declared, "You are my Son, the Beloved; with you I am well pleased" (Luke 3:22). The Holy Spirit descended upon him. In baptism, God makes us God's beloved children by joining us to Christ's death and resurrection, anointing us with the Holy Spirit, and empowering us to live as God's people. By remembering our baptism, we can find the comfort and assurance that Jesus loves and forgives us and the courage and strength to live as his people.

Many Christians, baptized as adults or teens, can vividly recall the event of their baptism; they may regularly return to the water where they were baptized. Yet many other Christians find it difficult to grasp what it means to come to the water, to explore the deep and joyful waters of baptism, or to draw water from the wells of salvation, because they cannot remember their own baptism. They may not even remember the details of their children's baptisms. I once heard a preacher admit in a sermon, "I can't find my children's baptismal certificates. I don't know where the dress is that my daughter wore or the little suit that my son was in. I can't remember the sermon that either pastor preached on those days."[2]

That preacher's admission was so powerful, because she spoke for
so many faithful Christian parents. Asking people to remember
something they cannot is silly. Yet, pastors do it all the time; at
least I do.

"We need to actively remember our baptism," I repeatedly
insisted with a smile in sermon and conversation. As you would
expect, the people of St. Timothy's Church responded with blank
stares. My claim that we need to celebrate the Lord's Supper every
Sunday for a while before we try to explain and to understand why
weekly communion is important may have initially sounded crazy
to my congregation. Yet, nothing I said struck them as more outra-
geous than my insistence that we remember something we simply
did not remember. The members of St. Timothy's Church were
baptized as babies. They knew that baptism happened to them
when they were infants, along with being born and getting im-
munized. Most did not know the date of their baptism. Few had
been told any details of the day. One or two had looked at pictures and seen themselves in a baptismal gown. One or two more
knew where their baptismal certificate was. Some kept a baptismal candle, usually from one of their children's baptisms, tucked
away on a shelf. But they couldn't recall their baptism. "How can
we actively remember what we cannot remember?" they asked.
Explaining baptism didn't help. Understanding is different from
remembering.

What Does It Mean to Remember?

Pilgrims journeying to the Holy Land see all the "exact spots"
where Jesus was at important moments in his life. They kneel at a
star on the floor of a cave in the basement of a church in Bethlehem, the "exact spot" where the Christ child was born. They stand
next to a stone slab in the Church of the Holy Sepulcher in Jerusalem, the "exact spot" where the body of Jesus was laid after his
crucifixion. They go to two tombs, both claiming to be the "exact
spot" where Jesus rose from the dead that first Easter. Many pilgrims report that after a while, standing on all those "exact spots"
feels silly. Then they come to Galilee and the lake.

"Now you will feel close to Jesus," their guide promises as they board a boat. "The churches weren't there when the Lord walked the earth, but this lake was. This is the lake where Jesus walked on the water. This is the lake where Jesus quieted the storm. This is the lake where the disciples went fishing after the resurrection and encountered the risen Christ." The guide might select one of those Bible stories to read, perhaps the one where the disciples took Jesus with them in the boat, "just as he was" (Mark 4:36).

> A great windstorm arose, and the waves beat into the boat, so that the boat was already being swamped. But [Jesus] was in the stern, asleep on the cushion; and they woke [Jesus] up and said to him, "Teacher, do you not care that we are perishing?" [Jesus] woke up and rebuked the wind, and said to the sea, "Peace! Be still!" Then the wind ceased, and there was a dead calm (Mark 4:37–39).

As I sailed the Sea of Galilee and listened to our guide read that story, I didn't feel close to Jesus. Yes, I made an intellectual connection—"Wow. I'm in the same place that Jesus was!" But I didn't really feel close to the Christ. Even though I know the stories, even though I understand everything Jesus did on that lake, I wasn't there when Jesus quieted the storm, walked on the water, and appeared after the resurrection. Spending time on the Sea of Galilee was like trying to remember baptism. I could understand what Jesus did and make the intellectual connection that Jesus does the same thing for me, but I could not remember what Jesus did on the Sea of Galilee as my own experience, as my own memory.

Remembering baptism—exploring the deep and joyful baptismal waters and drawing water from the wells of salvation—is different from recounting facts and recalling details of something that happened to us long ago. Remembering baptism is more like deepening our appreciation for what someone, namely Jesus, did for us, even if Jesus did it a long time ago. The way we remember our baptism, by deepening our appreciation for what Jesus did for us, often has nothing to do with the details of what happened when we were baptized. In fact, God often uses other details and places to help us remember our baptism. God regularly uses the event of worship to deepen our appreciation of baptism; sometimes, God uses something else.

Whenever I hear the story of Jesus calming the storm, I think of baptism. I think of Jesus coming to us in the water, speaking a powerful word, and silencing the storms of sin, death, fear, and isolation that so often rage in our lives. Yet, I do not think of the Sea of Galilee. I don't think of a baptismal font. I think of one of Michigan's eleven thousand inland lakes. I experience the risen Christ coming to me, calming the storms that engulf my life, and inviting me into the power of the resurrection on that Michigan lake. Just as the disciples returned to the Sea of Galilee after Easter, my family has been returning to that lake in Michigan for more than seventy years. While we might not always name it in biblical terms, we can all name the clarity and the calm, the awe and the wonder of confronting something greater than ourselves that quiets the storms in our lives as we spend time on those waters. My brother Don tells of fishing with our dad and uncle as a kid and hauling perch into the boat faster than they could bait their hooks (John 21:1–14). My brother Brian, who inherited the passion for fishing and has caught more fish in more places than I can name, swears there is nothing better than throwing a line in that lake. My own sense is that my younger brother's passion for that lake runs deeper than fishing. There on the lake a few years ago, Brian and I spoke of life direction, of vocation. There on the lake, Brian, successful in business but unhappy in life, shared with me a desire to take a new path, to do something different, to return to school, to join the Peace Corps, to make a difference. Brian's adventure began a few years later, and the storm in his spirit settled (Matt. 4:18–22).

My own lake story is a bit different. When I was eight years old, I decided that I wanted to learn to ride a two-wheel bike. That is somewhat extraordinary, even ridiculous, for a kid who is legally blind. More than forty years later, with a daughter of my own, I can only imagine the fear that I could not see in my mother's face. But my parents never let on. They didn't say, No! They taught me to ride a two-wheel bike. First two training wheels, then one, then wobbly, then riding. Sailing down the sidewalk, I didn't see the crack. The bike stopped; I didn't. My face collided with the con-

crete. The bloody bump above my left eye was the size of a soft-
ball. There were cuts and bruises throughout my body. My bike
was battered, and I was afraid to ride it. After a trip to the doctor
to assure my mom that I was okay, we set off for our annual trip
to the lake. Two weeks swimming and splashing with my brothers and cousins, fishing with my uncle and dad, and playing cards
with my mom, aunt, and grandma. And the lake did its work. The
water and the love of my family healed me. The cuts scabbed over,
the swelling shrank, and I grew strong. And early one morning, my
dad woke me to say that we were going fishing all by ourselves.
And out on the lake we talked about my bike. We decided to get
new handlebars and a banana seat and that I would try to ride it
again when we got home. And the storm in my soul was still (2
Kings 5:1–14).

A few summers ago my family was out on the lake again, in
the midst of another storm. Out on that lake, aboard two pontoon
boats piloted by Presbyterians, we commended my dad to God
and committed his ashes to the lake he loved. He had died in June
of that year after a long night of battling the storm of cancer. We
returned to the lake to spread his ashes, knowing that as surely as
the disciples encountered the risen Christ on the Sea of Galilee, as
surely as all those times we have met God on the water and felt
the storms in our lives settle, the risen Christ has come to my dad,
stilled the storm, and brought him safely to the shore of new life.
Remembering the promise of baptism not as an isolated event that
happened to us long ago, but as one more drop in the flood of the
reconciling river of God's love, we returned to water where we
experienced Christ as near to us, trusting that Christ would come
to us once again.

That my family and I could be on the water that day was co-
incidental, serendipitous, or, in my opinion, miraculous. The previous spring I met a Presbyterian minister named Thomas whose
church—let's call it St. Zebedee—was nestled on the shore of the
very lake my family and I returned to year after year. As we talked
about that lake, I told Thomas that my dad was fighting cancer
and that we hoped he would be able to go to the lake that summer. I explained that we had a small fishing boat, which my dad
wouldn't be able to get into, and wondered if Thomas knew some-

one with a larger boat who could give him a ride. Thomas understood that this was something I could do for my father and assured
me it wouldn't be a problem. When my father died a month before
we were supposed to make our annual trip to the lake, I called
Thomas and told him that I would still need the boat ride, that
there would be a few more passengers, and that the purpose of our
trip had changed.

The boat ride was arranged for a Sunday afternoon. Thomas
invited my family to worship with the congregation that morning
and graciously asked me to preach. In worship God lovingly surrounded my family and me with people we did not know but who
received us as their own. We heard God's word and prayed together; the congregation included an intercession for my family. I chose
to preach on Jesus calming the storm and named their lake as the
place where my family and I encounter God. The worship service
concluded with a blessing of tartans, the distinctive plaids worn
by Scottish clans. With this blessing, the congregation invited my
family into its own family ritual of remembering, caring for, and
asking God to bless loved ones who had gone before. In worship
God made us one community gathered around God's word to ask
God's blessing on loved ones who had died.

That afternoon, people we had worshiped with crossed the lake
in pontoon boats and picked up my family and me. They brought
us to my dad's resting place, in the same way that congregations accompany parents as they bring children to the baptismal font and
the bereaved to the cemetery. Once again, we worshiped together,
this time on pontoon boats floating side by side. We celebrated the
service of committal together, hearing God's word, offering our
prayers, entrusting my father to God, and releasing his remains to
the lake. Jesus was with us in the boat, speaking a powerful word
and stilling the storm of death that surrounded us. "How can we
ever repay you?" I asked Thomas and the two pontoon boat captains afterward. "Being here was payment enough," one captain
replied. "This was a privilege," the other said. "Besides," Thomas
added, "in baptism, God makes us one family. This is what brothers and sisters in Christ do for each other."

Some Christian traditions teach that Christ hallowed all water
when he was baptized in the Jordan. By being baptized in water,

Jesus blessed it and set it apart as a life-giving flood that washes away sin. On the boat ride home, I realized that, at least for that afternoon, Jesus turned that lake into a baptismal font, because Jesus did the same thing on that lake that Jesus does at the font. Jesus gathered the church on that lake in the same way that Jesus gathers his people around the font; we heard God's word. As in baptism, some of us faced death and received Christ's promise of new life. Others of us heard Christ's call to serve and minister to others and responded. For that afternoon, Jesus made us a tangible expression of Christ's body and a witness of Christ's love for all to see.

Jesus came to all of us on the water and taught us what it means to remember baptism. Remembering baptism is not so much about recalling the day or recounting the facts. Remembering baptism is about returning to or accompanying others to a place where God stilled our storms, where we encounter God who, once again, stills the storm that surrounds us. Sometimes that place is worship. Sometimes that place is somewhere else. Sometimes we need help connecting God's saving activity in baptism to the place where we experience God in the storm. In other words, we need help remembering baptism. In worship God reminds us of baptism so that we recall and trust in what God did for us in baptism—the promise God made to be with us—when we are surrounded by storms.

Surrounded by Storms

Often, we are not as ready to remember baptism in worship as we are when we are surrounded by storms. Like Jesus's first disciples, we know moments when, beaten by the waves and swamped by the storms, we fret over finding Jesus asleep in the stern, seemingly oblivious or unconcerned that we are in peril. In those moments, our knowledge, understanding, and accomplishments all fail us. Like Job, we carefully craft our questions about life or our circumstances or about God's silence or apparent absence based on all we hold to be true. And, if God answers at all, God's response often feels like the same *slap* God used to answer Job. From the storm that surrounds us, God seems to spit and sputter, "How dare you

question me?" "Who is this that darkens counsel by words with
no knowledge?" (Job 38:2). When we spend too much time asking
Why?—Why me? Why this? Why now?—what we get is smacked
by the storm.

Worse than rendering our knowledge of God, life, and the
world useless, the storm robs us of our experience of God. All
those times when we have felt so close to God seem to abandon
ship. All those moments of grace that we can so easily name are
forgotten. All those instances when we have experienced God active in our lives and in our world feel long ago and far away. Like
the first disciples, who saw Jesus heal the sick, heard Jesus teach
with authority, and witnessed Jesus restore to wholeness, we, too,
have seen the power of Christ at work in those around us. Like the
first disciples, we, too, still have no faith, if by *faith* we mean recalling facts and recounting details. Often we cannot even conjure
in ourselves enough trust that God will save us to keep our fear at
bay. In those moments of weathering the storm, as the wind howls
around us and the water rises from around our ankles to above
our knees, the last thing we need is a meteorological analysis of
conditions on the lake. The last thing we need are instructions
shouted from the safety of the shore. This is how you steer the
ship! This is how you bail the boat! Surrounded by the storm, we
need someone in the boat with us. We need someone to rouse Jesus
from sleep and to call upon Jesus to rebuke the wind, to speak to
the sea, and to say, "Peace! Be still!"

When we find ourselves surrounded by the storm, one way we
can hear that voice rousing Jesus is to return to a place where we
powerfully experienced Jesus in the boat with us and stilling the
storm. For whether the boat is a manger, a cross, a tomb, a family,
a congregation, a classroom, a world at war, or a heart seeking
peace, Jesus is in the boat with us, and Jesus will quiet the storm.
We need to return to the place where we experienced Jesus in the
boat with us, the place where we heard God proclaim that, regardless of whether the storms be "afflictions, hardships, calamities,
beatings, imprisonments, riots, labors, sleepless nights, hunger"
(2 Cor. 6:4–5), and even death, "the wind and the sea obey him"
(Mark 4:41).

Jesus promises that for all Christians, baptism is a place where Jesus encounters us and stills our storms. In the water of baptism, Jesus stills the storm of death, brokenness, and separation from God by claiming us as his own. Jesus calms the storm of isolation by making us part of his body. Jesus calms the storm of aimlessness and meaninglessness by calling us to share his work of reconciliation and service. When we find ways to return to a place of baptism, a place where we experienced Jesus in the boat with us and calming whatever storm we were facing, we actively remember our baptism and draw water from the wells of salvation. We also discover that remembering baptism is different from recalling the place where we were baptized.

As God's people, being in the boat together is our privilege. Rousing Christ for one another and for the world is our privilege as we come together in worship to hear God's word, to call to Jesus in prayer, and to meet Jesus in the water. Congregations actively remember baptism when their worship is such a place.

Making Worship a Place to Remember Baptism

The ship is an ancient symbol for the church tossed on the sea of chaos, doubt, the world's cares, and even persecution, but finally reaching a safe harbor. Part of the imagery comes from 1 Peter's comparison of baptism to the ark, which saved Noah's family during the flood. Part of this symbol comes from Jesus protecting the boat and the disciples on the stormy Sea of Galilee (1 Pet. 3:20–21; Mark 4:35–41). The people of St. Timothy's had no difficulty thinking of their church as a ship beaten by the waves and already being swamped. We were small and struggling. The storms from their lives that members brought with them to worship were generally known and empathically shared by all who gathered. The congregation also battled many of the storms common to small churches—shrinking attendance, limited resources, the same volunteers doing everything and getting worn out. Both individually and corporately, we needed to experience Jesus in the boat with us. We needed someone to rouse Jesus from sleep. We needed God-given moments of calm in the midst of the storms and confidence that Christ would bring us safely to shore. We needed to be reminded of baptism so that we recalled and trusted in God's baptismal promise when we were surrounded by life's storms. In short, we needed to make worship a place where we actively remember our baptism.

Our first opportunity to really remember our baptism presented itself when two members of the congregation—a couple—requested that their granddaughter be baptized at our church when their children brought the baby home for a visit at Christmas. I explained to the couple that baptism is a congregational event as well as a family celebration; God's people surround those being baptized and commit to care for them in their life of faith. The baptism would be part of a worship service and not something private. Also, since the parents and child did not live in our community, we would find ways to baptize the baby in partnership with the church she and her parents attended. That pastor offered to provide instruction prior to the baptism. The child and her parents were also remembered in prayer during that congregation's worship.

The people of St. Timothy's Church were so excited about a baptism that we decided to have it on Christmas Eve. The first thing we needed to do to get ready for the baptism was to find our baptismal font. It wasn't actually lost. Rather, our baptismal font had fallen into a state of disuse. It was tucked away in a corner of the chancel, the part of the church near the altar, like a revered relic we used once upon a time rather than a focal point of our worship space. We moved the font halfway down the center aisle so that everyone could turn and have a good view of the baptism and to suggest that God surrounds the child being baptized with the love and support of the Christian community. After Christmas, when we were taking down the tree and decorations and putting things away, I asked that we not return the baptismal font to its place in the corner of the chancel. Instead, we placed our baptismal font in the back of the church near the center aisle, so that everyone passed it as they entered worship. I then explained in a sermon that passing the font as we enter worship is one way we actively remember that we entered Christ's family, that Christ made us members of his church, when we passed through the waters of baptism.

The best way to actively remember baptism in worship is with a baptism. A long time had passed since the congregation celebrated one. The details of the service that Christmas Eve were soon forgotten; its impact on St. Timothy's Church was not. Standing at the baptismal font with that baby girl, her parents, and grandparents, the congregation experienced God acting in its midst. God was passing on the faith and extending the church to another generation. Once again, God promised forgiveness and new life. Preaching helped make God's activity explicit. "As Jesus shared our humanity in the manger, so we share the very life of Christ in the font," I said to the congregation. When it came time to sing "Silent Night," we lit our candles from the paschal candle, the tall candle often placed near the baptismal font as a reminder of our dying and rising with Christ. Some might say we were confusing Christmas and Easter. Perhaps we were. We were also finding ways for everyone to participate in this baptism as a way of remembering his or her own.

When Easter rolled around and we didn't have a baptism to celebrate, we decided to remember our own. One historic way to remember baptism is to recommit to the promises made at baptism by rejecting sin, the devil, and all those forces opposed to God and to confess the Apostles' Creed. Often, as the congregation confesses the creed, the pastor dips an evergreen branch into the baptismal font and sprinkles the congregation with water. That was a bit much for the people of St. Timothy's Church. Besides, the bowl in our baptismal font was so small that little more than the tip of an evergreen branch would fit in it. Instead, we agreed that after we said the creed together, I would invite the members of the congregation to come to the font. When they came, I would dip a thumb into the baptismal water, mark a cross on each person's forehead, and say, "Remember that you are baptized, and share the life of the risen Christ." As we sang an Easter hymn, the people formed a line down the center aisle to the baptismal font. They came to the water.

On the Sundays following Easter, I chose to preach on baptism as our participation in Christ's death and resurrection. "Do you not know that all of us who have been baptized into Christ Jesus were baptized into his death?" the apostle Paul asks. "Therefore we have been buried with him by baptism into death, so that, just as Christ was raised from the dead by the glory of the Father, so we too might walk in newness of life. For if we have been united with him in a death like his, we will certainly be united with him in a resurrection like his" (Rom. 6:3–5). During one sermon, I walked down the aisle to the baptismal font, pulled the small metal bowl out of its stand, held it up for the congregation to see, and declared, "Sometimes we have trouble realizing how big and important our baptism is because the way we celebrate baptism is so small." Soon after I preached that sermon, the pitcher and basin we used on Maundy Thursday started appearing in church on those rare Sundays we had a baptism and on other Sundays when we wanted to remember baptism. We set the basin on top of the baptismal font and poured water into it from the pitcher. Compared to the tiny bowl, baptism became big, dramatic, and something worth remembering.

In another sermon, I invited the members of St. Timothy's Church to make the sign of the cross as a way of remembering baptism, and a few of the members tried it. I never convinced the congregation to take the cover off the font and keep the little metal bowl filled with water so that members could dip their fingers in and make the sign of the cross as they entered and left worship. Yet, when we found ourselves in a storm that threatened the life of our church, we remembered that we were baptized. Remembering that Jesus was in the boat with us freed and empowered the people of St. Timothy's Church to listen for Jesus's powerful word and to dare to share his death and resurrection.[3]

As for dipping a finger in the baptismal water and signing one's forehead with a cross, I now do it almost every day. The baptismal font that we moved from the corner of the chancel to the entrance of St. Timothy's Church has a big sister in the seminary where I teach. Water flows like a fountain from a stone font to a pool in the floor. While the seminary may not be a baptizing community, it is a community that needs to remember baptism. I spend a moment at that font every day as I enter and leave worship, and I am impressed by how many others do as well. We do not teach people to do this; the baptismal space does.

As we remember baptism in worship, as God reminds us of baptism in places where we experience the power of God stilling the storm, God assures us that we are never far from the water, which speaks to us of drowning and new birth, of healing and vocation, of a loving family and a generous God, of death and new life. In the water of baptism Jesus quiets the fiercest storm of our lives—the thunder of evil, the cyclone of death. Jesus also promises that no matter what other storms surround us, Jesus will be in the boat with us. Jesus will speak a powerful word that stills the storm and brings us safely to new life.

For Reflection and Conversation

- Where have you experienced Jesus calming the storms that surround your life? What Bible story involving water best reflects your experience?
- How do you remember baptism? How does your congregation remember baptism? What does baptism mean to you?
- How has remembering baptism calmed storms in your life and in the life of your congregation and community? How has God's presence in a storm helped you remember baptism?

Chapter 3

Welcome Kids

"At that same hour Jesus rejoiced in the Holy Spirit and said, 'I thank you, Father, Lord of heaven and earth, because you have hidden these things from the wise and the intelligent and have revealed them to infants; yes, Father, for such was your gracious will'" (Luke 10:21). Hiding the things of God from the wise and intelligent and revealing them to infants continues to be God's will and God's way. Or at least that seems to be something God regularly does in worship. Of course, the wise and intelligent frequently fail to notice what God is doing and to learn from it. Instead, they—we—often assume that the wise and intelligent understand what God is doing and not only must teach infants and children, but also make certain that they properly understand before they are permitted to fully participate in worship.

That is certainly standard operating procedure in many congregations when it comes to kids in worship. I once led the weekly worship service at a Christian school. "The peace of Christ be with you always," I declared, smiling broadly and extending my arms. "And also with you," the kids mumbled in response, arms at their sides and eyes downcast. "Let's try it again," I said. "The peace of Christ be with you always," I said again, this time a bit more exuberantly. The kids' response was about the same. "Come on!" I said, "This is great news! This is Easter joy! The peace of Christ be with you always!" "And also with you!" the student body shouted in response, looking up at me. "Now!" I exclaimed, heading down the center aisle and shaking children's hands, "turn to your neighbor and come out of your pews and greet one another with a sign of Christ's peace." Things were great for about two minutes. Then I heard the school principal following me down the aisle; she was shushing students and shooing them back into their places. "That's *not* how we behave in church," she scolded the children and sneered at me.

The wise and intelligent are usually subtler than that principal. Congregations have many strategies for removing children from worship until they are deemed ready to participate. I grew up in a congregation where worship and Christian education ran simultaneously; parents went to church and kids went to Sunday school. In other congregations, kids are in worship through the children's sermon, and then march off behind a youth minister or volunteer "to do something fun and exciting." Some congregations provide professionally staffed childcare centers and pagers for parents. In many congregations, tensions flare and people stare whenever a child behaves unexpectedly in worship; if the child misbehaves too often, someone reminds the parents that a cry room is available.

So imagine what happens in some congregations when children come to the communion rail and extend their hands, fully expecting to receive the Lord's Supper. For centuries, Christian traditions, particularly those that consider Holy Communion a sacrament, said that we need to know and do some things before we are ready to receive the Lord's Supper. We need to diligently examine ourselves, humbly confess our sins, and genuinely hunger and thirst after righteousness. We need to receive the Lord's Supper in remembrance of Christ and give Christ thanks and praise for his saving death and resurrection. We are to love one another as Christ has loved us and willingly take up our cross and follow.

Paul's warning regarding the Lord's Supper in 1 Corinthians has been of particular concern to the church. Paul cautions the Corinthian church not to receive communion "without discerning the body," so that they do not "eat and drink judgment against themselves" (1 Cor. 11:29). Over the centuries, the church took the phrase "discerning the body" to mean properly comprehending the doctrine of Christ's presence in the Lord's Supper. The church determined the age at which children can understand the church's teaching. When children reach this age, they take first communion classes, are properly indoctrinated in the meaning of the Lord's Supper, and can then receive communion. Younger children and infants, and in some places those deemed not to be intelligent enough to understand the church's teachings, receive a blessing. My own Lutheran tradition baptizes infants and professes that in baptism God joins us to Christ's death and resurrection and makes us full members of Christ's body—the church. Yet, rather than welcoming these full members of Christ's body to the communion table, Lutheran pastors have compared receiving the Lord's Supper to voting; while we receive the right to share in the Lord's Supper at baptism, we do not exercise this right until we are old enough to understand.

Kids at the Lord's Table

For years, I knew exactly what to do when kids came to the communion rail, particularly when I was a visiting pastor and did not know the children. Unless I was told otherwise, I blessed rather than gave communion to younger children and infants. Most kids are cooperative, even very helpful. They extend their hands to receive the bread and fold their arms to receive a blessing. Other kids leave the pastor to guess. They enjoy playing a game with the visiting pastor, as if the pastor is a substitute teacher in school; they extend their hands even though they know they are not allowed to receive communion, just to see if they can get away with it. A word or gesture from a parent prevents the pastor from making a mistake. The "problem" comes from baptized children who take seriously what the church teaches them: they are beloved children of God and members of Christ's body—the church. Even though the church says they are not old enough or ready to receive the Lord's Supper, these children of God know they are. Everyone else knows it, too. You can see it in these kids' hopeful expressions when they come to the communion rail; you can sense it in their disappointed spirits when they receive a blessing rather than the Lord's Supper.

I encountered one of those kids in a congregation where I was a visiting pastor. This little girl, about four years old, extended her hands reverently and, without thinking, I gave her the bread, saying, "The body of Christ given for you." The little girl's mother shook her head no sadly. The communion assistant, a stern looking man who I knew to be a member of the congregational council, came alongside me and whispered loudly, "She is too young. Take it back." And in that instant, I made one of the biggest mistakes of my ministry: I removed the bread, the body of Christ, from that little girl's hand. She began to cry and pulled her head away as I extended my hand to bless her. Then she began to scream as her mother physically removed her from the altar rail. "I want Jesus! I want Jesus!"

In another congregation, a little boy wanted communion but knew he was too young to receive it. The boy's big brother knew it, too. When they came to the communion rail with their parents, the little boy dutifully folded his arms and received a blessing. Then, when I went to break the bread for his big brother, the older boy whispered, "Make it a big piece." I was intrigued and dutifully broke off a large piece of bread and placed it in his hand. Taking the piece of bread in both hands, the older boy tore it in two and gave half to his little brother, saying, "The body of Christ, given for you." Then the brothers ate the bread. Looking back at me, the older boy explained matter-of-factly, "My brother needs Jesus, too."

At Epiphany Church, a girl in second grade—let's call her Katie—and her mother made an appointment to see me. Katie had a question her mother couldn't answer. "Why do I have to wait until I am in sixth grade before I can receive Holy Communion?" In keeping with the congregation's policy, I explained to Katie that we need to understand and believe certain things before we can receive communion. I then asked Katie why she wanted to receive communion and what she knew about it. After listening to her talk about Jesus being in the bread and wine to forgive her sins and make her part of his family, I couldn't come up with a satisfactory reason why Katie had to wait, either. My conversation with Katie and her mother occurred before my denomination approved permitting infants and younger children who are baptized to commune. In fact, children like the ones I am telling you about and conversations like the one I had with Katie motivated my denomination to change its policy. But at that time, sixth grade was the accepted practice, and there wasn't much room for pastoral discretion. So I asked the church council if we could lower the communion age, at least for this one child. The council was not comfortable doing it. For some members, children communing before they were confirmed still didn't seem right. Others were uncomfortable with one so young drinking wine. Still others were afraid of making an exception for one child or breaking the rules and getting in trouble. I told Katie that she would have to wait until sixth grade to receive communion and that I was sorry. By the time she reached sixth grade, Katie had lost her enthusiasm for church.

Shortly after I delivered the disappointing news to Katie, I was the guest preacher in a congregation where kids were asking for communion, and the church council likewise said that children need to be in sixth grade before they could receive it. Children in that congregation wanted to know why. As I had done, the pastor had talked with the kids about the Lord's Supper and could not find a satisfactory reason why they shouldn't receive communion. I asked the pastor how he was handling the situation, and he told me that I would see.

During the worship service, when the time came for the children's sermon, the pastor called the kids forward and produced a plate with a dinner roll on it and a cup full of grapes. "I want to tell you a story about Jesus," the pastor began, "about what Jesus did on the night before he died on the cross." Lifting the dinner roll, he said, "On the night when he was betrayed, Jesus took a loaf of bread, and when he had given thanks, he broke it and gave it to his disciples, saying, 'This is my body given for you. Do this in remembrance of me.'" Lifting the cup of grapes, the pastor explained that Jesus had a cup of wine at the Last Supper and that wine comes from grapes. Then he continued, "In the same way he took the cup, gave thanks, and gave it for all to drink, saying, 'This cup is the new covenant in my blood, shed for you and for all people for the forgiveness of sins. Do this in remembrance of me.' We remember Jesus when we celebrate communion in church, and that Jesus gave his life for us because he loves us." Then the children extended their hands, as if they had done this before, and the pastor broke off a piece of the dinner roll and gave it to each child, and after that a grape, saying, "The body of Christ, given for you. The blood of Christ, shed for you."

After worship, I said to the pastor, "You gave the kids communion." "Did I?" he asked, smiling a knowing smile. "I told them a story about Jesus. In this congregation, children are not permitted to commune until the sixth grade, and communion is wafers and little glasses of wine. So I tell them the story of the Last Supper and give them bread and grapes." "How often?" I asked. "Once a month," the pastor answered, "and everyone thinks it's great."

What Do We Need to Know?

Like many other parents, pastors, and teachers, I have studied the arguments for and against communing baptized children and infants—the need for worthy reception, discerning Christ's body, knowing ourselves to be sinners, believing in the real presence, responding with thankful hearts and faithful lives. I learned that when Paul warns the Corinthians not to receive communion "without discerning the body" so that they do not "eat and drink judgment against themselves" (1 Cor. 11:29), Paul meant that people are not to eat and drink the Lord's Supper without love for the Christian community, the body of Christ of which all who commune are part. Paul was not at all concerned with properly understanding a doctrine. When people argue that children must nevertheless comprehend Christ's presence in the Supper before they can receive it, I often muse about how many adults who regularly receive the Lord's Supper understand the difference between "transubstantiation" and "consubstantiation" and could say whether they believe either doctrine.

I share the legitimate concern that if we do not have proper appreciation, understanding, and awe, and necessary, serious self-examination, we might trivialize the Lord's Supper or reduce it to some sort of magic. I wholeheartedly agree that children need to make a free and voluntary decision regarding church membership and participation in Holy Communion. I want children to approach the Lord's Table with an awareness of sin and the genuine desire for forgiveness and amendment of life. I consider this eucharistic piety or spirituality a lifelong process and hope children

will respond to the Lord's Supper *in ways appropriate for their age
and spiritual awareness.* Increasingly, I wonder whether the church
holds children to standards many adults do not meet, rather than
instructing children in the faith according to their capabilities at
each stage of their development. Experts in psychology and education widely assert that children's attitudes and feelings are created
and formed through experience and by reflecting on experience.
Instruction teaches them to understand. If the church's goal is that
children love God and value the Lord's Supper, and not merely understand its meaning, then the church needs to reconsider the assumption that children must be fully prepared intellectually before
they receive Holy Communion.

More to the point, if in baptism Christ joins us to his death and
resurrection and makes us members of his body—the church—
before we can understand, what more do we need to be welcome
at Christ's Table? Of course, using baptism as the criterion for
receiving communion makes the Lord's Supper about what God
has done and is doing, rather than about what children—and we—
must know and do. Experiencing the church at worship as the
continuation of God's saving activity and a sign and foretaste of
God's kingdom, which we are told is promised to all, leads many
children, parents, and congregations to feel uneasy about exclud-
ing baptized children—and, in fact, all people—as God gathers
people together to witness to and participate in God's work in the
world through sharing in the Lord's Supper. For these Christians
and congregations, welcoming baptized children to the Lord's Table better reflects God's determination to gather people from all
cultures, races, classes, and ages. Since the community that God
wills is inclusive, and by its very nature transcends human barriers,
these Christians argue that when baptized children do not receive
the Lord's Supper, worship emphasizes exclusion rather than God
gathering God's people. This is especially true when communion is
celebrated frequently and families worship together.

If loosening the requirements for receiving the Lord's Supper
might trivialize it, I wonder whether not admitting baptized children to the Lord's Table until they are of an age at which the church
considers them able to fulfill certain conditions gives greater importance to what people must know and do than to what God is

doing. Congregations that stress worship as the participation of all the people gathered together rightly press for ways children can participate in the service. They argue that rather than creating and adding things to the worship service especially for children, the church does better to welcome children into the heart of its worship.

In 1997 the Evangelical Lutheran Church in America (ELCA), the church of which I am a pastor, joined a growing ecumenical movement to welcome baptized children at the Lord's Table and approved a statement on sacramental practices, which asserts that "admission to the Sacrament is by invitation of the Lord, presented through the Church to those who are baptized."[1] According to this statement, receiving the Lord's Supper is the birthright of all who are baptized. If children are baptized, they receive communion. Unfortunately, the church's instructions are not that straightforward. Like all Christian denominations, the Evangelical Lutheran Church in America weighs historical and pastoral considerations along with its theology when determining practice. So, the statement continues: "Customs vary on the age and circumstances for admission to the Lord's Supper. . . . Baptized children begin to commune on a regular basis at a time determined through mutual conversation that includes the pastor, the child, and the parents or sponsors involved, within the accepted practices of the congregation. Ordinarily this beginning will occur only when children can eat and drink, and can start to respond to the gift of Christ in the Supper."[2] In determining their "accepted practices," different congregations weigh historical, pastoral, and theological considerations, including the church's statements, differently.

In some congregations, baptized children now commune at a very young age. Other congregations continue the practice of welcoming children to the Lord's Supper when they are in fifth or sixth grade, after a period of instruction. In still other congregations, children do not commune until after they are confirmed. But things are even more complicated. In congregations that commune children at a very young age, parents may decide that their children should wait; in congregations that do not permit children to commune until after they are confirmed, parents may decide that their children should start communing earlier, particularly if they were previously members of congregations in which their children could receive communion. Out of mutual respect among congregations of the church, these children are often received as communing members, sometimes as an exception to the congregation's general policy.

I found myself negotiating the chaos the statement created as I led worship in different congregations as a visiting pastor. In time, I came to see all this chaos as a sure sign that the Holy Spirit works through children who come to the communion rail to change the heart and mind of the church so that baptized children can receive communion earlier, even at the worship service at which they are baptized. I began to explain to the congregation where I preached that the Holy Spirit might be working through children. My practice also changed when children came to the communion rail. Rather than blessing younger children and infants, I gave them communion, unless someone told me not to. When I was told that children do not receive communion, I blessed them. Once I became convinced that I knew what God was doing in worship, I unknowingly became one of the wise and intelligent from whom God hides things.

The Lord's Supper Is God's Wisdom

A few years ago, I spent several months preaching in a congregation that held that children need to *know* some things before they are ready to receive the Lord's Supper. As a visiting pastor, I respected and did my best to abide by the congregation's policy. Children like Katie and the two brothers I told you about were present in the congregation and, more than ever, when they came to the communion rail, it saddened me not to give them the Lord's Supper; blessing them felt like a consolation prize. Then one week as I prepared my sermon, the voice of God's wisdom, speaking in the appointed Old Testament reading from Proverbs, caught my ear. "'You that are simple, turn in here!' To those without sense she says, 'Come, eat of my bread and drink of the wine I have mixed'" (Prov. 9:4). According to Proverbs, laying aside immaturity, living, and walking in the way of insight—the things the church required before children can share in Christ's Supper—seem to *result* from eating the bread of God's wisdom.

As it happened, I once again found myself in the lectionary year when the Gospel readings are taken from Jesus's discourse on the Bread of Life (John 6). As I prayed over and studied these passages alongside the reading from Proverbs, I noticed that Jesus did not give the crowd in the wilderness a four-Sunday discourse on the Bread of Life (as congregations that follow the lectionary receive) until *after* they have eaten their fill of the loaves and fishes. Jesus did not make the five thousand sit on the grass and give them a lecture so that they understood before he "took the loaves, and when he had given thanks, he distributed them to those who were seated; so also the fish, as much as they wanted" (John 6:11).

I began to think about all the Bible stories in which God feeds someone. In Scripture, God always provides food to accomplish something greater than satisfying physical hunger, and people never know what that something is until *after* they have eaten. Jesus multiplied loaves in the wilderness as a sign of God's abundant love. God provided manna in the wilderness as a sign of God's faithfulness. The angel of the Lord served Elijah bread in the wilderness to provide God's strength for the prophet's journey. Jesus, the bread that came down from heaven, the incarnate Word who entered the world, God-made-flesh who joined us in the wilderness of human existence, even the wilderness of death on a cross, gives us his body and blood in the bread and wine of the Lord's Supper to forgive our sins and assure us that our lives and God's gifts are eternal.

With the words from Proverbs pounding in my ears, I recalled these Bible stories for the congregation when I preached that Sunday. Then I asked, "Since the voice of God's wisdom bids us to eat her bread and drink her wine in order to become wise, couldn't Jesus, the Bread of Life on which we feast, also be God's wisdom for us when we are lost in our foolishness?" I reminded the congregation of our Lutheran teaching that in, with, and under the bread and wine of Holy Communion, which we believe is nothing other than Christ's body and blood, God does many things. Jesus nourishes faith, forgives sin, and calls us to be witnesses to the gospel. Then I wondered aloud, "Couldn't Jesus also give us God's wisdom, which surpasses our knowledge?" Then I recalled the children I told you about earlier. Katie, the two brothers, and the little girl who screamed she wanted Jesus knew that they were ready to receive Holy Communion, even though the church said they were not. I said that we all know children, in this congregation, who are just like those kids. Then I suggested that in the Lord's Supper God gives our children the knowledge and wisdom they need to receive the Lord's Supper. The point seemed obvious; Jesus welcomes children at his table. After worship, a young mother reminded us that when people were bringing little children to Jesus so that he might touch them, and the disciples sternly ordered them not to do it and Jesus saw this, he was indignant and said to them, "Let the little children come to me; do not stop them; for it is to such as these that the kingdom of God belongs" (Mark 10:13–14). She added, "I've never understood why the church keeps them away."

Children Are Our Teachers

Though *I* was convinced that God was working through children to change communion practices, God had something more in mind, at least in that congregation. God was using children to redefine who was wise and intelligent, both in the church and in the world. The sermon did not lead the congregation to immediately lower the age at which baptized children could receive communion. Instead, the young mother's comment after worship sparked conversation among members who previously attended, or who had friends and relatives that attended, congregations where infants and young children commune. They shared how much infants and young children *taught them* about the meaning of the Lord's Supper.

In the New Testament, Jesus does more than command that disciples must not hinder children from coming to him. Jesus makes children a model for adults. Jesus makes children our teachers. Jesus set a child in the midst of the people as an example (Matt. 18:2–5; Mark 9:36–37; Luke 9:46–47). Jesus teaches that unless we turn and become like children, we will not enter the kingdom of heaven (Mark 10:15; Luke 18:17). Jesus asks adults to become more like children, which means we who are wise and intelligent need to learn from them. Learning from children requires humility, willingness to watch and listen, honest and undogmatic openness, and perseverance. When adults are willing to learn, children free them to enjoy and grow from new experiences and gain new insights.

In one congregation, a mother told me that when she carries her infant daughter to the communion rail, she is aware that her baby is completely helpless and dependent on her. Looking down at her daughter, the mother smiles. "That's how we all are when we come to communion," she muses, "totally helpless and dependent on God." Then she laughs, recalling the night before, when her baby went from fussy to demanding and no one in the house slept much. "Sometimes she thinks she's the center of the universe," the mother says. "Isn't that what it means to sin?" This infant is teaching her mother about both sin and grace.

In another congregation, certain children seemed to fill their pockets with the snacks served at the coffee fellowship following worship. They came to church every Sunday without their parents; after worship they loaded up on whatever there was to eat. "What sort of child behaves so disgracefully?" someone asked and sat the kids down and gave them a good talking-to. "What sort of child behaves so disgracefully? Hungry children," someone else answered. The congregation quietly learned that the kids were taking food home to the rest of their family. Children's selfishness and disobedience, what we call sin, are frequently open for all to see and help adults understand more of both their own behavior and the ways children's behavior reflects adult society and values. At the same time, children are also open to giving and receiving forgiveness and can teach adults what it means to be reconciled. When the pastor sought the children out and apologized that someone had scolded and embarrassed them, they readily extended their forgiveness and resumed their place in the congregation, something many adults find difficult to do. These children not only taught the congregation about forgiveness; they also helped the congregation understand that sin is more than personal conduct. Sin is the state of a society in which children come to church hungry and need to take food home to the rest of their family.

"How do you know Jesus is in the bread and wine?" I asked second-grader Katie, who wanted to know why she had to wait until sixth grade to receive communion. "Because Jesus says so," Katie giggled. "This is my body. This is my blood." And she pretended to lift the bread and the cup, as she saw me do in worship. Children's openness to and ability to reckon with the reality of the unlikely and the invisible challenge adult notions of what it means to be ready to participate in God's kingdom. As models and teachers of God's kingdom, children help adults understand what it means to be children of God. Katie reminded me that God's children don't have all the answers. God's children believe the words of Jesus and trust his promises.

When children extend their hands to receive the bread and wine without understanding what the wise and intelligent think they need to know, they teach us that God's wisdom surpasses our knowledge. They remind us that God's wisdom is not as much comprehension as it is relationship. In worship, God works through children to show us that eternal life does not come through believing the right things. Eternal life is being in close communion with Jesus. Eternal life is to remain in Jesus and to have Jesus remain in us. As children of God, we take Christ's body and blood into our mouths, into our stomachs, into our bodies so that Christ remains in us and we remain in Christ. As we eat and drink the Lord's Supper, Christ moves us closer to himself. Christ moves us closer to the very life of God, so close that we are as intimate with Jesus as the Father is with the Son. In worship, as in the Bible, Jesus uses children to teach us.

Of course, if God works in worship to transform children into models and teachers of the kingdom, we might consider what other relationships God transforms in worship, and in the world, as God hides the things of the kingdom from those considered wise and intelligent and reveals them to those considered infants. After all, Jesus said, "The last will be first, and the first will be last" (Matt. 19:30; 20:16; Mark 10:31). Jesus declares that the greatest in God's kingdom will be the servants of all and the least of all (Matt. 23:11; Luke 9:48; 22:26). Both the beatitudes (and woes) and Mary's song are even more vivid and concrete (Matt. 5:1–12; Luke 6:20–26; 1:46–55). Mary sings, "[God] has scattered the proud in the thoughts of their hearts. He has brought down the powerful from their thrones, and lifted up the lowly; he has filled the hungry with good things, and sent the rich away empty" (Luke 1:51–53).

Sometimes when I distribute the bread at the Lord's Table, I remember the child who told me that communion is like Thanksgiving dinner at Grandma's house. All are welcome, everyone has a place, and all get enough to eat. As the river of God's reconciling love flows out of the church and into the world, perhaps God is transforming the way the world distributes food and other resources so that all our tables resemble Jesus's table. More than declaring the Lord's Supper to be divine wisdom, more than making children teachers and models, perhaps God is radically transforming relationships when children come to the Lord's Table. Perhaps God will transform the world when the church's response to kids is to welcome them.

For Reflection and Conversation

- What is your congregation's practice of children taking communion? Are you comfortable with this practice? Why or why not?
- How do you experience God when you take communion? Is it more of a head or a heart-based experience?
- What does welcoming children at communion tell you about God's relationship with us? What does including children tell you about our relationship to each other? What does it say about these relationships when we don't include children?
- What other relationships might God be transforming in and through your congregation's worship?

Chapter 4

Touch and Anoint

A reporter once asked if I believe in the power of prayer. "No," I replied, "I believe in God, and so I pray."[1] As people of faith, we believe in God. We rely upon God. We trust God, and so we pray. It is just what we do. We come to worship to pray. We often come to worship because we need to pray. Jesus knows our need for prayer. "Then Jesus told them a parable about their need to pray always and not to lose heart. He said, 'In a certain city there was a judge who neither feared God nor had respect for people. In that city there was a widow who kept coming to him and saying, "Grant me justice against my opponent"'" (Luke 18:1–3).

I cannot hear Jesus's parable of the widow and the unjust judge without thinking of Sandy. Not a widow, Sandy was a wife and a mother and a grandmother, a maker of stained glass, and a collector of cows. Sandy accompanied me on my hospital visits; we usually stopped along the way for chilidogs. One afternoon Sandy called to say that she couldn't drive me that day. She had a sore throat and had lost her voice. Weeks later she wasn't much better. Sandy went to the doctor to have her throat looked at, then to the hospital. The CT scan revealed cancer in Sandy's vocal cords and lungs, and probably in her brain. The doctors said there wasn't much they could do.

When I walked into her hospital room, Sandy greeted me with, "Well, Pastor, what do we do now?" Sometimes I speak before I think. "We have two choices," I said. "We can give up or we can get mad." "I'm mad as hell!" Sandy answered. "So what do we do?" I could feel Sandy, her family, and members of Epiphany Church looking at me as if I had a plan. "Pray!" I answered. What else are you going to say? "Pray!" It's what we do. And pray we did, starting right then. We made the medical staff round up some olive oil for us. We gathered around Sandy, everyone laid a hand on her, I anointed her with oil in the sign of the cross, and we prayed. We prayed for wholeness and healing. We prayed that the cancer would be driven from her body. The doctor walked in and Sandy's daughter made him lay his hand on Sandy and join us in prayer, the nurse too.

We kept praying. First, members of Epiphany Church and I went to visit Sandy every day in the hospital and then once a week at her home. In time, five or six of us gathered at the church on Thursday mornings to encircle Sandy with prayer and touch and oil. We read Scripture together, usually a healing story of Jesus. I gave a very brief homily; the message was always the same. "God's will is for our wholeness and healing." Then as Sandy sat in a chair, we stood around her. Everyone placed a hand on her head or shoulders. I would ask, "How can we help you in prayer today?" Sandy would tell us. As the pastor, I always offered a prayer; others sometimes did as well. As the final petition, I dipped a thumb into the olive oil and prayed, "O God, the giver of health and salvation: As the apostles of our Lord Jesus Christ, at his command, anointed many that were sick and healed them, send now your Holy Spirit, that Sandy, anointed with this oil"—and I marked a cross on her forehead—"may in repentance and faith be made whole; through the same Jesus Christ our Lord."[2] Then we prayed the Lord's Prayer together.

The doctors decided that they might try radiation. We touched and anointed and prayed through that. There was a possibility of chemo. We touched and anointed and prayed through that. They thought they saw remission. We kept touching and anointing and praying. "How can we help you in prayer today?" I asked each time we gathered. Sandy's prayer was always the same. Not for a miracle, she wanted more time. She demanded more time. First a few more days, then a week, then one more month, then two. Sandy told God that God owed her 'til spring and another trip to Cape Cod, then Christmas, and then Easter. Then she demanded another year, then a second, third, fourth, and fifth, asking one day at a time. Along the way Sandy and I made hospital visits again and ate chilidogs. In time I left Epiphany Church with Sandy's blessing. The group with its new pastor gathered with olive oil and kept praying. Then one morning after weekly prayers and breakfast, Sandy was feeling bad and asked to go to the hospital. The cancer had spread. Sandy kept praying, but not for more time. Her daughter told me that Sandy was ready. In those days Sandy prayed asking God how long "this" would take and demanding to know why God didn't just hurry up and get it done. Two days later Sandy died at home in her chair. Her perspective, it seems, had changed. She was a new person. We believe in God and so we pray. It's just what we do, and God does the rest.

Our Need to Pray

One of the Thursdays on which we came to church to pray with, lay our hands on, and anoint Sandy was Thanksgiving Day. Epiphany Church had a worship service on Thanksgiving morning, so we agreed to meet in the fellowship hall an hour before the service was to start. As I was putting on my robe, someone slipped into my office to tell me that rather than the usual five or six, more than thirty people, parishioners and Sandy's family and friends, were waiting in the fellowship hall. After a scripture reading and my usual declaration that God's will is for our wholeness and healing, the congregation made what looked like a football huddle around Sandy. After we laid our hands on, prayed with, and anointed Sandy, and before we prayed the Lord's Prayer, someone asked, "Are the prayers just for Sandy, or can anyone sit in that chair?" A knowing smile crossed Sandy's face as she quickly gave up her seat. As people took turns sitting in the chair and the congregation surrounded them with touch, I asked, "How can we help you with prayer today?" We learned that our need for prayer was bigger than we imagined. That morning, people coming to church on Thursdays to pray changed from something we did for Sandy to a ministry of Epiphany Church.

Like Sandy, we all know moments of illness or weakness or exhaustion or frustration when all we can do is pray. We have spent long nights like Jacob's night by the river Jabbok (Gen. 32:22–32). There Jacob wrestled with God until dawn and came away wounded with a limp. We have offered prayers like Moses must have offered when he looked over the cliff, saw only the Red Sea, and knew there was no escape (Exod. 14:10). "Where do we go from here, God?" Moses must have prayed. We have spent long nights like Jesus's night in Gethsemane. Like Jesus, we struggled to do God's will—to forgive evil, to temper our hate for those far from God's will, to release our desire for vengeance. "Father, if you are willing, remove this cup from me; yet, not my will but yours be done" (Luke 22:42). We have known that three o'clock hour, when the pain is so acute that, with Jesus, we cry with a loud voice, "Eloi, Eloi, lema sabachthani? . . . My God, my God, why have you forsaken me?" (Mark 15:34). We have all offered the prayers Paul talks about. Paul writes, "Likewise the Spirit helps us in our weakness; for we do not know how to pray as we ought, but that very Spirit intercedes with sighs too deep for words. And God, who searches the heart, knows what is the mind of the Spirit, because the Spirit intercedes for the saints according to the will of God" (Rom. 8:26–27).

In those moments, we come to our God with empty hands and broken hearts. Laden with doubts and questions, outrage and anguish, we futilely fumble as we form our words. In truth we fail at finding the words to say, at finding the words to pray. We are so numb, or so empty, or so confused that we simply cannot find the words. We just don't know what to say. We do not know how to pray as we ought. With the disciples, we ask Jesus, "Lord, teach us to pray" (Luke 11:1). Jesus does. In worship Jesus uses touch and oil to teach us to pray. The Spirit uses touch and oil to intercede for us, to help us to pray, to pray for and with us. And God does more than teach and help us to pray. When we do something as simple as lay on our hands and mark a cross of oil on forehead or hands, God hears our prayer and God responds.

More Than a Cure

I vividly remember times when I could not imagine myself laying hands on people and anointing them with oil as a gesture and expression of God's will for healing and wholeness. I once visited a congregation where the laying on of hands and prayers for healing were an integral part of worship. I attended the worship service as a student of Christian worship and not as someone seeking healing. But there I was, a person who is legally blind at a worship service intended to cure whatever ails you. Although I remained in my seat when the minister invited those who desire healing to come forward for prayer, I did not go unnoticed.

The worship service had just ended when the minister of healing approached me. He wanted to heal my eyes. He said it much the same way that someone would say, "I'd like to take you to lunch." "I want to heal your eyes." Everyone in the place had turned to watch us. The pressure was on, so I agreed. Putting his hands on my eyes, the minister of healing began to pray, "Feel the cooling power of Jesus. Feel the healing power of Jesus. You can see. You can see!" I noticed that what the minister of healing was saying was less a prayer to God and more instructions to me. When he removed his hands from my eyes, I was tempted to quote the man in Mark's Gospel who, when Jesus asked him, "Can you see?" looked up and said, "I can see people, but they look like trees, walking" (Mark 8:24). Instead, I said that I saw as I always had. The minister of healing tried to heal my eyes three times, each attempt longer and more intense, and it didn't work.

After the first attempt, the minister of healing was surprised and concerned. After the second attempt, he was frustrated. As he began to pray the third time, I realized that his reputation in the congregation was on the line. The issue was no longer healing my eyes; the issue was this minister saving face. I knew how these things typically play out, because I had been here before. The minister would declare that I lack sufficient faith to be healed and lament the fact that either I will not let go of my sin or I do not love and trust Jesus enough to allow Jesus to make me see.

As the minister prayed the third time, I quietly asked if it was possible that Jesus might intend more for me than a physical cure, since, in fact, I had not come to worship that evening seeking one. I whispered that I cherish the story in John's Gospel where Jesus tells the disciples, "Neither this man nor his parents sinned; he was born blind so that God's works might be revealed in him" (John 9:3). I told him that like Paul, who appealed to the Lord three times that his affliction would leave him, I need God's grace to be sufficient as I live with this "thorn . . . in the flesh" (2 Cor. 12:7). The minister of healing kept praying as he listened closely. Shortly after I finished whispering, the minister of healing stopped praying. Looking up at the congregation, he declared, "God, in his infinite wisdom, has determined to heal this man inwardly." The congregation was elated. A healing had occurred.

I couldn't disagree. Though I was not cured, the Spirit was certainly working in that prayer and conversation. Jesus said, "Do not worry about how you are to speak or what you are to say; for what you are to say will be given to you at that time; for it is not you who speak, but the Spirit of your Father speaking through you" (Matt. 10:19–20). I found Jesus's assurance to be genuine as the Spirit gave me the words that diffused what could have been a tense and embarrassing situation, both for me and for the minister of healing. I could have been called a sinner; the minister of healing might have been labeled a failure, even a fraud. The Spirit provided a way forward in which neither of us was embarrassed or shamed.

The tension and embarrassment I so wanted to avoid that day had nothing to do with prayer that includes touch and anointing. People are embarrassed in worship when a minister singles them out and a congregation scrutinizes them, rather than allowing people to choose whether or not to participate. Tension occurs when the church assumes or decides what people need, rather than asking them. When Bartimaeus son of Timaeus, who was blind, came to Jesus, Jesus asked him, "What do you want me to do for you?" (Mark 10:51). Prayer is misguided when the needs of the one who is praying take precedence over the one being prayed for. Like so many things in worship, prayer that includes touch and anointing can be done in ways that invite and expect God to act, and in ways that attempt to manipulate God and make God's people passive participants or even props in what worship leaders determine to do.

Curing disease through prayerful touch and anointing with oil is surely within God's power. That is, God can certainly use touch and anointing as doctors use procedures and medications—to treat a perceived change in a biological or mechanical function of the body, to relieve pain, and to return functioning. Yet, I am not convinced that curing disease is the sole or even the most important thing God does when Christians lovingly lay their hands on brothers or sisters, anoint them with oil in the name of Christ, and pray for the needs of people's hearts and lives, as well as their bodies.

Jesus's ministry certainly included healing. In fact, roughly one-fourth of the Gospels deal in some way with Christ's healing activity. People came from all over to be cured of their sufferings, and Jesus healed them.[3] There was no sickness or weakness that Jesus could not master. Yet, Jesus's healing was not an end in itself. Along with preaching and teaching, his mission was to proclaim the nearness of the reign of God. Jesus stated specifically that his healing was a sign of the in-breaking of the kingdom or reign of heaven (Matt. 11:1–6). Jesus was firmly convinced that his Father's purpose for humanity, and all creation, is wholeness and salvation. Jesus understood sickness as a destructive and evil force. He never once supported the Old Testament concept of disease as sent by God. Instead, Jesus disavowed entirely both the idea that sickness is divine punishment and the belief that the sufferer ought to remain ill in order to acquire courage or learn patience. Jesus was opposed to sickness, because it was not an established part of the divine order, but caused needless suffering, and so Jesus stopped it.

Jesus was interested in much more than providing a physical cure. While Jesus was always concerned to heal the sick in body, he invariably paid close attention to the mind and spirit of the sufferer. When Jesus talked with people who were sick, he tried to uncover a deficiency in the relationship between the sufferer and his or her environment. In this way, Jesus always sought to heal persons, not conditions. More than simply curing disease, Jesus healed so that the power of God might break through into the lives of people, that they might know God's love and be made whole. Then Jesus set about teaching them.

If the healing ministry of Jesus is an indication of God's activity, God wants to do more than to cure. God desires to create or restore a state in which body, mind, and spirit are united in wholeness and well-being for the individual, which extends beyond the individual to his or her relationship with the environment, community, world, and, ultimately, with God. Such a state of unity, balance, and harmony of personality and relationship is holy, because it is God's will and God's gift. This state of health was intended by God in creation, lost in the fall, made possible in the cross of Jesus Christ, and is finally to be accomplished in the resurrection. This state of health is what Scripture means by *salvation*. Rather than sending sickness as punishment, rather than being content with a physical cure, God wills and intends that we live in a state of wholeness.

As followers of Jesus, we pray, touch, and anoint in obedience to Jesus's command, following Jesus's example, and as an extension of his own ministry. As Jesus used a threefold ministry to announce the coming of the kingdom of God, so the church preaches, teaches, and heals to proclaim the power of the gospel to all creation. Since prayerful touch and anointing is part of the church's greater mission of proclaiming the good news of God's love in Christ, it may not always involve curing. More important than the relief of pain or the return of functioning, which the medical profession can often provide, is a right relationship with God. By asking people their needs, the church looks beyond the symptoms of the disease to the meaning of the illness in the sufferer's person and relationships. This form of healing is neither alternative medicine nor a desperate attempt at a cure. Prayer in the name of Jesus, which includes touch and anointing, serves as a tangible sign of God's will for wholeness and healing and power to bring life, as well as God's unconditional love and never-ending presence.

God Brings Wholeness through Touch and Anointing

Thursday healing prayers at Epiphany Church never turned into a revival or a rally. During my tenure as pastor, attendance never again matched the thirty who came that Thanksgiving Day. A core group attended every Thursday to pray and be prayed for; others from the congregation and community came and went, depending on their needs. "How can we help you in prayer today?" we asked everyone who sat in the center chair. They all had their own answers. Sandy's was, "More time." Sandy wanted more time to do things she needed to do and come to the wholeness God intended for her. After describing their physical symptoms, others asked for forgiveness, for help letting go of their anger, for strength, for the lessening of pain or the ability to manage it while they did something they wanted or needed to do, and to feel God's presence. No one ever asked for a miracle. I don't recall anyone asking for only a physical cure. We prayed, touched, and anointed, and word of what we were doing spread.

One afternoon the church office received a telephone call from our community's AIDS clinic. They had heard about our "healing prayers," and the woman on the phone wondered if the congregation would sponsor an evening healing service, with touch and anointing, for people who are HIV-positive. In those days, before much research and public education about HIV or AIDS had been done, church members were panicked over becoming infected by drinking from the same communion cup or exchanging the peace in worship with someone they didn't know. People with AIDS were also stereotyped and stigmatized as somehow deserving the disease. Sponsoring this service would be a major, even controversial, step for the people of Epiphany Church; holding the service without the congregation's support could have a negative impact on those who attended. I told the caller that I would present the request to the church council.

The church council raised many crucial issues. They named the fear that this service would cause some of our members and the unspoken belief among some people that AIDS is divine punishment for immoral behavior. Most interesting to me, some members asked what purpose prayers with touch and anointing might serve people who have a condition that is incurable. Were we offering false hope? They weren't sure we should have the service. Others said that the church is "a house of prayer for all peoples" (Isa. 56:7) and that if people want to come to our church to pray, we should welcome them. In what I later realized was a masterful compromise, the church council decided that Epiphany Church would host the service but not sponsor it. Members of the congregation were welcome but not obligated to attend.

On the evening of the service, a group of patients and staff from the AIDS clinic came to Epiphany Church, along with some members of the congregation. We sang hymns, said a litany, and read Scripture. I preached a sermon about God's unconditional love for all people and God's will for wholeness and salvation. We prayed for those who suffer, for recovery from sickness, for those in affliction, for those who minister in healing, for the ministry of family and friends, and for those making decisions. Then I invited people to come forward and kneel at the communion rail for personal prayer with touch and anointing. When they came, I asked them their name and how we could help them in prayer. As they knelt before me, I laid my hands on their heads and prayed for them. Then I marked a cross on their forehead in the name of the triune God. Most brought people with them to the communion rail, some of whom were staff members from the AIDS clinic, who laid their hands on them as well. Several embraced me when they stood at the conclusion of the prayer. When all who desired had come forward, we said the Lord's Prayer, sang a final hymn, and I offered a blessing.

A few days later, the director of the clinic called to thank Epiphany Church for the worship service and to say how much it meant to those who attended. She explained that one of the people we prayed for that night had died. She told me how much it meant to him to hear that God loves him, for the church to pray for him, and especially for the church to touch him. She said that he died peacefully and that God's healing power was certainly at work in the service. No one was cured. But God brought at least one to peace and a greater sense of wholeness.

Sometimes God uses prayer with touch and anointing to release us from anger that is consuming us. I once preached and led worship in a congregation on the Sunday after the funerals of two members who had been brutally and violently murdered. The appointed scripture passages included Romans 8:28: "We know that all things work together for good for those who love God, who are called according to his purpose." No one saw any good that morning. I preached that Paul does not mean that God wills and wants everything that happens. God most certainly does not. Paul does not mean that everything happens for a reason. Some things that happen are simply unreasonable and wrong. But God, who in Christ brings speech out of silence, light out of darkness, hope out of despair, and life out of death, brings good out of every evil, even the evil that this congregation faced in recent days. I went on to say that when evil and death have such a hold on us that we cannot speak, or hear, or understand, we need to find another way to let God get under our skin and into our hearts so that God can touch us with new life.

"On this Sunday," I continued, "when words escape us and simply do not suffice, we need to find a way to cry out to God. Might we permit the Spirit to intercede for us through the church's way of praying with touch and oil? In just a few moments, I'll invite you to come forward and to kneel before our God. A minister of Christ, acting as Christ's representative, will be here to meet you. You can tell that pastor your name, and you are free to tell that pastor anything else you want. The pastor will lay hands on your head and silently pray for you. Then, dipping a thumb in the oil, an agent of healing that dates back to antiquity, the pastor will mark Christ's cross on your forehead, as was done at your baptism. There is no magic here, no hocus-pocus, no miracles on tap. There is Christ's presence and power and will for our wholeness and healing. For Jesus wants to touch us when we are frail and feeble. Jesus wants to heal our hurt, to rekindle our hope, to strengthen us to live on, and to bring us to new life. On this Sunday when words fail us, we offer our empty hands and some simple oil. And the Spirit intercedes for us, commending us to God's care."

The people came forward, and you could see the change in their faces. Through prayer with touch and oil, God heard their unspoken shock, lament, and outrage. God healed them of their hurt. God healed them of their hate. God filled their emptiness and gave them hope. God strengthened them to get through the day and to begin another day tomorrow. In the process, anger subsided. The change was not instantaneous or miraculous or, dare I say, permanent. People would continue to experience moments of anger, bewilderment, violation, helplessness, and hate. But somehow they had experienced God in it with them, bringing good and life and wholeness.

Sometimes rather than healing individuals, God uses prayer with touch and anointing to bring wholeness to the body of Christ. I led worship in another congregation on the second Sunday after the pastor had been removed for misconduct, a charge the members of the congregation regarded as the church's overreaction to a litigious society. The previous Sunday, the visiting pastor preached on the sin of lust and, in effect, scolded the congregation as if *they* had done something wrong. I chose simply to tell the congregation that God loves them, and although their pastor is gone, God is still with them. This congregation included prayers with touch and anointing in their worship service once a month, and this happened to be the Sunday. "Only a few people come forward," the woman helping with the service told me. But when the time came for prayer, almost everyone in the room came forward. "I don't understand," my assistant whispered to me, "these people aren't sick." "But our church is ailing," someone in line whispered back. God was using prayer with touch and anointing to bring wholeness to the common life of the congregation.

I have come to regard prayer with touch and anointing as a "sacramental," something that makes explicit God's will and intention but that by no means is indispensable to God's will and action taking place. While different Christian traditions recognize a definite number of sacraments, usually two or seven, sacramentals abound in worship and life. The sign of the cross, a favorite hymn, and a stained-glass window are among the sacramentals God uses in worship. A homemade chocolate chip cookie, a card in the mail, and a sunset are among the sacramentals God might use in daily life. These things and so many more show us that God uses the ordinary stuff of this world to communicate and bless us with God's extraordinary love for us and for all creation. In the book *The Preaching Life*, which I read to my introductory preaching students every semester, author Barbara Brown Taylor says that God uses material things to reach out to us. "If, in touching or being touched by these ordinary things," Taylor writes, "we believe that we are being touched by God, then we can no longer draw a line between the secular and the sacred in our lives. Every created thing is a potential messenger sent to teach us more about our relationship with God."[4] The first and perhaps most important lesson is that in every circumstance, God is as near to us as touch and oil.

For Reflection and Conversation

- Can you think of a time when God changed you through your prayers? How did it happen?
- Describe a part of your congregation's worship where God brings wholeness and healing in a tangible way.
- Is there a "sacramental" that is particularly important or meaningful to you? What is it and what about it makes it important? Is there a story or experience connected to it?

Chapter 5

Light Candles

In many congregations, lighting candles is such an established, even central, part of the Sunday service that we might assume candle lighting has always been part of Christian worship. We light candles on altars, candles on Advent wreaths, and candles we carry into worship. Many congregations light candles on Christmas Eve. Some congregations light extra candles on Good Friday just to put them out, and then light even more candles on the night before Easter. In some congregations, couples light a candle at their wedding; in other congregations, candles are lit at baptism.

Despite all our candle lighting, we find in the Bible precious few references to lighting candles as part of worship. The description of the celebration of the Eucharist at Troas in Acts may be the only one. "On the first day of the week, when we met to break bread, . . . there were many lamps in the room upstairs where we were meeting" (Acts 20:7-8). The "many lamps" were undoubtedly necessary to provide light, since Acts tells us that Paul and his companions broke bread after midnight. Today, though churches are well illuminated by both natural and electric light, congregations continue to place great importance on lighting candles and lamps. Christians' use of candles and lamps in worship has taken on deeper spiritual significance. The particular meanings Christians and congregations place on lighting candles are often found in the way people expect candles to be lit.

"They're Not Lighting the Candles Correctly!"

The organist was playing the prelude as worshipers settled into their places. As usual, I was standing behind the choir in the narthex of Epiphany Church, waiting for the organist to begin the opening hymn and the procession to start. Mary, a short fourth grader, was at the altar lighting the candles. For the last few Sundays, some members of the congregation had complained that the service of our shorter acolytes, who had a hard time reaching the tall candles, didn't look reverent enough. Rather than imposing a height requirement on what was a small cadre of acolytes, certain members of the altar guild began covertly painting the altar candlewicks with finger polish remover. All the acolyte needed to do was place a lit taper near a wick and the candle burst into flames. That is what Mary did. Like clockwork, she reverently lit first one candle and then the other. I smiled to myself that we had solved the problem.

Just as Mary finished lighting the second candle and was stepping away from the altar, Agnes shot out of her pew and trotted up the center aisle toward me, as fast as her legs would carry her. Pushing her way past the eight members of the choir, Agnes stood before me, shaking her finger. "Pastor," she said, exasperated. "They're doing it wrong! They've been doing it wrong for weeks, and you haven't done anything about it. I want to know why not." Having just watched Mary reverently light the candles, I had no idea what Agnes was talking about, so I asked her. "Who isn't doing what right?" My question made Agnes even more animated. "The acolytes!" she exclaimed loud enough for everyone to hear. "They're lighting the gospel candle *before* the epistle candle!"

In the next few days, I learned that a former pastor's wife taught the congregation that the candle on the pulpit side of the altar is the "gospel candle," and the candle on the lectern side of the altar is the "epistle candle." In the same way the epistle reading precedes the gospel reading in the worship service, the epistle candle is lit before the gospel candle. The gospel candle is *never* to be lit before the epistle candle, which I was letting the acolytes do. I didn't learn this particular candle lighting rubric, either in my seminary education or my doctoral studies in worship. In fact, I never heard of gospel and epistle candles. I suspect that naming the candles was originally a clever mnemonic device designed to ensure that the candles were lit uniformly. Over time, lighting the candles in the proper order took on ritual, even theological, significance in the hearts and minds of some of the members of Epiphany Church. Regardless of where the rule came from, lighting the epistle candle before the gospel candle was common knowledge to Agnes and some others, who were incensed that the acolytes lit the candles incorrectly and the pastor didn't do anything to correct them. For Agnes, lighting candles at the beginning of the service is a way we come before our God, become aware of God's presence, or even ask God to be present. There is a right way—and a wrong way—to do it, and Agnes wanted to make sure we did it right.

Agnes is not alone. In another congregation, people fussed so much about how the candles were and were not being lit that my pastoral colleague and I felt as though we spent more energy in worship coaching and correcting the lighting of the candles than leading the rest of the service. "It's too slow," people said; then, "It's too fast." "They forgot to bow at the altar before lighting the candles," we heard; and, "They blew them out instead of using the taper," which the acolytes sometimes did. When Pentecost Sunday came and went, and we noticed that our acolytes' fancy turned from lighting candles to summer vacation, my pastoral colleague and I decided to give ourselves a vacation and "bench" the entire team, eliminate a formal candle-lighting ceremony from the service for the summer, and start over after Labor Day. "The ushers can light the candles before the service and put them out after," we explained. Some members of the congregation were very concerned that the service would be wrong or incomplete without lighting and extinguishing the candles and volunteered to serve as acolytes during the summer. However, we decided that giving the candles a rest for the summer might help us think about why they are so important that the way they are or are not lit can, in effect, ruin the rest of the service.

We wondered, what is missing when we don't formally light the candles at the beginning of the service and put them out at the end? The acolytes found that they missed having something to do and began to appreciate assisting in worship as a privilege. That made training them easier in the fall. The adults talked about how watching the candles being lit helped center and quiet them as they became mindful that they were in God's presence. Everyone agreed that the single handbell, which a member of the bell choir always

rang seven times after the prelude, went from a signal to stop talking to a powerful experience of the Spirit quieting and centering
the congregation and preparing it to worship. People were nevertheless glad when the acolytes resumed lighting the candles again
in the fall and were a bit more tolerant of their ministry.

When I began serving as their pastor, the people of St. Timothy's Church had already done away with acolytes altogether, in
part because children and teens did not attend worship consistently. A seventy-something-year-old man, whom I will call John, was
responsible for lighting and extinguishing the candles. Each and
every Sunday during the first verse of the first hymn, John marched
up the center aisle, a lit taper in hand. Pausing and bowing before
the altar, John then stepped forward, lit the candles, stepped back,
bowed before the altar a second time, turned, and marched down
the center aisle to take his seat in the last pew on the left. During
the last verse of the last hymn, John repeated the process to put
the candles out. When members of the congregation suggested that
encouraging children and teens to be acolytes might help members persuade their children to bring the grandchildren to worship,
John told us all the reasons why only he could properly light and
extinguish the candles.

For John, lighting and extinguishing the candles was his niche,
his ministry, his role in and service to God and the congregation,
and John wasn't going to let anyone or anything prevent him from
carrying it out. We learned this firsthand one Sunday. I was standing at the altar pronouncing the benediction, when I heard an
enormous thud and felt the church building as it shook beneath
my feet. It seems that sometime during the worship service, someone came in late and sat in the aisle seat in the last pew on the left.
As I was giving the benediction, John looked around and realized
that someone was blocking his way to the center aisle. John knew
that we were about to sing the last hymn and it was time for him to
extinguish the candles. Rather than asking the person in the pew
to allow him to pass by, John stood up, turned to face the back of
the church, put his hands on the back of his seat, and attempted to
vault over the last pew. The loud thud and shaking church resulted
when John's foot hit the back of the pew as he attempted to jump
over. Managing to land safely, John marched up the center aisle, a

taper in hand, as we stared through the last verse of the last hymn. Pausing and bowing before the altar, John stepped forward, extinguished the candles, stepped back, bowed before the altar a second time, turned, and marched down the center aisle. John had a job to do, a service to perform for God and the congregation, and nothing was going to stop him.

I once preached in a congregation that did what some members of St. Timothy's Church suggested and used the candles as a way to keep young people coming to church. "The acolyte is on his way," the congregational president told me five minutes after the service was scheduled to start, "but we might as well get started." I took my place in the chancel and we began the service. The candles on the altar were not lit and no one made any effort to light them. We had finished the first hymn and were well into the scripture reading when a young man in his late teens wandered out into the chancel from behind the altar. He was dressed in jeans, a white T-shirt, leather jacket, and sneakers. The young man went to light the first candle and the taper he was carrying went out. Looking out at the congregation, he smiled, reached into a pocket, produced a butane lighter, and lit the candles. Slipping the lighter back into his pocket, the young man sat down next to me, sliding the taper under the pew. Turning to me, he extended his hand and said, "Hey, Preach, how's it going?" No one seemed to take notice of any of this, even the man standing at the lectern reading Scripture. After worship, the congregational president told me, "Lighting the candles gets the young people to church once in a while, and the congregation is so glad when they're here."

Can the Church Enlighten Us about Candles?

For many Christians, placing candles on the altar and lighting them is an important way of entering into God's presence and even calling God's Spirit. For others, lighting candles is an important ministry of the church that needs to be cherished and respected. For still others, lighting candles is an important way of remaining connected with people on the fringes of the church's life. Yet, for more than a thousand years of Christian history, the church did not normally place candles on the altar. Instead, candles were carried in procession ahead of the bishop and his assistants or held up by an assistant standing next to the bishop at the altar as the bishop elevated the communion host. Some think these practices came from the secular culture, where the emperor and other notables were preceded by people carrying lights. The candles functioned like a spotlight, shining on what was important. In a way, the church's use of candles was provocative in that it implied that the bishop is a notable person, and that Christ, who was understood to be present in the Eucharistic host, is as important as the emperor.

The only clear teaching that the church offers on the meaning of candle lighting does not involve altar candles. Instead, the church has historically placed greatest importance on the paschal candle, a large and special candle on its own stand or candlestick. The lighting of this candle is one of the principal parts in the vigil service on the eve of Easter.[1] Congregations that celebrate an Easter Vigil often begin the service outside by gathering around a bonfire or, in the city, a charcoal grill. In preparation for this service, the congregation extinguishes all candles and lamps in the church, either as part of the stripping of the altar on Maundy Thursday or a tenebrae service on Good Friday. In the Easter Vigil service, the rekindling of the fire, the light breaking the darkness, and the lighting of the large paschal candle symbolize Christ rising in glory and triumphing over sin and death.[2]

The church makes a big deal when the paschal candle is lit at the Easter Vigil. Using a long stick or taper, the pastor lights the paschal candle from the fire while singing, "The light of Christ, rising in glory, dispel the darkness of our hearts and minds."[3] Light from the paschal candle is then passed to everyone gathered around the fire, all of whom are carrying hand candles to receive and share the light of Christ's resurrection. The congregation then follows the paschal candle, carried by a minister who repeatedly sings, "The light of Christ," into the darkened church. The paschal candle is placed in its stand, and worship leaders light the candles in the church. Standing near the paschal candle, the person who carried it into the church then sings a special chant, called the "Exultet." The music is long and laborious. The words include biblical allusions to the passover and the crossing of the Red Sea, which are presented as foreshadowing Christ's cross and resurrection, his passover from death to new life that rescues us and all creation from evil and the gloom of sin, renews in grace, and restores us and all creation to holiness. Sometimes five grains of incense are inserted into the candle during the singing, to symbolize the five wounds of Christ. The paschal candle might even be plunged into the baptismal font to suggest that in baptism we share in the light and life of Christ's resurrection.

At the first few Easter Vigils I attended, I found the candle-lighting ceremony—gathering around a fire, following the paschal candle into a darkened church, and listening to someone attempt to sing a lengthy, archaic, Christian chant—somewhat odd. One year when I was leading the service, I plunged the paschal candle into the baptismal font and a woman pulled me aside to quietly explain that what I just did has explicit sexual overtones. "I'm sure you didn't want to communicate *that*," she said. "Well," I answered, "I think that's *exactly* what the church is trying to communicate, that baptism is the womb of resurrected life." "Ooh," she said blushing. Another year, I attended an Easter Vigil where the fire and smoke set off the sprinkler system, and the fire department showed up as we shared the light of the paschal candle in the darkened church. I would have been fine with skipping the candle lighting and moving straight to the scripture readings.

Then one Easter I really listened to the person trying so hard to sing the long and difficult Exultet, and the church's ancient Easter hymn spoke to me. It says that the burning candle reflects the light of Christ's resurrection. It reminds us of the pillar of fire, which led Israel out of slavery, through the wilderness, and into the land of promise. Like the candlelight, the Exultet declares the glory of Christ's resurrection is not diminished, even when its light is divided and shared. Watching the paschal candle and its light passed and shared until every member of the congregation's hand candle was lit, I experienced what the cantor was singing. We were symbolically receiving and sharing the undiminished light of the risen Christ. In fact, Christ's light grew brighter as we shared it!

Receiving Christ's Light

So what if all candle lighting in worship—altar candles, the paschal candle, hand-held candles, even wedding candles—is about receiving the light of Christ's resurrection and, once we have received it, sharing it with others? That is certainly the message in many baptismal services, when a representative of the congregation presents people who have just been baptized—or the parents of infants and younger children who have just been baptized—with a lighted candle. Usually, the person presenting the candle reads or recites one of two Bible verses, either Jesus's declaration, "I am the light of the world," and promises that those who follow Jesus will have the light of life (John 8:12), or Jesus's teaching that in the same way we put a lamp on a stand so that it lights the whole house, so we allow the light of Christ we received at baptism to shine in our lives as a witness of God's love to others (Matt. 5:16). Both Bible verses connect the gift of baptism with receiving and sharing the light of Christ's resurrection. The promise in the first Bible verse is more about receiving the light of Christ; the encouragement in the second Bible verse, to let Christ's light shine in good works, is more about sharing the light of Christ. Receiving and sharing the light of Christ's resurrection is enhanced when, as part of the presentation, the representative of the congregation lights each candle from the paschal candle and then gives it to the newly baptized. Sharing the light of the paschal candle recalls the Easter Vigil and connects baptism and the resurrection of Christ.

I learned to appreciate lighting candles as a way of receiving and sharing the light of the risen Christ during my years at the University of Notre Dame. The campus features a grotto, which is dedicated to Our Lady of Lourdes. People come to the grotto from across campus, as well as from throughout the country and around the world, to pray and light a candle, whether for themselves, someone else, or a situation or condition in the world. At first I visited the grotto out of curiosity and because my daughter enjoyed lighting a candle. During those visits, I watched as obviously faithful people lit their candles and knelt to pray. I was initially reluctant to participate in any sort of prayerful or spiritual way; my Lutheran "baggage" made me nervous about doing anything that smacked of "works righteousness," doing something in an attempt to appease God's anger or to merit God's favor. Over time, however, lighting candles with my wife and daughter had a profound effect on me. I came to understand that, though some people may visit the grotto and light candles to influence God, many more visit the grotto and light candles to be influenced by God. Approaching the grotto and seeing rows and rows of flickering lights, especially in the evening or at night, and lighting candles myself, inspired me to think about ways God gives individual lives and the life of the world the light of Christ's resurrection, and how lighting candles at the grotto is a way of sharing the light we receive. I was drawn into the powerful reflection of the risen Christ in the candlelight, as I had been at that Easter Vigil. I understood that some came to the grotto to receive the light of the risen Christ themselves; others came to the grotto to share the light of the risen Christ with others. Throughout my years at Notre Dame, whenever I needed to feel connected to Christ's death and resurrection, or to share the power of Christ's resurrection with someone and I didn't know how to do it, I went to the grotto and lit a candle. If my experience is any indication, the ebb and flow of receiving and sharing the light of the resurrection changes with each candle we light. In the process, Christ encounters all in a way they need through the simple act of striking a flame to a wick.

Since leaving Notre Dame, I have lit candles in Lutheran cathedrals in Uppsala and Stockholm, the monastery in Germany where Martin Luther was a monk, the Duomo of Milan, and St. Peter's Basilica in Rome. In each place, as I looked upon the rows of lit candles and then lit my own, I was aware that I received and shared the light of Christ with Christians from across the ages and throughout the world. Lighting candles has become so important to me that I requested that candles be included in the prayer chapel at the seminary where I teach, and I keep oil lamps on my desk in the study where I write. When I need to receive and share the power and life of Christ's resurrection, I light a candle. My oil lamps burn as I write these words and pray that, through these pages, I might share the light of Christ's resurrection with you who read them. One Sunday, when the preacher harangued other Christians for clinging to their candles and boasted about us Lutherans who don't need candles because we cling to the word of God, my daughter leaned over to me and whispered, "Dad, you light candles all the time." She was right. Now I do, and I encourage others to light candles as well.

At St. Timothy's Church, we celebrated All Saints' Sunday by lighting candles. For a congregation whose membership was shrinking, some observers might say that as the congregation was dying, finding ways to remember those who gave their lives to the church became increasingly important. People were aware that they might lose their connection to their history and to deceased loved ones who were church members. They wanted to do something more than read the names of those who died in the past year. We decided to remember everyone that anyone wanted remembered. As we prayed the names of those who had died, either a loved one or the person who submitted the name came forward and lit a votive candle placed on the altar. By the time we were finished naming the names, the altar was symbolically ablaze with the light of those saints who, although they have parted from us, continue to share Christ's Table with us. Standing at the altar to celebrate the Lord's Supper, I was aware of the communion of saints, that great "cloud of witnesses" (Heb. 12:1), which surrounds us and whose lives brighten our path as we walk through this world by faith.

The light of those candles reflected the light of Christ's resurrection by reminding us that Christ's Table has one end here on earth and one end in heaven, or one end in this world and the other in the world to come. Even though people move from one end of the table to the other, they remain at Christ's Table with us. In the Eucharistic meal, God joins us with saints of every time and of every place. When we receive the bread and the wine, we sit at the same table with biblical biggies, with loved ones who have gone before us, saints who will come after us, and with Christians of all nations and denominations. The barriers of time and space, life and death are broken as this taste of the kingdom of God breaks into our world and into our lives. God gives us a real and delicious foretaste of the feast to come. God provides a hint of what the fulfillment of the kingdom of God will be like, when the pains of this world are destroyed and we live forever with God and those we love. At Christ's table, we bridge the distance between life and death. We traverse the gulf between this world and the next as we participate in God's own life by eating the risen Christ's body and drinking his blood. In Holy Communion, heaven and earth are united; death and life become one as we sit at the banquet table of God's kingdom with Jesus and all the saints.

Our experience at the table with Jesus and the saints made things clearer for the people of St. Timothy. We could assume that Jesus loves us and not that he was angry or disappointed that our congregation was shrinking. We could expect to live with Jesus forever, regardless of what the future brings, because our fate was finished lovingly on the cross. And so what we do on Sunday, hearing the word and sharing the meal, is a foretaste, an appetizer of the banquet described by the prophet Isaiah, when the Lord of hosts will make for all peoples a feast of rich foods and well-aged wines. And God will destroy the shroud that is over all peoples, and swallow up death forever, and wipe away the tears from all faces. Those who lit the candles those All Saints' Sundays, and we who watched the candles as they were lit, both received and shared this light of the risen Christ.

If God uses candles in worship to reflect Christ's resurrection so that we receive and share the light of the risen Christ, perhaps we can learn something from the church's practice during the first thousand years of its life. Rather than placing candles on altars and then developing elaborate rituals for lighting them, the church carried lit candles in procession. In worship, when lit candles or torches are carried into the congregation as part of the procession, God reminds us that Jesus comes to us and we receive the light of Christ's resurrection, regardless of whatever darkness we may be in. As lit torches or candles are carried out of the church at the conclusion of the service, we symbolically follow the light of the risen Christ into the world, where God calls and invites us to share the good news. Perhaps it is not about how we light the candles, but about what we receive from God and share with others and the world when our candles are lit.

For Reflection and Conversation

- Can you think of worship practices in your congregation that not everyone understands? What are they?

- How are candles used in worship in your congregation? What meanings do they communicate?
- How do you receive and share the risen Christ in worship? What makes you aware of the communion of saints?

Chapter 6

Celebrate Vocation

Fred and Naomi, who were in their eighties, worked hard their entire lives. They farmed, took extra jobs to make ends meet, raised their children, and were known in the community for being very generous neighbors and willing volunteers. They still helped out at the senior citizens center. Between them, Naomi and Fred had done every job there was to do at St. Timothy's Church at one time or another. Fred still served on the church council. A quiet man, he didn't say much in meetings, but when Fred spoke, the conversation stopped and everyone listened. Naomi taught Sunday school for decades. Over the years, she had a hand in raising most of the congregation's children. She also coached the congregation's mothers. Fred and Naomi sat in the same pew, up front and on the right, every Sunday. Fred always wore his suit, and Naomi always wore a dress, even in the summer when it was hot and we told everyone to dress comfortably. "You don't need to wear a robe today, Pastor," Ardyce, the congregation's volunteer secretary, would tell me when we were together before worship in the office we shared. But we both knew that I would be wearing a robe. "If Fred's going to wear a suit, I'm going to wear a robe," I would always answer. "It just doesn't seem right not to." Ardyce would just shake her head.

Every Sunday in worship, the congregation collectively held its breath as Fred and Naomi held each other up while they hobbled their way down the aisle and over the chancel step to the communion rail. "We're happy to bring communion to you," I told them every once in a while. "Why would you do that?" They always responded, looking confused, first at each other and then back at me. Then Fred would explain, "We've been kneeling at this communion rail ever since we built the church. We don't see any reason to stop now. Besides, Pastor, you don't need to make a fuss over us."

Today, titles like *patriarch* and *matriarch* frequently have a negative connotation when it comes to congregational dynamics. The congregation's *patriarch* and *matriarch* are often power brokers and gatekeepers who exercise the right to veto anything and everything. This was not how the people of St Timothy's Church regarded Fred and Naomi. Naomi and Fred did not wield power. They were the congregation's patriarch and matriarch in an Abraham-and-Sarah sort of way. They followed God their entire lives, through change and uncertainty, good times and bad. They didn't talk about themselves much, but people who had known Fred and Naomi for years, and people who took the time to listen, knew that their faith had taken root in real life. Fred and Naomi considered the church a second home and the congregation part of their family. Once when Fred and I were talking about the future of St. Timothy's Church, Fred wondered aloud whether, if we gave the denomination our church building, they might build a senior living center on the property. "If they would," Fred declared, "Naomi and I would give them everything we have and move in tomorrow." Fred was so respected in the congregation that the council seriously investigated whether Fred's idea was possible.

The people of St. Timothy's Church were understandably excited when word spread through the congregation that Naomi and Fred would soon celebrate their sixty-fifth wedding anniversary. Everyone wanted to do something big to celebrate. In typical fashion, Fred and Naomi did not want people to make a fuss. "So how do we downplay their wedding anniversary in a meaningful way?" everyone seemed to be asking. People had all sorts of ideas of what we should do. Someone suggested that Fred and Naomi renew their wedding vows. Naomi seemed pleased with the idea; Fred wasn't so sure. This seemed like a bit of a fuss. Carol Ann, known for serving a special dinner every holiday on the calendar and regarded as an expert on weddings and such, came up with the perfect solution. Rather than fussing with a special event, Fred and Naomi could renew their vows as part of the regular worship service on the Sunday closest to their wedding anniversary. The congregation could do something extra at coffee hour, and Fred and Naomi's family could take them out to dinner afterward. Carol Ann's plan was special enough to satisfy everyone who wanted to make a big deal and enough like a regular Sunday to satisfy Fred and Naomi, who agreed to it.

During the sermon hymn that Sunday, Naomi and Fred helped each other as they walked up the aisle, stepped over the chancel step, and stood together before the altar. I led the congregation in prayer, thanking God for providing Fred and Naomi these sixty-five years together, and asking that they might continue to grow in God's love and faithfulness and to share with each other their joys and sorrows and all that life will bring. Then someone read those familiar words from 1 Corinthians; though Paul's discussion of love often sounds sweet and sentimental when read at weddings, it took on a certain strength and profundity that day. Love "bears all things, believes all things, hopes all things, endures all things. Love never ends" (1 Cor. 13:7–8).

Naomi and Fred then faced each other, joined hands, and repeated their vows in turn. "I have taken you to be my wedded wife (husband). I now renew my promise to be your loving partner, for richer, for poorer, in sickness and in health, to love and to cherish; until death parts us." We then prayed, asking God to bless Fred and Naomi with continued life together, signs of God's presence each day, and increasing love for God, each other, and the world. Fred then kissed Naomi, and the people of St. Timothy's Church, tears in their eyes, broke into applause.

When the congregation stopped clapping, I asked Fred and Naomi if they wanted to say anything, if they had some advice to offer or a perspective to share. Naomi thanked the congregation, her family, and especially their children for the special day and spoke of the importance of prayer and humor in marriage. "Well," Fred began when it was his turn to speak, "saying the vows means so much more the second time. You know what they really mean. You know what you've been through, the good and the bad, and you have an idea of what lies ahead. You have a much better appreciation that the other person said those vows to you, and you know you can't do it without God."

In worship that day, the people of St. Timothy's Church witnessed so much more than a man and a woman, married for sixty-five years, renewing their wedding vows. In Fred and Naomi, God showed us one particular human being living as the embodied expression of God's unconditional love, revealed in Jesus Christ, for another particular human being. We watched Fred and Naomi claim their Christian vocation. Their children were grown and had families of their own. Naomi and Fred were retired. They were not able to do some of the things they had done even a few years before. They could—and did—continue to love and care for each other. Loving each other as Christ loves them stood as Fred and Naomi's abiding Christian vocation, a vocation that inspired others and proclaimed Christ in the world. Fred and Naomi's marriage proclaimed God's love and faithfulness as their love for and commitment to each other overflowed into the lives of their family, neighbors, congregation, and community. That Sunday morning, St. Timothy's Church glimpsed the self-giving love with which Christ gave himself up for the world in Fred and Naomi. God powerfully connected everyday life and God's work of reconciliation and new life as we did our best to downplay their wedding anniversary.

Celebrating Vocation in Worship

"Now there are varieties of gifts, but the same Spirit; and there are varieties of services, but the same Lord; and there are varieties of activities, but it is the same God who activates all of them in everyone. To each is given the manifestation of the Spirit for the common good" (1 Cor. 12:4–7). The church teaches that *all* Christians—*all* people—are gifted by their Creator and called by the Holy Spirit to offer themselves in service as a way of giving thanks for all that God has done and continues to do for us in Jesus Christ. The church teaches that vocations, occupations, and professions are ways Christians proclaim and bear witness to Christ through loving service in the world. Occupations and callings are not higher or lower, better or worse, more or less connected to God's work of reconciliation. The plumber's work is as much a calling from God and an opportunity to serve as the preacher's. Paul compares the body of Christ to a human body and says, "The members of the body that seem to be weaker are indispensable, and those members of the body that we think less honorable we clothe with greater honor" (1 Cor. 12:22–23). The tasks and activities to which people devote the majority of their lives are Christian vocations, ways we thank and praise God through loving service in the world. The tasks of everyday life, and the work people spend most of their time doing, are signs of the Spirit's presence for the good of all. They are ways people participate in God's work of reconciling the world to Godself and bringing new life.

Yet, many Christians do not grasp this understanding of their work because, in worship, the church often uses these words of Paul to point to and celebrate ministries *within the congregation*— leading worship, teaching Sunday school or Bible study, singing in the choir, evangelism, stewardship, visiting the sick, and ministering to those in need, for example. In a sense, a congregation lifting up church work in worship is completely understandable. Congregations naturally celebrate the ministry that is most apparent, immediate, and essential to their life and ministry. As part of their worship, congregations rightly find ways to recognize all the ways people serve Christ's church as their participation in God's reconciling love at work *in the congregation*. For example, congregations regularly install church boards, publicly thank the choir on music Sunday, and pray for Sunday school teachers. Yet, congregations are often less intentional and explicit about publicly recognizing and honoring daily work as service to God. In fact, worship may deal with questions of life and death, heaven and hell, but never explicitly connect people's daily work to the Christian faith.

When in worship congregations point to church activities as Christian service, while neglecting to name other arenas of people's lives as ways they participate in God's work of reconciliation, they reinforce people's tendency to separate Sunday from the rest of the week, faith from the rest of life, and Christian service from the way we make our living. Christians may come to regard certain occupations, such as pastor, preacher, nurse, and teacher, as more connected to God's work and even holier than other occupations. After all, Jesus called Simon, Andrew, James, and John *away* from their boats and nets to do the work of the gospel (Matt. 4:18–22). Paul's naming of the gifts given to the members of Christ's body could be interpreted as suggesting that certain activities are more connected to God's work than others. People might decide that since they do not possess the gift of prophecy, administration, preaching, teaching, almsgiving, or a call to works of mercy as their primary vocation, they cannot serve God (Rom. 12:6–8). Paul's use of numbers to describe the way God set up the church—"first apostles, second prophets, third teachers; then deeds of power, then gifts of healing, forms of assistance, forms of leadership, various kinds of tongues" (1 Cor. 12:28)—may suggest to some a ranked order in which some gifts and callings are more important and essential to God's work than others. Christians who do not find these gifts in themselves might conclude that they do not have a role to play in God's work of reconciliation and new life in their daily lives. They may understand themselves to be serving God solely by volunteering at church. While this understanding of Christian service might be good for congregations, it suggests that serving God is something people do in addition to everything else they have to do, rather than the reason behind or motivation for everything they do.

To our benefit, God occasionally steps in and uses celebrations in worship, such as Fred and Naomi's renewal of wedding vows, to make the connection between faith and daily life, our everyday activities and our Christian vocation, unmistakable. Yet, I wish we had more intentionally connected faith and daily work in worship. I regret that we did not celebrate every member of the congregation's Christian vocation in worship the way we celebrated Naomi and Fred's. I wish we had found ways to name and honor the work people do outside of church as ways they participate in God's work of reconciliation in the world, and to thank and praise God for them. Even congregations that desire to connect faith and daily life in this way are often unsure of how to do it or even where to begin. Yet, sometimes all the Spirit needs is for someone to ask, "How does your faith inform your work? How does your work inform your faith?"

Making Wine

I was once the guest preacher at a church in California's wine country. As part of my visit to the congregation, the pastor and some members of the church took me to a small winery, where a member of the congregation was the vintner. As we toured the winery, he explained the science of winemaking, from growing and harvesting the grapes to fermentation and aging. Then, in the barrel room, we tasted wines at various stages in the process. As I walked around the winery that Saturday afternoon, I found myself thinking about Bible verses and stories that talk about vines, vineyards, and wine. For example, Jesus compares the kingdom of God to a vineyard, turns water into wine, and calls himself the vine and his disciples the branches.[1] Toward the end of our time together, I asked the winemaker what insights he might have about these stories, how growing grapes and making wine might help us understand them and how making wine informed his faith.

After protesting that he knew about grapes and wine and not the Bible and theology, the winemaker spoke of making wine as an experience of God's grace. Setting aside the exact science and precise calculation he had told us about as we toured the winery, the vintner talked about being totally dependent on God, because in the end making wine is a mystery. God grows the grapes, sends the rain, gives the harvest, and is the power at work in the process of making wine. The winemaker shares in God's work of creation. "We do our best," he said. "We offer what we have, and God takes it and does something special." The next morning in worship, when the ushers brought the communion wine to the altar as part of the offering, we who visited the winery experienced the church bringing what it has to God, who takes it and, in a mysterious way, does something special. We learned this lesson the day before from a winemaker who, when invited to think about it, understood that his job is his Christian vocation.

Perhaps the first step in intentionally celebrating people's primary occupations and everyday activities as Christian vocations is for the church to go to the places where Christians "live and move and have our being" (Acts 17:28), listen and learn as people explain their work, and urge them to teach the church how the river of God's reconciling love overflows in and through this place and activity. The church can then carry these insights back to its worship by naming them in sermons, lifting them up in prayer, and finding ways to embody and enact them using the forms and parts of the worship service. I have often mused over what God might do in worship if people came to church wearing the clothes and uniforms they wear to work every day. Imagine what God might do through the exchange of peace in a church where company officials and striking workers worship together and the preacher frames both labor and management as Christian vocations. What might God do for the care and education of children when congregations invite teachers and school children to tell them about their Christian vocation and remember them in prayer during worship? I have a dear friend who likes to say that we need to be ready to be God's answer to our prayers. When the church visits people's everyday lives to listen and learn, God will certainly transform our prayers into action.

Mother's Day

In worship, God reminds us that our daily work is not so much about us or the work itself as it is about responding to and sharing in God's work in the world. I have slowly come to understand that worship on Mother's Day and Father's Day can and ought to be about sharing in God's work rather than about motherhood and fatherhood themselves. I do not have a very good track record when it comes to preaching and leading worship on Mother's Day. Parents often want sermons that hammer home God's commandment to "honor your father and your mother" (Exod. 20:12). In one congregation, several mothers stopped by my office during the week before Mother's Day to tell me that my Mother's Day sermon should make their children feel guilty for not honoring and appreciating them enough. When I didn't preach that kind of sermon, but instead preached about the privilege of parenting, the women got mad. In another congregation, when I preached that the relationship between parents and children is more important than any single day, some mothers heard me telling the congregation that they shouldn't celebrate Mother's Day. Finally, one Mother's Day, I preached a tribute to mothers and to motherhood. Women who were unable to conceive and people who had terrible relationships with their mothers told me how much pain I inflicted upon them.

For a few years after that, I went on vacation on Mother's Day and left the preaching task to someone else.

In recent years, I have preached in congregations that honor mothers and fathers outside of worship. Mothers might be given a corsage as they leave the service, and dads given a boutonniere. Men might have kitchen duty at the coffee hour on Mother's Day, or children on Father's Day. These congregations do not celebrate *parenthood* in worship; the emphasis is not on children's duty to honor, serve, obey, love, and respect parents. The point is not to pay parents homage. Instead, these congregations celebrate the privilege and responsibility parents—and all who care for and about children—have to share God's love with those God has entrusted to them. Parents are to earnestly and faithfully provide for their children's material and spiritual welfare. They are to obey God themselves and raise their children to praise and honor God. Parents are to spare no effort, time, or expense to teach their children to serve God and the world. These congregations name fathers and mothers as the first and most important way God acts in the lives of children and invite parents to embrace their role as a way of sharing in God's work of loving both their children and the world. Rather than honoring fathers and mothers, they honor parenting as a Christian vocation. Children honor their parents because parenting is sharing God's work of bringing unconditional love and new life, first and foremost, to their children.

What is true for parenting is equally true for whatever daily work Christians do. Honor is not based on who we are and what we do. In fact, Jesus teaches that though in other communities the people recognized as leaders lord it over others and are tyrants, in the Christian community whoever wishes to become great must be the servant of all.[2] In worship God overturns our notion of status by reminding us that the way we participate in *God's* work is more important than who *we* are and the work *we* do.

Anointing Hands

Of course, if the church is to celebrate people's vocations as signs of the Spirit's presence and ways Christians share in God's work of reconciliation in the world, Christians will need to acknowledge that some occupations and activities are inconsistent with their faith. In the early centuries of the church's life, this is precisely what Christians did. The "Apostolic Tradition," a so-called early church order attributed to Hippolytus of Rome, purports to offer authoritative "apostolic" principles on moral conduct, worship practices, and church organization. This document includes a catalog of prohibited occupations.[3] It directs that as part of preparation for baptism, people are to be asked about their life and work. Some would have to give up occupations deemed to be inconsistent with the Christian faith or be rejected by the church. Occupations considered inconsistent with the Christian faith included pimping, prostitution, making idols, fighting in gladiatorial games, and driving chariots in warfare and competition. Soldiers were to do no injustice or extort any money, but were to be content with their wages. Teachers were to educate children not about the Roman gods, but only about the Father, Son, and Holy Spirit.

The challenge congregations face today is how, in a forum as public as Sunday worship, they can dare to even hint that some occupations and activities contradict the Christian faith. People are quick to remember that Jesus ate with outcasts and sinners. They seem to forget that these people were changed by their encounter with Jesus. For example, Jesus said to the woman caught in adultery, "Go your way, and from now on do not sin again" (John 8:11). The church has long said that Zacchaeus, a chief tax collector, responded to Jesus by declaring, "Look, half of my possessions, Lord, I will give to the poor; and if I have defrauded anyone of anything, I will pay back four times as much" (Luke 19:8). In worship, God can direct us away from what we are not to do, as well as lead and motivate us to embrace our Christian calling.

During one of the first worship services of the school year at the seminary where I teach, the worship leader calls first-year students forward to stand before the seminary community. After prayer, the appointed seminary representative, perhaps the dean of students or the dean of the chapel, marks a cross of oil in the palms of each student's hands. The person doing the anointing might say something like, "May Christ be known in the work you do" or "Christ blesses the work of your hands."

For many years, I regarded this service of anointing as a ritual in search of some meaning. Everyone thought it was a neat thing to do, but most people were unsure of why we did it. One year a senior professor preached that, in the anointing, the Spirit was setting students' hands apart for the work of this season of their lives and ministries. The professor explained that, during these years of seminary, there will be many calls for helping hands and many kinds of work students will want to do. Yet, the Spirit's call in this season of life is study and preparation. During these years, the work of our hands is to open books, to write papers, and to manipulate keyboards. Our hands will do more praying for the world than serving in the world. This work is not separate from ministry. Our hands are set apart to minister to those we will one day serve in congregations by faithfully studying Scripture, diligently learning the faith, intentionally growing in spirit, and passionately practicing the arts of ministry. The point is that when the Spirit sets our hands apart *for* important work, the Spirit also sets our hands apart *from* other equally important work. The Spirit also sets our hands apart from activities that conflict with the work to which the Spirit calls us, such as acts of violence and injustice and self-centered behaviors.

The sermon was controversial. It challenged students' tendency to distinguish between the academic and practical, between learning the tradition and engaging in mission. In the anointing of hands, God called students in seminary to engage in certain tasks and activities, to refrain from other tasks and activities, and to postpone still other work until another season of life. In the anointing, God set limits and determined priorities. What is true for seminarians is also true for all Christians and congregations. Despite the many needs and much work to do in the world, in worship God calls us to undertake certain tasks, to refrain from others, and to set still others aside until another time and circumstance. In worship, the Spirit shapes and directs how Christians and congregations will carry out their Christian vocations in the world.

God Calls and Equips

Most important perhaps, worship can be a place where God calls and equips the members of Christ's body for various ministries in the world as people discover their gifts, take on new roles, and gain confidence. "I'm a behind-the-scenes person," Judy explained to me. "I'm happy to serve on the altar guild, but I don't want to do anything up front. I won't assist with communion or read Scripture." One Sunday we needed someone to help distribute communion and somebody asked Judy. "Just this once," she said, and then she discovered that she liked doing it. When I asked Judy to visit Anna, a homebound member of the congregation, she told me that she couldn't do that; she wouldn't know what to say. Judy did agree to drive me to visit Anna. At first Judy didn't say much more than hello during those visits, but slowly she started to talk. After Judy and I visited Anna together for a few months, Judy decided that I wasn't going often enough and started visiting Anna on her own. When Anna mentioned that she might like to receive communion more than when I brought it once a month, Judy helped the congregation begin a ministry in which members take communion to the sick and homebound on Sunday after worship. Now Judy works in a senior living center, visiting "complete strangers" and being their advocate with the administration. Judy says that her adventure seems to have begun in worship when someone invited her to step out of her comfort zone, imagine herself in a new way, and help distribute communion. The love for seniors Judy discovered in church is now the way she serves in the world. Sometimes God calls and equips people as they discover new gifts and gain new confidence by taking on leadership roles within the congregation's worship. Gaining skill and experience in worship then leads and empowers them to undertake similar or corresponding work in the world.

Worship can also be a place where God helps us release responsibilities, leads us to take on different roles, and guides us into new seasons of life. Lee had been a member of the church council for decades, including serving several terms as its president. Lee's health was failing and his hearing was going. He knew that he could not serve another term as president, and he was having a hard time letting go of the job. "We don't need you to be president anymore," the pastor told Lee. "We need you to do something more important." Lee looked shocked. What could be more important than serving as president of the church council? The pastor continued, "We have kids that want to help out in worship.

We need someone to take them under their wing." We soon found Lee ushering with ten-year-old kids. Lee was their coach and their cheerleader. The congregation could not have planned a better intergenerational activity. No longer a president, Lee had become a mentor, the congregation's elder statesman, at least as far as the kids were concerned.

To facilitate the Spirit's calling and equipping people to participate in God's work of reconciling the world to Godself, congregations should plan worship that calls forth the gifts of as many congregational members as possible and requires the participation of all. Congregations should find ways for the pastor and people to share worship leadership. Members of the congregation read Scripture, sing, play music, and lead prayer. They serve as ushers and greeters; they prepare and serve at the altar. Most important, worshipers participate by confessing their sin, singing hymns, responding in the liturgy, confessing the creed, giving an offering, and coming to the table. This approach to worship is completely opposite from the pastor doing everything while the congregation watches. Yet when it happens, Christians enter into worship as a place where God uses their different callings, gifts, and abilities as the river of God's reconciling love flows out from the congregation and into the world.

For Reflection and Conversation

- How does your congregation honor and celebrate significant events in people's lives in worship?
- How does your congregation celebrate people's church work in worship? How does your congregation celebrate people's daily work in worship? How do these ways of celebrating compare? What might that suggest about the Christian faith?
- How does faith inform your job, occupation, or daily work? How does your job, occupation, or daily work inform your faith? How is your work a response to God's love for you in Christ and a way you participate in God's work of reconciliation and bringing new life?

Chapter 7

Pick Hymns

Many churchgoers regard music, and especially congregational singing, as the most important and powerful ingredient of Christian worship. In every congregation I served, certain members became so agitated over hymns they didn't like that I decided it was safer to preach heresy than to pick an unpopular hymn. So, because I am not particularly gifted in music, and not wanting to shoulder all by myself the responsibility for what hymns we sang, I learned to rely on church organists and choir directors and to collaborate with congregational worship and music committees.

Then I came to St. Timothy's Church. The musicians—a pianist some Sundays and an organist the rest—picked the hymns. "The B-I-B-L-E," we sang many Sundays, along with "Jesus Loves Me" and other songs I learned as a child. Singing Sunday school songs struck me as somewhat odd, since my daughter was frequently the only child in worship. The worship service was completely different on the Sundays an organist was with us. The hymns were selected to correspond to the Scripture readings and the time of the church year. It took me months to figure out that we sang Sunday school songs in worship on piano Sundays, because they were what the pianist knew how to play. "Make a joyful noise to the LORD, all the earth," the psalmist declares (Ps. 100:1), and we most certainly did.

Things went along fine until the Sunday before Christmas. I was sitting in front of the congregation after preaching the sermon when the pianist launched into "Silver Bells." The congregation was singing, "Strings of street lights, even stop lights, blink a bright red and green, as the shoppers rush home with their treasures." I'm told that I turned white as snow as the shock swept over my face. Then I flushed Christmas red as the congregation continued, "Hear the snow crunch, see the kids bunch. This is Santa's big scene. . . ." Immediately after the service, Linda, our one-woman worship committee, informed me that starting next Sunday I would be picking the hymns. "We can't have you flipping out in front of the congregation," she said smiling. "Besides, the songs should have something to do with God, don't you think?" So I took on the task of selecting hymns that were appropriate to the Scripture readings and the church year, that the congregation would enjoy singing, and that the musicians could play. I came to regard picking hymns as among the most important parts of worship preparation, not because people would get mad if I made a bad choice, but because God does wonderful things in worship through music and singing.

Be Filled with the Spirit as You Sing!

"Worship the LORD with gladness," the psalmist proclaims, "come into his presence with singing" (Ps. 100:2). "Be filled with the Spirit," the apostle Paul encourages, "as you sing psalms and hymns and spiritual songs among yourselves, singing and making melody to the LORD in your hearts" (Eph. 5:18–19). Hymn singing has a rich scriptural history. Moses, Miriam, and the Israelites sang to the Lord after God brought them safely through the sea. Tradition holds that Mary sang what we know as the Magnificat when the angel Gabriel told her that she would bear the Messiah. On the night before he died, Jesus and the disciples sang a hymn in the upper room before going to the Mount of Olives. Even in prison, Paul and Silas sang hymns to God. The writer of Revelation reports that in the heavenly throne room, he heard "every creature in heaven and on earth and under the earth and in the sea, and all that is in them, singing, 'To the one seated on the throne and to the Lamb be blessing and honor and glory and might forever and ever!'" (Rev. 5:13).

Most often, we think of singing in worship as the congregation praising God, and, in fact, it is. "Beautiful Savior" and "Lord, I Lift Your Name on High" are certainly songs Christians sing to praise God. Sometimes, rather than offering our music and singing to God, singing hymns is a way we proclaim to others who God is: "I love to tell the story of unseen things above, of Jesus and his glory, of Jesus and his love." Sometimes, rather than anything we do, God uses music and singing to do amazing things for us. In worship, God works through music and singing to increase our faith, build up the congregation, help us pray, and speak to us directly.

God works through singing hymns to *teach and nurture faith*. A congregation's singing a hymn—"Holy, holy, holy, merciful and mighty! God in three Persons, blessed Trinity!"—is a far more effective way of teaching about God's nature than a congregation's listening to lectures and lessons on the doctrine of the Trinity. Singing hymns teaches Christians, including children and those new to the faith, the story of salvation. On Easter, for example, we learn the story of the resurrection by singing, "Jesus Christ is risen today!" Songs that employ different images for God and God's gifts teach the congregation that God's nature and blessings are bigger than we imagine; they are even boundless. Singing hymns helps me think of God as both "strong mother God, working night and day," and "warm father God, hugging every child."[1] God is both old and aching, gray with endless care, and young and growing, eager, on the move. God is the sculptor of the mountains, the miller of the sand, the jeweler of the heavens, and the potter of the land. God is the nuisance to Pharaoh, the cleaver of the sea, the pillar in the darkness, and the beacon of the free.[2] Unlike sermons, most prayers, and instructions in the faith, lyrics do not change; they therefore provide one of our most consistent sources of theology. Hymns also have the power of repetition and reinforcement when they are sung over the course of weeks, seasons, years, and lifetimes. By this repetition and reinforcement, God not only teaches faith through singing hymns but the Holy Spirit also nurtures and strengthens our faith. Singing "O God, our help in ages past, our hope for years to come, our shelter from the stormy blast, and our eternal home" helps us to have faith in God, to trust God to help us.

The Holy Spirit also uses hymns to provide us with words with which we can *express our faith*. Singing in church is a way we witness to Christ and share our faith with those around us. Perhaps most obvious to us, church choirs express their faith through the anthems they sing. Outside of worship, when we find ourselves in situations where we need to speak of God or share our faith and we don't know what to say, recalling a favorite hymn or a song that seems especially meaningful often gives us the words we need. Many families report that when they are in a hospital room or nursing home or when they are facing the death of a loved one, singing hymns is the way they express their faith, hope, and trust in God.

In addition to increasing individuals' faith and helping them to express it, the Holy Spirit uses singing hymns to reinforce the communal nature of worship by uniting members of the congregation and the whole church. Though the congregation is made up of many individual voices, the congregation sings in one voice. Singing together both prepares the congregation to worship as a community and provides a way for that community to respond to God's activity in the service. The hymns a congregation sings most frequently and sings really well reinforce and reflect the congregation's identity, who the congregation is as a faith community. What and how a congregation sings also creates and reflects its attitude and mood. Singing hymns well can support a spirit of joy and festivity or permit a spirit of sorrow and lament. In fact, many worshipers regard the enthusiastic participation of the entire people of God in song as a sign of the Spirit's presence and an assurance of Christ's love.

God also adds a congregation's song to the song of the church throughout the world and throughout the ages. God uses songs a congregation loves or that have a history in the congregation to make us aware that the Christian community is part of the gathering of God's people of every time, including all of the saints that ever worshiped in a particular congregation, and to connect us to the communion of saints. God uses newer songs, particularly those that come from beyond the congregation's culture and from other parts of the globe, to strengthen the congregation's connection to the church throughout the world. Singing the songs of other parts of Christ's body may even help to deepen a congregation's concern for the lives of saints in other parts of the world and motivate a congregation to work for the well-being of those faraway saints.

As surely as God uses music and singing to create communal identity, God also uses congregational singing to form and strengthen communal memory. Hymns sung in worship are among the most powerful ways faith remains with people throughout their lives; in later life and as they approach death, people often remember hymns when they have forgotten almost everything else. Songs also return us to moments when God was close and powerful in ways no other expressions of faith can. We sing "Silent Night" holding a small candle on Christmas Eve and are connected to everyone we have ever shared Christmas worship with, as well as those who will light candles and sing this carol on Christmas Eve after we have joined the heavenly chorus. A communal memory can be so strong that singing a particular song makes members of a congregation weep uncontrollably and unexpectedly. They don't understand why until they remember that they sang it together at a significant moment or transition, whether in the life of an individual or in the life of the congregation. The hymns we sing at baptisms, confirmations, weddings, funerals, incidents of great tragedy, and occasions of great joy are especially powerful ways God creates communal memory.

Singing hymns is an especially powerful way the Spirit helps the congregation pray together. Rather than one person giving voice to the congregation's petitions and intercessions, singing hymns allows the entire congregation to address God with one voice. Most often, the congregation uses hymns to call upon the Holy Spirit or to ask God to be present in worship. We might sing "Come, thou almighty King, help us thy name to sing; help us to praise; Father all glorious, o'er all victorious, come and reign over us, Ancient of Days."[3] Sometimes hymns give congregations the words with which to ask God for what they know they need: "change and decay in all around I see; O thou who changest not, abide with me."[4] Sometimes sung prayer is more general. "Kyrie eleison," we sing. "Lord, have mercy."

Sometimes God uses hymns to speak to a congregation in its own voice. A hymn a congregation sings in worship might be God's answer to prayer, God's assurance or challenge, or God's call or commission. God speaking to the congregation through its own singing is perhaps evident when hymns are taken from Scripture:

"'Comfort, comfort, now my people; tell of peace!' So says our God." "Have no fear, little flock; have no fear, little flock, for the Father has chosen to give you the kingdom." "Go, make disciples, baptizing them, teaching them. Go, make disciples, for I am with you till the end of time." Sometimes, rather than the words of a hymn, God speaks through the emotions or mood that comes over the congregation as the people sing together. We often think that in worship, we offer our prayers. Singing together reminds us that God answers our prayers in worship as well.

So much happens when we sing praises to God in worship! God uses our singing to teach and nurture our faith and help us share our faith with others. God creates communal identity and strengthens communal memory. God helps us pray and speaks to us in our own voice. Since God does so much in and through what we sing in worship, picking hymns the congregation sings with faith and confidence is an important part of worship planning and preparation. I came to understand this in a new way when I attended a gathering of my denomination's bishops and teaching theologians and found myself unexpectedly agitated during a worship service because of a hymn someone had selected.

Closing the Hymnal

I did not expect to be starstruck when I attended a meeting of my denomination's bishops and theologians that teach in colleges, universities, and seminaries, but when I got there I found that I was. I wasn't so much in awe of those in attendance as I was amazed to be in their company. When I graduated from seminary more than two decades before, I don't think anyone could have imagined me being part of such a gathering and, if they did, they never told me. While no one ever quoted these verses from Leviticus to me, back then much of the church seemed to operate according to this scriptural proscription: "The LORD spoke to Moses, saying: Speak to Aaron and say: No one of your offspring throughout their generations who has a blemish may approach to offer the food of his God. For no one who has a blemish shall draw near, one who is blind . . . or [has] a blemish in his eyes . . . shall come near to offer the LORD's offerings . . . ; since he has a blemish, he shall not come near to offer the food of his God" (Lev. 21:16–21).[5]

As graduation was approaching and I was seeking a church, a representative of the denomination gave me what I now realize was an honest and realistic assessment of my prospects and the best pastoral advice he could offer. "Expect to wait three years for a church," he said. "And if you get one, don't mess up, because you won't get another." When asked to consider me to be their pastor, several congregations responded that people with disabilities are meant to be ministered to, not ministers. One congregation offered to hire me for several thousand dollars below the minimum salary because I am legally blind. After a year of waiting, I began my pastoral ministry as a part-time assistant pastor. I was—and still feel—extremely grateful both to that congregation and to the saints that sustained me while I waited to get there. Back then I never imagined being part of a gathering of bishops and teaching theologians. Throughout the years, whenever I took a step that would eventually bring me from being a part-time assistant pastor to a seminary professor—a journey I didn't plan—the church responded with a certain level of caution, nervousness, even uneasiness. So, yes, I was somewhat amazed to be at that meeting.

I am always a bit conscious of being legally blind when I attend conferences. Negotiating unfamiliar surroundings, interacting with people when everyone is wearing nametags I cannot read, and making my way through buffet meals requires energy and concentration. But one of my seminary professors graciously joined me at the opening reception, introduced me to people so that I did not need to read nametags, and guided me through the buffet line. So I was thinking about John 9 rather than Leviticus when I entered opening worship. "As [Jesus] walked along, he saw a man blind from birth. His disciples asked him, 'Rabbi, who sinned, this man or his parents, that he was born blind?' Jesus answered, 'Neither this man nor his parents sinned; he was born blind so that God's works might be revealed in him'" (John 9:1–3).

Sitting in the worship space and listening to music prior to the service, I felt as if I was back in seminary. I was sitting next to my academic advisor, and several of my professors were also in the room. A guy who was a year or two behind me in seminary, now a bishop, played piano, just as he had when we were in school. A few other classmates, now bishops and professors, were also in the congregation, as were several of my own faculty colleagues. The worship leader was a thoughtful, sensitive fellow whom I consider to be a friend.

Feeling just a bit nostalgic, I guess I let my guard down. When I worship with a congregation I don't really know, and some congregations I know really well, I tend to brace myself just a bit so that I am not caught off guard by anything in worship that strikes me as—or is—insensitive. I learned to do this the hard way. Once, a congregation asked me to participate in a dramatic presentation of the story of the man born blind, as the man born blind, of course, and then introduced PowerPoint into worship. Everything was on the screen, so I was not able to actively participate in the service. In another congregation, the preacher declared that we need to "translate the healing stories of Jesus, since, in our society, handicapped people are no longer discriminated against." Most often, the word *blind* serves as scriptural and ecclesiastical shorthand for sin, the lack of faith, and willful indifference to the needs of the world. So I brace myself just a bit so that I am not surprised. I guard my heart so that I don't get hurt, but I didn't brace myself that night. As I recall, one of the scripture readings at that opening worship service, taken from the lectionary, was the story of Ananias coming to Saul of Tarsus and laying his hands on him so that he might regain his sight (Acts 9:10–19). We sang "Amazing Grace": "I once was lost but now am found, was blind but now I see." Under the circumstances, the song left a bit of a sting.

The next evening, worship surprised me, or at least my reaction to the service did. The liturgy was meticulously sculpted to include everyone. For example, since some people experience masculine names for God as exclusive and even oppressive, the worship planners did not use the traditional name for the triune God—Father, Son, and Holy Spirit. Once again, we heard about Ananias coming to Saul of Tarsus and laying his hands on him to cure his blindness. Then at the end of the service we sang, "We are called to be hope for the hopeless so hatred and blindness will be no more."[6] Thoughts raced through my mind as I sang: "They're equating blindness with hatred. . . . Is God calling us to eliminate this thing that is so much a part of who I am? The church can be sensitive to everyone else, but not people with disabilities. Nothing has changed in all these years." Closing my hymnal, I stopped singing as tears welled up in my eyes.

At the worship service the next morning, I listened attentively as the presiding bishop presented a laundry list of things our church should be involved in and concerned about. Correcting the notion that disabilities are a sign and consequence of personal sin and God's judgment, ministering with persons with disabilities, and lifting up the gifts of people who live with disabilities and feel called to public ministry were not on his list. I have not been able to sing the hymn calling us to eliminate blindness since.

God Works Even When We Don't Like Worship

For months after that worship service, I asked myself—and I asked God—what God was doing in worship that weekend. I chose to assume that God was present and acting in those worship services, rather than deciding that since one hymn affected me so negatively, God must have been absent that day. Assuming that God was working in and through those worship services, even though I didn't like them, changed my strong negative reaction to a hymn selection into a question about what God was saying to me or calling me to do. So, the first thing this experience taught me is that when I assume God is involved in worship I do not appreciate, God keeps me from getting trapped in my negative reaction to the service and dwelling too long on myself. I cannot dismiss worship that I do not like and that I may even experience as insulting and injurious. Instead, the Spirit empowers me to be in conversation with God and, sometimes, with others.

I also learned that we bring as much to worship as we get out of worship, and that what we bring to a worship service frequently determines what we get out of a worship service. Hymns are a powerful tool with which the Spirit uncovers and puts us in touch with what we bring to worship. They can touch our hearts and cut through our defenses in ways other parts of the service do not. Sometimes the context influences how a hymn affects an indi-

vidual or the congregation. Sung in the context of a congregation
of my denomination's bishops and teaching theologians, a hymn
that, to me, equated blindness and hatred caused me to experience and name my ambivalence over being a leader in a Christian
church that in my experience does a poor job of ministering with
people with disabilities. In another setting, this same hymn may
not have affected me this way. Those who planned the service had
no way of knowing that the hymn would affect me as it did, since
I could not predict this myself. That day, neither I nor the worship
leaders realized the significance of what I brought to worship—my
experience of being a person who lives with a disability in my denomination. Yet now as I plan worship, I increasingly find myself
questioning whether the words and images used, particularly in
hymns, might negatively affect anyone who attends the service,
especially those whom the church has historically portrayed negatively. As I reflect on my experience, I believe that this is something
Jesus would want worship planners to do.

I am also convinced that the words and images of both Scripture and the prayers and hymns we use in worship have a cumulative effect—positive or negative. For example, repeatedly hearing Paul's declaration "that neither death, nor life, nor angels, nor
rulers, nor things present, nor things to come, nor powers, nor
height, nor depth, nor anything else in all creation, will be able to
separate us from the love of God in Christ Jesus our Lord" (Rom.
8:38–39), particularly in times of fear, doubt, loss, and tragedy, is
comforting, life giving, and empowering. On the other hand, as
much as prayers, hymns, and even Scripture remind and reinforce,
their repeated use can distract and discourage. A given word or
image often has less influence—positive or negative—when it is
only used once in a worship service than when it is employed repeatedly throughout the worship service or consistently in worship
from week to week. For example, over time, congregations that
describe the church exclusively as *family* will find that some members of the congregation feel excluded and even orphaned, because
they need the church to be something other or more than family.
Congregations then need to find songs that describe the church
in other ways. At the gathering of bishops and theologians I attended, reading the story of Ananias coming to Saul of Tarsus and

laying his hands on him so that he might regain his sight, at three consecutive worship services had a cumulative effect on me.

When they are aware of the cumulative effect of words and images, God may call congregations to sing songs that challenge and correct rather than echo and reinforce the prevailing images that the congregation, church, and even Scripture use. In this way, God uses hymns to help us question and challenge our faith, as surely as God uses hymns to teach and to nurture faith. When I was growing up, in Sunday school we regularly sang, "Onward, Christian soldiers, marching as to war, with the cross of Jesus going on before." Over the years, the church's reflection on a militaristic Jesus and times in Christian history when the church acted like an invading army caused this once-popular hymn to fall into a state of disuse in many parts of the church. Today we may sing, "Lord, Make Us Servants of Your Peace,"[7] a hymn that reminds us that we are called to be peacemakers. Reflecting on my experience of how the words *blind* and *blindness* are used in worship, I keep hoping for a hymn that celebrates how blindness frees people from the first impressions and stereotypes that seeing often reinforces so that people can experience each other as brothers and sisters in Christ. When people become agitated over what is sung in worship, the Spirit may be using hymns to help the church question and reexamine expressions of the faith the church at one time took for granted.

Earlier, I said that the Spirit uses hymns to create community, cultivate communal memory, and connect the congregation or worshiping community to the church of all times and places. My experience reminded me that the community the Spirit creates and the church to which the Spirit connects the congregation is authentic rather than idyllic; the communal memory the Spirit fosters is honest and not romanticized. As the congregation sings together, the Spirit recalls times of sorrow as well as great joy, occasions of despair and occasions of hope, moments when the church shone like a city on a hill and moments when the church hid its light under a bushel. All these memories of the church's life are real and true; one aspect of the church's story does not deny or negate another. I can recall times when the church rejected my gifts because I am legally blind and times when the church celebrated my gifts as pastor, teacher, and leader, sometimes even naming the contribution I bring because I live with a disability. All these experiences are true of Christ's church. In fostering communal memory, the Spirit uses some memories to comfort and assure and other memories to challenge and correct. Yet, the Spirit does not ask the church to embrace some memories and deny others.

Last, the Spirit might challenge or correct our faith by using the discomfort and agitation people sometimes experience on account of the hymns sung in worship—and, in fact, any part of the service—to motivate them to bring about change or to work for justice. In the months following that conference, my experience of singing with my denomination's bishops and teaching theologians a hymn that pairs blindness and hatred renewed and increased my commitment to use my privileged position to be an advocate for and stand with persons with disabilities, particularly those who understand themselves as called by God to the public ministry of the church. So, though I left that worship service agitated and upset by the hymn we sang, perhaps God is using that experience to call me to a kind of prophetic ministry, something for which I wasn't really looking.

Of course, discovering what God might be doing when a congregation sings, especially something that agitates people, requires that people move beyond their likes and dislikes and consciously reflect on how God might use the hymns, and indeed any aspect of a worship service, to communicate Godself and God's will. When worshipers, worship leaders, and those who plan worship are both willing to reflect on their experience in this way and able to share their reflections together, congregations find the ways God is present and acting in hymns, prayers, sermons, and worship services that some people object to and may even find painful. Rather than responding to people's likes and dislikes, picking hymns and planning worship become another way the people of God respond to God in their midst.

Many months after that meeting of bishops and teaching theologians, I was the keynote speaker and preacher at a conference. The worship planning team wanted the congregation to sing, following my sermon, the hymn that agitated me so. I shared my problem with a song that equates hatred and blindness and asked the committee to select something else. At our next meeting, a member of the planning team said, "I've given what you told us a lot of thought and decided it's not a bad hymn. It's a good hymn with a bad line. Could we sing it this way? 'We are called to be hope for the hopeless so hatred and *violence* will be no more.'" We sang the hymn that way and I joined the song. I'll sing it that way from now on.

For Reflection and Conversation

- Name three of your favorite hymns and the reason each hymn is special to you.
- What hymn was the first you learned to sing by heart? How has that hymn informed or shaped your faith?
- Can you recall a time when God spoke either to you or to your congregation through a hymn? What did God say?
- Is your congregation a singing church? What does the way your congregation sings say about it as a faith community?
- Is there a hymn that makes you close the book and stop singing? Why? What might God be doing or telling you when the congregation sings it?

Chapter 8

Preach Christ

"But we proclaim Christ crucified," the apostle Paul declares, "a stumbling block to Jews and foolishness to Gentiles, but to those who are the called, both Jews and Greeks, Christ the power of God and the wisdom of God" (1 Cor. 1:23–24). Paul calls the proclamation of Christ crucified, which in worship is most obviously (though not exclusively) expressed in preaching, "the power of God and the wisdom of God." That is an audacious claim. Yet, Paul is not alone in making it. Martin Luther, for example, wrote that "faith is produced and preserved in us by preaching," and the faith produced by preaching results in new life.[1] St. Ambrose preached that through baptism and the preaching of the Lord's passion, God opens the eyes of people's hearts so that they see with eyes of faith.[2] Preacher and author Barbara Brown Taylor calls preaching "a process of transformation for both preacher and congregation alike, as the ordinary details of their everyday lives are transformed into the extraordinary elements of God's ongoing creation."[3] While Paul, Luther, Ambrose, and Taylor are four of my favorites, sentiments like theirs about preaching are found throughout church history and, more important, in every congregation. Even in congregations where preaching is poor, certain people show up for worship week after week hoping this will be the Sunday when they experience God's power in preaching. Despite evidence to the contrary, they agree with Paul that the proclamation of the gospel is God's wisdom and not foolishness.

Yet, Paul's audacious claim that preaching is the power and wisdom of God is not universally held. My experience, from both listening to sermons and talking to churchgoers, tells me that many preachers and listeners have three problems with Paul's pronouncement. First, Paul makes it sound like *we* do it all, whether preaching and listening to sermons in worship or conversing about Jesus in our world. Paul says, "But *we* proclaim Christ." The problem comes when we become so focused on ourselves that preachers worry too much about how well they preach, parishioners judge a message's value solely according to what they get out of it, and Christians insist on having every answer and knowing exactly what to say before they will utter a word about Jesus. When this happens, the voice of Christ, the power and wisdom of God, which is the real speaker in proclamation, never gets heard.

The church finds power and wisdom by trusting that when Scripture is read in worship, when sermons are preached in church, and when faith is shared in the ordinary and extraordinary moments of life, ultimately God is doing the talking. The church also finds power and wisdom by expecting that God has something worthwhile to say. How often a parishioner thanks the pastor for something said in a sermon that was particularly important and meaningful, even quoting it back to the pastor, and the pastor never said it. How often Christians talk about the impact particular people had on their faith, and those people were simply being themselves, living their own lives, completely oblivious to the difference they were making. God was doing the talking, and God had something important to say.

A second problem with Paul's pronouncement about proclaiming Christ concerns sermon content. Paul says we preach "Christ crucified." Yet, so many other issues, topics, agendas, and concerns want to be preached, or perhaps preachers and their hearers want sermons to be about so many things besides Christ crucified. Congregational concerns, social issues, global situations, and life's questions all need to be addressed in preaching, and they should be. Following Jesus's own example as a preacher, we learn that every issue is fair game for preaching; no topic is out of bounds. To say otherwise is to conclude that there are areas of life where Jesus has no place.

The problem with addressing anything and everything from the pulpit comes when the way issues and topics are included and addressed in sermons is not appropriate to Christian preaching. Since we preach Christ crucified, the issue is what Jesus or God has to say. Every issue and topic that gets included in a sermon must be grounded in and related to the biblical story of God's work of reconciliation, particularly the life, death, and resurrection of Jesus Christ. In fact, I wholeheartedly agree with venerable preachers like Gardner C. Taylor, the friend and mentor of Martin Luther King Jr., considered by many to be the dean of American preaching. I once heard Taylor remark that the gospel has not been preached until the gospel is connected to the issues and concerns of the people hearing the sermon. Some preachers, congregations, issues, and topics more than others demand that the connection between sermon content and gospel proclamation be stronger and more explicit. When people cannot miss the relationship between even the most difficult or controversial issue or sensitive topic and the gospel, when the connection is inescapable, when they are convinced that God has something important to say, preachers and congregants may well feel uncomfortable, but most will listen as God speaks to and through them.

When I am stuck or dissatisfied with a sermon, or when my listeners tell me that a sermon hasn't worked, I search through my manuscript looking for Jesus. Nine out of ten times, Jesus just isn't there, or I have shined the spotlight on something else and left Jesus in the shadows. The sermon's language is beautiful. The way the sermon moves or is laid out is innovative. The manuscript is well crafted. All I forgot is Jesus, the good news of God's love and life that preachers are charged to preach and people come to church to hear. Without Jesus, whatever I talked about became my opinion, my agenda, words from me rather than the word of the Lord.

I found a way to check myself; I invite the children to hold me accountable. One of the first children's sermons I always give in a congregation is about preaching. I ask the kids what a sermon is and what sermons are supposed to be about. I learn a lot about the kind of preaching that has gone on in that parish. I then tell the kids that I understand my job as a preacher is to talk about Jesus, to tell the congregation what difference it makes that Jesus lived, died, and rose from the dead. I tell them that regardless of what I preach about (and I will preach about everything under the sun), they should hear about Jesus in every sermon. If they don't, I want them to tell me, and I will treat them to ice cream. More than creating a quality control mechanism for myself, I cue the congregation—the children and everyone else listening in—to how they should listen to sermons, at least the sermons I preach.

Some preachers and congregants argue that insisting on an explicit statement about Jesus in every sermon is unnecessarily confining and inappropriately exclusive. For example, some correctly note that the Old Testament is the story of God's reconciling love and saving activity, and the Old Testament makes no explicit reference to Jesus Christ. Others argue that insisting on an explicit statement about Jesus in every sermon tacitly invalidates other faith traditions. I could argue that Jesus introduced a Christ-centered interpretation of the Old Testament when he said to the disciples, "'These are my words that I spoke to you while I was still with you—that everything written about me in the law of Moses, the prophets, and the psalms must be fulfilled.' Then [Jesus] opened their minds to understand the scriptures, and he said to them, 'Thus it is written, that the Messiah is to suffer and to rise from the dead on the third day, and that repentance and forgiveness of sins is to be proclaimed in his name to all nations, beginning from Jerusalem'" (Luke 24:44–47).

I hold that Christian leaders preaching to Christian congregations, and Christians sharing their faith, proclaim Jesus Christ and not another faith tradition. Yet, as I preach Christ crucified and as I share my faith with others, I embrace the admonition in 1 Peter that "all of you must clothe yourselves with humility in your dealings with one another, for 'God opposes the proud, but gives grace to the humble'" (1 Pet. 5:5). Even those who disagree with me about including an explicit statement about Jesus in every sermon can hold themselves accountable to preach about—and listen for—God's reconciling love and saving activity, and can pay attention to the way issues and topics are connected to God's work in the world—in every sermon.

A third problem with Paul's pronouncement about preaching is that many Christians, both preachers and hearers, do not regard and trust the gospel, what Paul calls the proclamation of Christ crucified, as the power of God. Instead, we often think that we need to exercise some other power, some power of our own, if things are going to change or anything is going to happen. So, rather than talking about

Jesus, preachers may undertake to persuade, convince, motivate, or cajole people to do something. Some parishioners might want the preacher to instruct, correct, decree, or direct, usually someone other than themselves. Threats, guilt, and shame may even become the motivating force of a message that, according to Paul, is supposed to be about God's reconciling love in Jesus Christ. That we substitute some power of our own for the power of the gospel is not surprising, since we frequently want to exercise power we can control. We want to exercise power that brings clear, instantaneous, profound, and lasting results and not the slow, subtle, small, and patient change that the power of God brings. When the gospel is preached and nothing seems to happen, some preachers end up feeling powerless, and some parishioners decide that preaching is meaningless.

One of my best preaching students called me a year and a half after graduating from seminary and beginning parish ministry. "I've lost it," she said. "I can no longer preach. I was hitting them out of the park. Now I'm afraid to step up to the plate. What books should I read?" "Your bag of tricks is empty," I said. "Now you're ready to preach. It's time to open the Word with your people, to listen to their hearts and to listen to your own. It's time to trust the power of God at work in the gospel, rather than trusting yourself. When was the last time you took a day off? When was the last time you heard a good sermon?" My student hung up the phone disappointed. I hadn't given her a book to read. A few months later she called back. "I hate you," she said, with the spunk in her voice that I remembered. "How did you know?" she asked. "I've been there," I answered, knowing too well the times I had lost track of the power of God's grace in my life and stopped noticing God at work—in the congregation and in the world. I had to discover again that though the power of God may not work at the pace and in the manner we desire, proclaiming Christ crucified is nevertheless full of God's power. The trick is not to miss it.

Power or Foolishness?

When I came to St. Timothy's Church, some of the other congregations in town were among the first things that caught my attention.

They were active and growing. One congregation was purchasing property because its leaders knew that, in time, the congregation would need to expand its facilities. This church was right down the street from St. Timothy's. I wondered why the members of my little flock didn't join one of these other churches. So I asked the leaders why St. Timothy's Church needed to exist. Were they attached to their building? Were they afraid to let go of what was familiar? Were they reluctant to give up their strong sense of community and become part of something different? Yes, they told me, and something more. The leaders of St. Timothy's Church were convinced that they and their community needed a Christian proclamation of the gospel that presented the life, death, and resurrection of Jesus Christ as God's unconditional, all encompassing, reconciling love. They needed to hear that Jesus brings life out of death. They and their community also needed a place that tries to embody that love and life for all people. The unspoken subtext was that at least some of our members had not found this gospel proclamation and kind of community elsewhere.

So I did my best to preach God's love and mercy, and St. Timothy's Church did its best to live it out. For four years, we proclaimed the gospel, enriched our worship, and welcomed the stranger. Visitors genuinely appreciated the preaching and worship and the warmth of the congregation. Then they asked about Sunday school for their children, activities for their teens, and programming for adults. At St. Timothy's Church, Naomi, an eighty-something-year-old saint who had taught for decades, was Sunday school. Naomi told Bible stories and shared treats with whatever kids showed up; many Sundays the class consisted of Naomi and my daughter. We didn't fair as well when it came to activities for youth and adults. When visitors learned that St. Timothy's Church was unable to offer the programs they were looking for, they soon moved on, often apologetically. Rather than welcoming new people, we watched as our members got older, our attendance got smaller, our budget got tighter, and our building started showing its age. More than asking why St. Timothy's Church should exist, we began to wonder whether St. Timothy's Church could continue to exist.

Congregational leaders decided to contact the bishop's office and schedule a meeting with the staff member responsible for evangelism. "What can a congregation like ours do to grow?" they asked. The outreach officer told us to do two things. First, we had to make our worship service more "user friendly," which meant me giving directions verbally. "We begin our worship service with the order of confession and forgiveness," I was to say, "which is found on page fifty-seven in the green hymnal. The worship service is in the front part of the book, and page numbers are small and in the lower corner of the page. Will you stand, please?" Then, after we confessed our sin and I declared God's forgiveness, I was to say something like, "We continue our worship by singing, 'Lift High the Cross,' hymn 377 in the green hymnal. Hymns are in the back of the book and numbers are large and in the upper corner of the page. Will you please remain standing?"[4] I was to talk the congregation through the entire service in this way, until we reached the benediction and closing hymn. The second thing we were to do was bake bread so that when visitors worshiped with us, someone could go to their house on Sunday afternoon, present them with a loaf of bread, thank them for worshiping at St. Timothy's, and express our hope that they would worship with us again. After doing these things for a couple months, all we ended up with was a freezer full of bread and complaints that my instructions interrupted the flow of the service and made it longer. "Besides," a member observed, "when people show up and look lost, whoever is sitting next to them helps them find their place in the book."

What were we to do? First, we decided to go back to doing things the way we had, which meant no more running commentary in worship. Then we decided that we needed to listen carefully to God's Word, particularly what we heard in worship, and be fervent in prayer. Different passages started resonating, first with me and then with the leaders. More and more, we began to hear Scripture's message of death and new life directed squarely at us. One Sunday in the autumn of our fifth year together, we heard, "Then Jesus told his disciples, 'If any want to become my followers, let them deny themselves and take up their cross and follow me. For those who want to save their life will lose it, and those who lose their life for my sake will find it'" (Matt. 16:24–25). That changed how we understood our situation and brought out into the open possibilities we were afraid to talk about. We began to wonder together what it meant for St. Timothy's Church to deny ourselves and take up our cross and follow. We also began asking if we were working so hard to grow because we wanted to save our life. I began to raise these questions in sermons.

"We could hang in there, struggling to survive, staying open until that fatal Sunday morning when no one showed up and we breathed our last," I said in one sermon. "Then we could quietly and painlessly fade into oblivion. Or we could complete our ministry while we still have assets that can be used to further the work of God's kingdom. We could complete our ministry at a time when we can still look after and care for each other, and especially our homebound members. We could complete our ministry in a way that makes us a part of the future, both individually and corporately by providing a real legacy for our congregation. We could complete our ministry in ways that proclaim the good news we believe our community needs to hear: that the cross could not keep Jesus down, that God raised him from the dead, and that because of him, there is life even in the midst of death. We could testify to the truth that the death of a congregation will not keep God's people down, that God in Christ will raise them up, and that the death of our congregation will bring new life to Christ's church."

Sermons about closing our church were difficult to preach and undoubtedly more difficult to hear. Talking about closing our church was painful. But I kept preaching about Christ bringing life out of death by embracing rather than avoiding the cross. Overall, people kept listening, and the congregation continued to pray and talk together. After six months of hard words and heartfelt feelings, of listening intently to the Word and clinging desperately to our baptismal identity as God's beloved children, and of Christ's presence in bread and wine, we came to believe that closing our church was the right thing to do, that it was what God was calling us to do. We decided that the best way we could witness to the good news that in Christ there is life beyond death was to die—to complete our ministry, close our doors, and give everything we had to two mission congregations just getting started.

On Pentecost Sunday, the people of St. Timothy's Lutheran Church denied themselves and literally took up their cross. They took up their cross from the altar. With it they took their Bible, their candlesticks, their communion plate and cup, and their baptismal pitcher and basin. They carried them out of the church. They gave them all away. They gave everything away that day. Over dinner after our final worship service, every member received a keepsake, a memento of St. Timothy's. The congregation gave me an antique pitcher and basin so that I could continue to wash feet. My wife received the congregation's silver coffee service so that she could extend the congregation's hospitality. My daughter, then eight years old, was given an adult cross, because she had served as an adult leader in the congregation by, among other things, helping to count the offering and assisting at the altar. With every gift came a story, a memory. Finally, they gave the bishop's representative the congregational records, the keys to the church, and what was left of the congregation's savings. And with those things they gave away their church. They gave themselves away. And in that death, in that selfless giving, they found the eternal legacy of their congregation. The death of St. Timothy's Church gave life to two mission congregations.

The members of St. Timothy's Church were faithful, courageous people who chose to take seriously what it means to deny themselves, to take up their cross, and to lose their lives for the sake of Jesus and the gospel. They knew and trusted the proclamation of Christ crucified as the power and wisdom of God that brings life out of death. Many people outside the congregation appreciated what St. Timothy's Church did that day as the gospel proclamation we intended, but not everyone. Some, both inside and outside our church, could only see closing a congregation as failure, foolishness, and a stumbling block to the furthering of God's kingdom. Two or three of our members became so disillusioned and disappointed by the decision to close the church that they up and quit. More than once we heard, "It's a shame about St. Timothy's. It's so sad that they're closing up shop. I used to go there. But there were problems, and I fell away." Then there was the pastor who called me a failure and implied that I was faithless.

In the weeks following Pentecost, the people of St. Timothy's Church and I went "church shopping" together. We worshiped with a different congregation each Sunday and met with the pastor after the service. Some members of St. Timothy's Church hoped that they would find a congregation everyone liked and that they would all join together. In reality, different members had different needs and joined different churches. One couple enjoyed visiting different churches so much that they decided to spend a year "shopping around" before settling into their next congregation. The congregations we visited were overwhelmingly warm and welcoming, and the pastors gracious and inviting. One pastor, however, took a decidedly different approach.

"You must be feeling very guilty," the pastor responded, when I telephoned to tell him that we planned to visit his church on Sunday and to ask if he could meet with us after the service. "Guilty about what?" I asked. "Being a failure as a pastor. Letting your congregation down, not to mention the church and the Lord," he answered. "Don't worry. Your members can join here." When we met with the pastor after worship that Sunday, the pastor explained that, since our churches were doctrinally close, he expected that the members of St. Timothy's Church would join his congregation. He would make pastoral visits on our members and ask them some questions. When he was satisfied that they properly understood the Christian faith, they could take communion. Until then, they shouldn't.

I was sitting between two of my members, women in their seventies. "Pardon me?" one interrupted the pastor. "We can't take communion? We're baptized Christians. What makes you think we don't understand the Christian faith?" "I'm sure your pastor meant well," the pastor responded carefully, "but your church did close. . . ." "We're leaving," the other woman said, standing and cutting the pastor off. The women sitting next to me headed for the door, followed by the rest of our group. "Let's calm down," I said, standing up and attempting to be diplomatic. "Pastor Craig," one of the women responded, "I said we're *leaving.*" I felt like I had been reprimanded by my mother. Saluting the pastor, I turned and followed them out the door. That pastor's response to the people of St. Timothy's Church and to me convinced me that the apostle Paul is right. What some people regard as God's power and wisdom is likely to be dismissed as foolishness by others. So how do we discern the difference?

A Place of Grace

As Christians preach and listen to sermons and then endeavor to faithfully respond to the word of God proclaimed and heard in worship, we do our best to distinguish between wisdom and foolishness, between God's power and a stumbling block. As I said earlier, a clear and honest connection between the issue at stake and the life, death, and resurrection of Jesus makes discerning easier, as do preparing, preaching, hearing, discussing, and responding to sermons in conversation with the Christian community.[5] Christians are also better able to experience God's power and receive God's wisdom when they hear and preach sermons from a place of grace.

I regularly tell preachers that when they sit down to prepare sermons and certainly when they stand in the pulpit to preach, they do well to put themselves in a place of grace. More and more, I also tell churchgoers that putting themselves in a place of grace is the best way to listen to sermons. By a *place of grace*, I mean a place within us where God can speak and we will hear and listen. It is a state of mind and heart in which we are keenly aware of both our need for God's grace and God's gift of unconditional love, forgiveness, acceptance, and a second chance. I sometimes describe a place of grace as that chamber or room in our hearts where we come face-to-face with ourselves and with God. A place of grace might be a memory of a time when we experienced God's grace as real, tangible, and immediate. Most important, perhaps, places of grace stick with us, even years later. When we recall and return to them, both our need for and God's gift of grace remain vivid and real. Places of grace might be monumental or profound experiences, though they need not be, as long as the experiences are true to us. In fact, one person's place of grace may seem silly to another.

When I was a teenager, my dad yelled at me whenever I misplaced something. The more important the thing I misplaced (wallet, keys, eyeglasses), the louder my dad yelled. Looking back, I can understand my father's motivation; it is not good for someone who doesn't see well to misplace things. Today, I rarely lose anything of importance. But back then, misplacing anything made me angry at myself and panicked over being yelled at. As many kids do, I internalized my father's yelling and, after I left home, I yelled at myself and became panicked whenever I lost something. The more important the thing I misplaced, the louder I yelled, and the more panicked I became.

So imagine how frustrated and frantic I became when, on Christmas Eve during my year as a seminary intern, I dropped the keys to the church in a snowbank as I was hurriedly walking home to get ready for worship. Down on my hands and knees cursing myself, I dug through the snow and couldn't find the keys. When at last I gave up and went home, I nervously called my supervisor, a wise pastor named Bernie, at home to tell him what had happened. "I . . . I . . . d-dropped the keys to the church in the snow," I squeaked. "Oh," he said, "and you're late for dinner. Get ready and get over here." When I arrived at my supervisor's house, everything was Christmas cheer. Bernie and I sat down together and talked about that evening's worship services. I was very nervous about the keys. I convinced myself that my supervisor was toying with me, giving me time to contemplate how badly I messed up before letting me have it. Bernie was still talking about worship; I was preoccupied and not paying attention. Finally, he looked at me and asked, "Craig, what's wrong?" "I dropped the keys in the snow!" I blurted out. "Oh, yes," Bernie said, smiling, "the keys. I suppose I have to yell at you. Yell, yell, yell, yell, yell." Then, reaching into a pocket, Bernie produced a duplicate set of keys, handed them to me, and said two words: "Snow melts." "Craig," Bernie continued gently, "the snow will melt, and we will find the keys." To anyone else, that is common sense. But to me, that was grace. When you mess up and know that you deserve to be shamed and don't deserve to be trusted, and instead you are welcomed, cared for, and given a second chance, that is grace.

Of course, places of grace can be profound, even universal experiences. I am a lectionary preacher. On Sunday evenings, I read the appointed scripture passages for the next Sunday as the first step in preparing my sermon. On a Sunday evening not long ago, I read these words of Jesus: "For truly I tell you, if you have faith the size of a mustard seed, you will say to this mountain, 'Move from here to there,' and it will move; and nothing will be impossible for you" (Matt. 17:20). In all honesty, I was not impressed. The next evening as I was walking home after teaching an evening class, I experienced what I thought was a bad case of heartburn. Pressed by both a late afternoon and an early evening class, I had sped home to eat a quick supper of baked ziti and garlic bread and then rushed back to school. Walking home from the evening class, I told myself I had to slow down and eat healthier. Then I felt the heartburn making its way into my throat and traveling down my left arm. I found it hard to walk. I called my daughter and told her I needed help carrying my briefcase. When I arrived home, I called upon a neighbor who is a nurse. She wasn't home, and so I took it easy. After about a half hour, I felt fine. When my neighbor stopped by a few hours later, I apologized for having bothered her. "Just for fun," she said, "can I listen to your heart?" "Just to be sure," she said, "let's call your doctor." "Just to be safe," my doctor said, "you need to go to the emergency room." So off I went, convinced that I would spend several hours waiting in the emergency room and then be told that nothing was wrong.

But when I arrived at the ER, my neighbor said something I didn't understand, and I was taken immediately to the head of the line. "We're going to proceed as if you're having a heart attack," the emergency room doctor said as he slipped nitroglycerin under my tongue and attached things to my chest. "Am I having a heart attack?" I asked. "We're going to proceed as if you are," the doctor responded. In the next few hours, I learned that I wasn't going home that night. Lying alone somewhere in the emergency room, waiting for my heart to heave as the doctors tried to bring my blood pressure down, I was scared. My wife, who was attending a class that evening, had no idea what was happening. Certain that nothing was seriously wrong, I left our daughter home alone to wait for her. Suddenly, I was overwhelmed by the possibility that I might never see them again, that I might die that night, that one day I will die, and that I was not ready. I still had things to do, responsibilities to keep, and people I wasn't ready to leave. "God," I whispered, "I can't handle this. I don't have enough faith." A voice in my head answered, "All you need is faith the size of a mustard seed, and I give you even that." God also gave me a cardiologist who took the time to talk with me and seemed to move mountains to get me diagnosed, treated, and on my way home as quickly as possible. The heart attack I experienced was extremely mild. Thanks to my neighbor and my daughter, who insisted I go to the hospital, I have no permanent damage. I received grace in their persistence, in the skill and care of physicians and nurses, and in the realization that even my faith is God's gift.

When I sit down to write a sermon, when I stand in the pulpit to preach, and, increasingly, as I settle in to listen to others preach, I return to Bernie's house on Christmas Eve or to a hospital bed in the emergency room in the late hours of a Monday night. Once again, I know my need of God's grace, and I experience God freely offering that grace. Then I am ready to preach or to listen to a sermon. When we prepare, preach, and listen to sermons from such places of grace, God's power and wisdom are palpable, and so God's power and wisdom become palpable in the proclamation of Christ crucified. Sometimes God's power and wisdom are up front and center, and all we need to do is receive them. Sometimes we pull God's power and wisdom from the shadows and bring them into the spotlight. Sometimes we provide the missing pieces, fill in the gaps, and preach to ourselves what might be missing from a sermon—Christ crucified, the power and wisdom of God. Whatever we do, we do it expecting God to speak and have something important to say, since we have heard God speak to us before in those places of grace from where we are listening or preaching. Whether we sit in a pew or stand in a pulpit, God speaks power and wisdom to us in and through the foolishness of our crucified Christ.

For Reflection and Conversation

- Is your congregation concerned with growing? If so, why does your church want to grow? Could it be to save your congregation's life? What might losing your congregation's life for the gospel free your church to do or be?
- How do you prepare yourself to listen to or preach a sermon?
- What is your place of grace?

Epilogue

Tell Stories

The best part about telling stories of times when God speaks through worship is that they usually inspire other stories. In response to the stories I tell about worship, people often say, "That's nothing. You ought to see what God's doing at my church!" I ask them to tell me a story and they are right. Their stories of God speaking and acting through worship are often better than mine. As you read this book, perhaps memories and stories of God acting in worship came into your mind. Perhaps your tears or laughter connected you to a worship service you attended or led. Don't keep these experiences to yourself. When you see God acting, hear God speaking, and feel God catching you or someone else in the current of the river of God's reconciling love as it flows through worship and overflows into the world, talk about it. Tell someone about it. Tell stories about it.

Stories about God speaking and acting through worship do not need to be dramatic or earthshaking. As I said in the introduction, the best stories are small and unassuming. Large and dramatic stories about God speaking through worship may strike some people as fantastic, unbelievable, or at least unlikely to recur. Small, unassuming stories attest to God's pervasiveness and point to God's will to be present in and transform the most common activities— washing feet, touching, lighting a candle. Most important, small and unassuming stories spark a new story in the mind of the listener. This new story, which listeners create for themselves, connects with them emotionally and leads them to act. In fact, this new story becomes a story they live by.

You don't need to have the story's meaning figured out before you tell it. You probably won't be able to unequivocally declare what God is saying and doing. The church has been telling the story of Jesus's death and resurrection for two millennia, and I am not convinced that we have its meaning completely figured out. Christians usually figure out what God is saying and doing through prayer and conversation together; God seems to prefer it that way. Yet, someone has to initiate the prayerful conversation by telling the story. Let that someone be you!

Of course, to have a story to tell, you will have to pay attention in worship. Notice what you and others are *doing*, because worship is action. Encountering and being encountered by God as we worship happens in the doing. "Preach the gospel, administer the sacraments, teach the faith, visit the sick, bury the dead," my bishop wrote. I would add a few more pieces to my bishop's "disappointing advice"—*give* God the first word, *remember* baptism, *welcome* kids, *touch* and *anoint*, *light* candles, *celebrate* vocation, *pick* hymns, and *preach* Christ. Though I didn't set out to do it, I have created a collection of verbs, a list of action words that can be summarized by the verb *worship*. The things of worship—what is written in books or projected on screens, for example—are not as important as the covenant relationship God initiates and God's people respond to as the church worships. All that relationship requires is God and people *doing* together. The things, words, gestures, and places people frequently associate with worship are merely catalysts and tools. They are to worship as a script is to a play. Even the Bible is just a book unless it is *read* and *heard*; bread and wine, just food unless they are *shared* in Jesus's name. Worship is all in the doing.

Since worship is all in the doing, Christians and congregations do well. They worship well. By *well* I do not mean "correctly" or "excellently" according to some standard. We do not worship to worship. Nor do we worship to entertain, to celebrate ourselves, or to instill values, support causes, raise issues, and push agendas. We certainly do not worship to placate, appease, or persuade God. We worship *well* when we worship joyfully and expectantly because we trust that God will speak and act through worship. We worship vigilantly because we are eager to hear what God is speaking and to participate in what God is doing. Whether we are worshipers or worship leaders, we prepare ourselves to worship. One way we can prepare ourselves to worship is by putting ourselves in a "place of grace," a place within us where God can speak and we will hear and listen. We worship with our whole selves—head, heart, body, and spirit, as well as with all the gifts and abilities the congregation brings. We worship well when we risk, perhaps washing a foot, allowing hands to be laid on us as part of prayer, or taking a leadership role outside our comfort zone. We worship well when what we do in the world informs what we do as we worship, and what we do as we worship shapes what we do in the world.

As you notice what you are doing, pay attention to the particulars. We tend to forget that worship is very particular. Worship in general does not exist. Worship is always a concrete event at a specified place and time involving particular people who have their own way of doing things. Whenever I fill in as a preacher or worship leader, I ask my host if there is anything unusual or unique I should know about. "No," my host replies, "we do it like everybody else." "Okay," I answer. Then the service starts and I wait to get caught by the particulars. In one congregation, the acolyte looked at me aghast when I didn't extend my hands so that he could pour water over them before I presided at the table. In another congregation, I didn't say, "You may be seated," after reading the appointed Gospel, and the congregation remained standing well into the sermon. One Easter, members of a congregation were disappointed because I didn't "do what we always do" and hide a chocolate Easter egg in the sanctuary and tell the first one to find it to shout, "Christ is risen, indeed!"

When telling stories about God speaking and acting in worship, we do our best to communicate the specific, concrete event we experienced or witnessed. When I sit in a pew as opposed to leading the service, I increasingly find myself setting aside the hymnal and the worship folder so that I can fix my attention on the people. I am curious about how this congregation does the verbs we call worship. I notice, for example, people's postures as they pray—looking upward with open hands or head bowed and hands folded. I listen to the people around me as they sing. I wonder why people occupy the space the way they do. I pay attention to how things are said, how I feel, and the mood of the service. I like to ask children how adults look when they come back from communion. Have they been to a party or a funeral? In all this, I want to know how the congregation is responding to what God is doing as they worship.

Most important, pay attention to what God is doing, since God is more than the audience, the One to whom we address our prayers, praise, songs, and confession. God is the power at work in worship. In fact, God makes worship possible. God's saving activity flows like a river from the events of the Bible, particularly the life, death, and resurrection of Christ, through the worship of the church, into the life of the world. Worship, then, is not something we do. Worship is God's gift and activity for and with us.

Worship is also God's activity for and with more than us. God carries out God's mission of reconciling the world to Godself in worship, because that is who God is. "For God so loved the world that he gave his only Son" (John 3:16). God gave the Son, Jesus, the Christ, to save *the world*. God does more through worship than bring *us* into God's presence and life. Worship is how God gathers people to witness to and participate in God's work of reconciliation. Through worship, God continues to give Christ to save the world as God's people, the church, are formed to be the body of Christ, conformed to the mind of Christ, and transformed to live the life of Christ *in the world*. The body of Christ is broken for the sake of the world. The mind of Christ is "obedient to the point of death—even death on a cross" (Phil. 2:8). To be transformed to the life of Christ means taking up our cross and following Jesus, being united with him in a death like his, and, certainly, being united with him in a resurrection like his. Cross bearing, dying, and rising as the body of Christ are always for the sake of the world. God always speaks and acts through worship to reconcile the world.

The river of God's reconciling love does not flow from the cross into the church and stop. It continues to flow into the world. As it does, God gathers, forms, and carries Christ's body, the church, into the world. In the world, Christ's body witnesses to God's unconditional love for the world by giving its life away as a sign of the nearness of God's reign and the certainty of God's promise to bring life out of death. Through worship, God forms, empowers, and gives the church to the world, as witness to and participant in God's own purpose of reconciling the world to God's own self.

God can certainly transform us and reconcile the world in dramatic ways, as God did when Jesus appeared to Saul of Tarsus on the road to Damascus, knocking him off his horse (Acts 9:1–22). The Spirit might use a powerful sermon, a beautiful piece of music, or the liturgical marking of a significant life transition. Yet, like the stories we tell, God's activity in worship is often small and unassuming. We therefore need to remain patient and to celebrate small changes.

The small and unassuming stories in this book are themselves indications that God is transforming the world through worship. In a North American context, to claim that worship is all about doing challenges our preoccupation with material things and our stance as consumers who come to church to be served. In a culture marked by individualism and celebrity, to claim that worship is all about God means acknowledging that we are not central. As we worship, we subordinate our identities, values, agendas, preferred style, and what we get out of the service to God. Our understanding of what God is *supposed* to do in worship and what is *supposed* to happen is not as important as what God is actually doing and what is actually happening. Attending to the small and unassuming ways God speaks and acts in worship liberates us from the cultural idols of self-help, quick fix, instant gratification, and innovation for its own sake. Worshiping for the sake of the world overturns our tendency toward self-preservation and notions of success as we struggle with the difference between participating in God's own work of reconciliation and saving, preserving and expanding congregations, church institutions, and denominations.

Because the church is the body of Christ, it always worships for the sake of the world. Filled with the Spirit and blessed by the Father at his baptism, "Jesus came to Galilee, proclaiming the good news of God, and saying, 'The time is fulfilled, and the kingdom of God has come near; repent, and believe in the good news'" (Mark 1:15). The church is filled with the Spirit and blessed by the Father as it worships, and Christ, through his body, continues to point to the nearness of God's reign, proclaim and invite trust in the gospel, and bring transformation to people's lives and to the world. Christ's mission happens gracefully when the church attends to and participates in what God is saying and doing through worship. One way we can attend to and participate in God's activity is by telling stories about times when God speaks through worship.

For Reflection and Conversation

- In what particular ways does your congregation worship?
- What does it mean for you to worship well?
- How does your congregation acknowledge God speaking and acting through worship?
- What story about God speaking and acting in worship are you most eager to tell? To whom would you like to tell it? Why?

Notes

Foreword

1. Reynolds Price, *A Palpable God* (New York: Atheneum, 1978), 3.

Preface

1. Craig A. Satterlee, *When God Speaks through You: How Faith Convictions Shape Preaching and Mission* (Herndon, VA: Alban Institute, 2007).

2. In this discussion, I draw upon the Web page of the Evangelical Lutheran Church in America. See http://archive.elca.org/communication/brief.html.

3. "The Augsburg Confession," in *The Book of Concord: The Confessions of the Evangelical Lutheran Church,* ed. Robert Kolb and Timothy J. Wengert (Minneapolis: Augsburg Fortress, 2000), 42–43.

Introduction: Disappointing Advice

1. I do not find *contemporary* to be a helpful way of describing worship because it does not tell anything about the service and implies that any other form of worship is antiquated. Personally, I find much liturgical worship is quite contemporary.

2. For a fuller discussion of the relationship of worship and mission as *mountain, plain,* and *river,* see Satterlee, *When God Speaks through You,* 50–53.

3. Craig A. Satterlee and Lester Ruth, *Creative Preaching on the Sacraments* (Nashville: Discipleship Resources, 2001), 17.

4. Alexander Schmemann, *For the Life of the World: Sacraments and Orthodoxy* (Crestwood, NY: St. Vladimir's Seminary Press, 1963), 27.

5. The language of "primary theology" or *theologia prima* to describe worship (as distinct from the *theologia secunda,* or "secondary theology," that constitutes formal or systematic theological reflection) is borrowed from Aidan Kavanagh, *On Liturgical Theology* (Collegeville, MN: The Liturgical Press, 1992), 74ff.

6. Mary Catherine Hilkert, *Naming Grace: Preaching and the Sacramental Imagination* (New York: Continuum, 2000), 44.

7. Ibid., 53.

8. See, for example, Stephen Denning, *The Secret Language of Leadership: How Leaders Inspire Action through Narrative* (San Francisco: John Wiley and Sons, 2007).

9. Craig A. Satterlee, *When God Speaks through Change: Preaching in Times of Congregational Transition* (Herndon, VA: Alban Institute, 2005), xi.

Chapter 1: Give God the First Word

1. Craig A. Satterlee, *Ambrose of Milan's Method of Mystagogical Preaching* (Collegeville, MN: Liturgical Press, 2002), 155–56.

2. William Harmless, *Augustine and the Catechumenate* (New York: Pueblo, 1995), 362ff.

3. Ambrose of Milan, *On the Sacraments and On the Mysteries,* ed. J. H. Srawley (London: SPCK, 1950), 74.

Chapter 2: Remember Baptism

1. *Invitation to Christ: Font and Table, a Guide to Sacramental Practices* (Louisville, KY: Presbyterian Church [U.S.A.], 2006), 5.

2. Nancy Douglas (sermon, ACTS Doctor of Ministry in Preaching program, Chicago, IL, June 20, 2008).

3. I tell that story in chapter 7.

Chapter 3: Welcome Kids

1. Evangelical Lutheran Church in America, *The Use of the Means of Grace: A Statement on the Practice of Word and Sacrament* (Minneapolis: Augsburg Fortress, 1997), 41.

2. Ibid.

Chapter 4: Touch and Anoint

1. Carol C. Bradley, "Craig Satterlee: Finding Light in the Darkness," *Notre Dame Magazine* 31, no. 2 (September 2002): 52.

2. Association of Evangelical Lutheran Churches, Lutheran Church in America, and The American Lutheran Church, *Occasional Services* (Minneapolis: Augsburg Publishing House, 1982), 94.

3. See Matthew 4:24; 14:14; 19:2; Mark 3:10; 6:56; Luke 5:15; 6:18.

4. Barbara Brown Taylor, *The Preaching Life* (Boston: Cowley Publications, 1993), 66.

Chapter 5: Light Candles

1. The Easter Vigil, also called the Paschal Vigil and the Great Vigil of Easter, is a service held in many Christian churches in the hours of darkness between sunset on Holy Saturday and sunrise on Easter Day, most commonly in the evening of Holy Saturday. As a vigil, it is a rather lengthy affair, consisting of four services—Light, Readings, Baptism, and Holy Communion. According to historical practice, people (especially adults) are baptized and received into full communion with the church during this service. The Easter Vigil is the church's oldest worship service, with the exception of the Saturday-Sunday vigil that was celebrated in New Testament times, like the one Paul and his companions observed at Troas, from which the Easter Vigil is derived. The Easter Vigil is considered to be the first celebration of Easter Day and includes both the first celebration of the Eucharist during the Easter season and the first use of the acclamatory word Alleluia, which is a distinctive feature of the liturgy of the Easter season after having been

eliminated from the liturgy at the beginning of Lent. Many who attend this service find worship on Easter Day to be anticlimactic.

2. I acknowledge that the biblical metaphors of darkness and light are problematic and painful for many because of the history of slavery in the United States and ongoing cultural racism. For my further reflection on this issue, see Craig A. Satterlee, "Living by the Word: Groping in Darkness," *The Christian Century* 123, no. 8 (April 18, 2006): 20.

3. Evangelical Lutheran Church in America, Evangelical Lutheran Worship (Minneapolis: Augsburg Fortress, 2006), 267.

Chapter 6: Celebrate Vocation

1. Matthew 21:33–46 and parallels; John 2:1–10; John 15:1–5.

2. Mark 10:42–44 and parallels.

3. Paul F. Bradshaw, Maxwell E. Johnson, and L. Edward Phillips, *The Apostolic Tradition: A Commentary* (Minneapolis: Augsburg Fortress, 2002), 88–89.

Chapter 7: Pick Hymns

1. Brian A. Wren, "Bring Many Names," in Evangelical Lutheran Church in America, *Renewing Worship Songbook* (Minneapolis: Augsburg Fortress, 2003), R216.

2. John Thornburg, "God the Sculptor of the Mountains," in Evangelical Lutheran Church in America, *Evangelical Lutheran Worship* (Minneapolis: Augsburg Fortress, 2006), 736.

3. Source unknown, c. 1757.

4. Henry F. Lyte, "Abide with Me."

5. Though I edited these verses to speak directly to my own experience, the Levitical Code prohibits those with any sort of disability or "blemish" from functioning as priests.

6. David Haas, "We Are Called," in Evangelical Lutheran Church in America, Evangelical Lutheran Worship, 720.

7. James Quinn, S.J., "Lord, Make Us Servants of Your Peace," in *The Presbyterian Hymnal* (Louisville, KY: Westminster John Knox Press), 374.

Chapter 8: Preach Christ

1. Martin Luther, "The Freedom of a Christian," in *Three Treatises* (Minneapolis: Augsburg Fortress, 1990), 293.

2. Satterlee, *Ambrose of Milan's Method of Mystagogical Preaching*, 189.

3. Taylor, *Preaching Life*, 85.

4. I refused to say "if you are able," because I experience these words as the church feigning hospitality rather than seriously welcoming and accompanying people who are not able.

5. For more on preparing, preaching, hearing, discussing, and responding to sermons in conversation with the Christian community, see Satterlee, *When God Speaks through You.*

Chapter One:
Divine Decision

I saw it from the beginning.

Before the great disasters and wars that now have Humanity cowering in a corner, before the Seals were opened, before any of you had an inkling of what might be going on, I saw it all. But far before that, I saw you crawling through the mud, rising up for civilization. I saw you in the ancient times, before the Flood, before anything.

Like I said, I saw it all from the beginning. And indeed I could not help but do so, for I am God's scribe, his writer. I am Gabriel, an angel of our Lord God.

But for this case I should be a lot more specific. For what has recently transpired, I was there to witness.

Humanity had been making of itself a greatly unruly child, filled with corruption and a seeming hatred of its own kind. Man was given many chances, particularly after Noah and the Flood, but now to see what Man has wrought across the world greatly saddens my Lord's heart.

So, He called me in and bade me sit with my scribe's pen to mark down a new record. No predictions this time, no revelations to give future generations warning, but rather an accounting of what was about to occur so that any future survivors would be aware of the true course of events.

I was to write the history of the end of Mankind.

I guess that makes me a reporter of sorts; a news reporter with wings. And so it has been my sad duty to take note of everything that passes, and in that function I have been given freedom to come and go to anywhere that I need to... even unto the deepest pits of where Lucifer himself dwells. I have been given immunity from any and all concerned, but neither can I interfere. I can only watch and record.

And weep...

Lucifer– or Satan as the world has long known him– lies imprisoned in his dark pit, trapped behind a series of seven seals. But, that does not mean he has been without his influence. He can still reach out with his mind to command his followers and tempt Mankind. Not that Man needs much tempting; indeed, that's sort of what this whole end-times thing is all about. At any rate, Satan does have a minion faithful to his cause, and that is his son. Oh, he's been known by many names throughout your history, but the name that concerns us right now is Ashtar. He's the guy that's behind all the world's satanic cultists, Satan's commander.

Of what I am to write, though, I suppose it begins with a meeting. A meeting in which the two Sons were summoned before the presence of the Lord. Jesus and Ashtar. No love lost between those two, let me tell you; Jesus smiles and Ashtar hisses.

It is said that one cannot look upon the face of God. Well, the reason for that is simple practicality: How can Infinity have a face? It's more like, anyplace that God decides to shift his focus, becomes his face. In this case a heavenly realm between worlds, a realm of clouds, sky, and golden light.

Ashtar wasn't liking any of it, but when the Big Man summons you, there is no choice.

They stood side by side, Ashtar with his golden-haired false countenance and dark heart, while I remained quietly off to the side to record it all.

He spoke not with a voice as you would know it, but more like feelings and images. For purposes of this record, though, I shall render that exchange into words that may be understood. Basically it began with a great rumbling from above, followed by an exclamation that had Ashtar bowing to his feet.

"I am greatly displeased!"

Jesus waited a bit while Ashtar cowered, the latter no doubt wondering if he was the target of the wrath. The rumbling carried on for a moment or two before fading enough for Jesus to quietly inquire.

"Father, what displeases you so?"

A moment in which Ashtar looks ready to cringe, but the answer when given has the son of Satan pausing with sudden hope.

"Man. Every chance I have given him has been thrown back in my face. Such suffering and misery as I see, and yet not only caused by his own hand but welcomed in the same breath with which he complains about it."

Ashtar hears this and gets a crafty smile upon his face before he speaks.

"It is just as I and my father have said. Mankind is not deserving of–"

"*Quiet! I know you and your father have had a hand in much of this, but it is not for this which I would punish the world, but rather the lack of willpower in not ignoring your words. Man has had plenty of opportunity to wake up, now I'm afraid it is time for some tough love.*"

"Father," Jesus begins, "you cannot mean–"

"*I have decided. Judgment time is at hand. Jesus, my Son, I had proclaimed that yours is the only hand that may break the first of the Seven Seals, thereafter the hand of darkness may breach the other six, and so it shall be done. It is time to bring everything out into the open; no more this battle amongst the shadows, let the battle-lines be more clearly drawn, for I would see an end to this. Let Satan's hand be allowed to sweep across the world to bring the signs of my wrath and the coming of the end. Then the two of you will go to the place of Satan's imprisonment to break the first of the Seals and signal the beginning of the end. Satan will be free to bring my judgment upon the lands. Let Man see the face of evil direct and judge for himself his own soul. That is my command.*"

The two bowed before him, then everything faded from around them until only the stars remained to hang suspended in a night sky…

I said I was given freedom to go anywhere I needed to record events, and that included eavesdropping upon any secretive exchanges, such as between Ashtar and Satan. Even as Ashtar and Jesus journeyed down to the dark pit to where are the Seals that bind Satan, there was another father-son conversation going on in private.

Father, Ashtar's thoughts inquired, *I bring news.*

Slow stirring, like the head of a great beast turning with a hiss to regard some intruder into its lair. The psychic voice rings with an accent of darkness as it perceives who addresses it.

Ashtar… what news do you bring your father?

The best. You are to be allowed to bring God's divine wrath across the world. Then we are to undo the Seals and free you at last. God has decided that you are to pass his judgment along to the world.

Slowly a psychic eyebrow raises, a vicious grin gradually creeping across the face of his thoughts before giving reply.

So, I am to be his judgment, is that it? The Old Man finally decided to give Man a spanking? Well, I'll do a lot more than that. You have been in psychic contact with our operatives on the Earth?

Constantly, father. I've been dangling little tidbits before them to keep them going.

Excellent. Then it's time to put my own plans into motion. I want you to contact my chief operatives.

The Illuminati Thirteen. They have their headquarters in London.

Tell that brotherhood of the coming tribulations, of my pending freedom to pass God's judgement. I want them to be prepared to make most creative use of those events.

To what end, my Lord Satan?

Here a pause, and I can just imagine the grin spreading itself across Satan's face as he relishes the moment.

Why, to make sure that Mankind flunks the judgment, of course. Any that fail the test fall to me by default. Souls to fill the ranks of my armies for the final assault upon Heaven. I shall strengthen my armies and destroy His favorite creation at the same time. And all because He ordered me to! I may not be able to destroy God, but maybe I can get him to destroy himself!

The telepathic laughter that then resulted was more than I could bear, and so I hope you don't mind if I just skip ahead a little.

———————

The great pit in which Satan is sealed away is at the very bottom of the Well Between Worlds; a realm between dimensions that looks much like a pathway through the stars, except there are no stars down there, only empty space. A void, at the bottom of which is a single rather massive door. Ancient wrought iron, double doors that split down the middle. Their hinges seem to hang onto nothing but empty space, and if one walks around it, you will still see nothing but empty space behind it. A door just hanging there in the middle of nothing.

And yet it is a door to where Satan has long slept.

The door is sealed by a series of seven seals embossed across its width. To open it up and unleash the hand of God's judgement is a judgement in itself, for the breaking of each seal unleashes horrors in themselves. A lot has been written about what will happen if these seals are broken, much of it rather metaphorical, but the reality is this: Those tribulations spoken of are no joke, and right now I fear for the world.

Jesus paused before the door, looking sadly at the Seals.

"If I do this," he said, "the world will greatly suffer."

"You heard your father," Ashtar snapped. "Now break the first Seal."

Jesus paused to look at the other. No malice in his heart, not even for the son of Satan, but there is a subtle determination flecking through his features. A quiet look but one from which Ashtar must nonetheless flinch.

"Know this: we may not fight in any but the mortal realm, but when we do I assure you that the reign of you and your father will be short."

"But that will only happen," Ashtar smiled, "if enough people call to you. And I assure you, it will not be *your* name they call. Now open the first seal!"

"You do not command me, son of a snake," he firmly but quietly replied. "I do this because it is the will of my Father... not because of any desire of your own. Now know your place!"

To the direct glare of Jesus, Ashtar more visibly flinched, then looked more relieved as Jesus turned his attention back to the Seals. A sigh then Jesus reaches out towards the First Seal, pausing for a moment a hair's breath before it.

"Let a measure of Satan's power be allowed to bring forth the signs for Man to see before this First Seal finally breaks."

A light touch of his forefinger and the First Seal begins to flicker, straining for release. But not yet will it break for this is only the beginning, as a rumble of thunder echoes throughout this featureless realm to signal the start of Man's trials.

The unleashing of Satan has begun.

Chapter Two:

The Illuminati Thirteen

London is a busy place under the best of circumstances, but busier still is the financial center located within the heart of the city. A full square mile where financial institutions from around the world have their headquarters. But the most notable is the ancient building towering above them all. A pinnacle of baroque architecture topped by a tower running up to a point, in the center of which hangs what looks like an old bell.

An old bell carved from stone, one that in the right light might even look sort of like a single large eye looking down upon the domain below. At the base of the tower, just beneath this bell, is emblazoned a coat of arms, symbol of the ones in control of this bank. The symbol of the Rothschild family.

A day seemingly like any other, the moist London air hanging heavy with morning dew. Businessmen coming and going through the many doors of the bustling complex as transactions large and small fill the labyrinthine corridors of the largest of banks. Bees in a busy hive, constantly in motion, shuffling billions of dollars around every day.

Looking down upon this busy hive of activity is a room above it all. An office that might be deemed as the business equivalent of a throne room. Large circular mahogany desk, but at this round table sit not the knights of old, but the lords and ladies of business. Dressed in the most expensive of suits and business attire, they are thirteen in all… with one seat kept empty by tradition; the seat where their king would sit were this the court of King Arthur.

The room has a high ceiling sporting a chandelier of diamonds and crystal, with wall sconces about the corners of the vast room. Two adjoining walls are paneled in smoked glass, affording a view of the city to the horizon. A short line of servants stands against one un-windowed wall awaiting commands from any of the thirteen, while the remaining wall has the single golden elevator that permits the only access to this vaulted chamber.

There are no name plates identifying any of the thirteen, and even in this sanctuary no names are used; they are well aware of what types of technology are now available that might be able to listen in through their windows despite the best of their precautions, and so take no chances even here. They address one another only by numbers.

"Number One," one of them speaks, "why have you called this meeting? I was very busy when you called."

The one addressed is old, white-haired, and looks a bit like a wrinkled potato. His voice, when he replies, sounds much like the creaking of an ancient door, though there is a strength behind it that seems to defy his age.

"It was not I who called this meeting."

As answer, Number One turns his head to look at the one chair left always empty. Immediately everyone straightens up, any conversations quelled, as all attention is given to that one empty chair.

It starts as a will-o-wisp, faint flicker of violet-hued light, growing stronger each second until it fills the chair, taking on the semblance to a golden-haired man.

"He comes in person!" one elderly woman gasps.

"For generations we have waited," another stunned man echoes.

As the image solidifies into the projection of an actual person, all heads bow in supplication, and not even Number One will speak unless bidden.

A moment to take in their supplication before uttering his first word.

"Speak."

It is Number One that speaks, his tone reverential as a knight before his king.

"My Lord Ashtar, long have we awaited your appearance. We have heard you in our dreams and in our thoughts, but never thought in our lifetimes to actually see you in person. This is a momentous day indeed, Lord Ashtar."

"More than you know," Ashtar replies. "I am here because the breaking of the first Seal is nigh; the Seal that has long restricted my freedom of movement in your world. Soon it will be completely gone and I will be able to come to you in the solidity of flesh."

"Then the times are upon us," Number One remarked. "The time when we will reign directly as kings upon the world under your rule."

"Yes," Ashtar said with a cunning smile, "but first there is some preparatory work that must be done. Before the Seven Seals are to be broken and the Four Horsemen released there will be a series of trials and tribulations for the world to face. Great disasters that will hit the world; ones which you are to take advantage of. The world must be primed so that when I arrive in my full glory, the world will readily kneel before me. Mankind must be made ready to accept that which they would never give thought to otherwise."

"What would you have us do, my Lord Ashtar," Number One asked.

"Oh, it's quite simple. We can start with engineering a global economic collapse."

"Another one?" one of the thirteen dared to ask.

"Not like any before," Ashtar replied. "For this one must leave the entire world in complete ruin. It shall be like nothing anyone has seen before." His voice began to rise as he continued, his features to darken as he spoke. "I want to see the world's greatest economies brought to their knees! I want to see scorched earth, smoke, and dust. I want to see billionaires crawling around on the ground digging through garbage for food. Do I make myself clear?"

His tone had risen to give the chandelier a shudder as all thirteen faces snap up with looks mixing fear and subservience. Looks exchanged all around the table, then settling on Number One as their chosen spokesman. Number One swallows a lump before daring to speak.

"If I may ask... to what purpose, my Lord Ashtar? We already control nearly everything worth controlling. The world's money supply is in our hands. We could easily–"

"I want economic destruction!"

Seething anger for a moment, and in that moment Ashtar's face flickering with an overlay of horns and demonic features, until he sees the true leaders of the world cowering before him and eases back into a calm demeanor and handsome features once again.

"It is all part of a larger plan," he continues in a smooth voice. "Each of the Seals will bring a different calamity upon the world, the intent of which is to render judgment upon the faithless and salvage those that remain. Before even the First Seal is broken, however, there are to be some preparatory signs meant to give Man a little warning and take heed. However, we're going to twist that a bit."

"How– How so, my Lord?"

The grin that grew across Ashtar's face held a cunning that gained the immediate interest of the Thirteen; enough so to quell their fears and listen most intently.

"The judgement is supposed to be pretty straight forward; if you've been bad then that's it, if you're good then you go to Heaven. But circumstances have been known to twist good people into performing deeds they otherwise would never contemplate. To that end, we're going to turn these little warning signs into great calamities in themselves; magnify them to bring the world into ruin before the First Seal even breaks! Something of biblical proportions, if you don't mind the pun. When the world is falling about you, everything in economic ruin, and it's a struggle to put food on the table for your family, how many people do you know that would then remain true to their beliefs? How many would do whatever it takes to survive? Murder, cannibalism, everything will be on the table as viable options. With the world in economic ruin, many of those that might have otherwise been judged as innocent will fall to the other side. By the time even the First Seal breaks—"

"The *entire* populace will be ready to receive you," Number One realized.

"We will control more than just their bank accounts," the elderly lady that had previously spoken put in, "we will control their hearts."

"*Now* you're catching on," Ashtar grinned. "There will be no one left willing to follow anyone *but* me… and my father. For whoever can lead them out of the darkness, all of Mankind will blindly follow to their doom."

"We will control the entire world without having to remain clandestine," another there stated. "Oh, under your hand of course, Lord Ashtar."

"Of course," Ashtar beamed. "Now, if you're quite finished emotionally ejaculating, I have some disasters of my own to set up."

"Have no fear, my Lord Ashtar," Number One promised. "We will have the world in a complete economic meltdown by the weekend."

"I will hold you to that."

A last cunning smile then the light begins to well up around him once again until it is nearly blinding. A moment later it dims and the chair is once again empty.

Number One took a moment to settle himself before addressing the rest, his subservient manner gone.

"Number Two," he said, addressing the elderly woman, "see that the interest rates on all loans are *doubled*. That should get things started in the right direction."

"Personal *and* commercial?" Number Two asked.

"Hmm... The commercial rates are already a bit lower than personal accounts... Better triple the commercial rates. At the same time let's see about dropping the return rates on investment accounts. That's good for a warm up, but... how much do we have built up in derivative investments worldwide?"

"About twelve hundred trillion, U.S.," Number Two answered. "It's the world's largest gambling scheme and every major investment firm on the planet has a piece of it. There's also another nine trillion in housing debt in the United States alone that we can add in, not to mention all the student loans."

"Excellent," Number One stated. "Then let's bring it all crashing down. Over twelve hundred trillion in derivative investments suddenly vanishing should get some people's attention. Now, Number Three..."

He spoke now to the first man that had addressed him when the meeting had begun. A middle-aged man of apparent Hindu lineage.

"...we could use some trouble at the manufacturing end of things. Something to send costs soaring."

"Simple enough," Number Three shrugged. "I'll just see to it that all sweat shops in China and India pay their factory workers more than the ones in the Western world get. No one will be ready for that."

"Indeed," Number One mused. "They'll have no time to adjust. Then what else... Number Seven, how's about a political crisis? Leak to the news outlets what's *really* been going on in D.C. and the Congressmen behind it."

"Abandon our allies?" Number Seven, a brown-haired man, asked. "After we spent so much time and effort entrenching them?"

"The repercussions will send the U.S. political elite into a tailspin," Number One replied. "Something that most people will enjoy, but coming at the same time as the economic turmoil we're about to engineer, there will be no one not in jail competent enough to handle it all. Now, about China…"

The meeting would continue for a couple hours after that, detail stacking upon detail, the net result of which would begin a progression of economic chaos. The details of who got affected worse by this madness and when did not matter. Sooner or later, all would succumb.

———

It happened just as they promised, literally overnight. Loan rates skyrocketed, the housing market crashed, and people found themselves suddenly unable to make their mortgage payments. Then came a new well-meaning law rushed through Congress that forgave *all* student loans, not just their interest rates, that had the banks that had made the loans desperately struggling to make up the difference. But that would only be the beginning.

When the derivatives investment market suddenly crashed, it took with it entire countries; twelve hundred trillion dollars does not die quietly. By the weekend newspaper headlines declared that Greece and Bulgaria were ready to declare bankruptcy if the United Nations would not act to help them, while the European Union had to quickly absorb the financial devastation of its member nations. Russia had no problem with enacting their own form of martial law, but the rest of Europe was not as quick to act. Overnight there were many nations faced with complete ruin if solutions could not be quickly enacted.

International banks that had been around for nearly two hundred years were forced to close their doors and forbid anyone from accessing their savings accounts until they could figure out what to do. Investment firms had the unenviable task of informing even their biggest investors that their portfolios had been completely wiped out. Soon a cry was heard around the world for the heads of those bankers responsible for this disaster. A few scapegoats were found and quickly arrested, but that did not stop the chain of events.

The financial domino effect raced across the world, where the eastern stock market completely collapsed and the giants of Japanese industry were faced with making very severe cutbacks or risk bankruptcy. China acted quickly and closed its doors to the outside world, which of course meant that the western trade it had become so dependent on suddenly dried up.

In the United States the DOW dropped a shocking twenty thousand points and echoes of the Crash of 1929 raced through the business world. Faced with utter ruins, executives jumped out of the windows of their high-flung Park Avenue offices, while company after company closed its doors. By the end of the second week, unemployment rates had crashed through the thirty percent barrier. Many had savings for just such emergencies, but with the banks in trouble no one could access them.

To save themselves from imminent disaster, many mortgage lenders called the bulk of their loans due in full. Needless to say this was not a tenable option for the bulk of home owners; the ones that could, took the banks to court, while many of the rest were threatened with ending up on the streets.

It was not long before there was a march on the nation's capitol for swift action, but even there the populace was stymied. For at the same time as the economy collapsed, evidence enough to indict half of Congress came into the light and the hallowed halls of government were littered with waves of subpoenas. With the Federal government effectively frozen from acting swiftly on the crisis, the United States' economy became like a heavy anchor that started to pull down the rest of the world along with it.

I walked the streets to see for myself how this first trial was affecting Humanity. I saw the homeless population exploding, while suburbs became battle grounds as families fought to keep their homes while figuring out how to pay for the basic necessities of Life. It wasn't long before trash began to pile up along the curbs as such civil services as trash collection began to fold.

The local and state governments acted quickly to save themselves, but their actions were predictable. Rather than work to reduce their expenses, they simply increased taxes and put an even greater burden on the citizenry. Inflation skyrocketed and the economy became even worse.

One action begets another. Where poverty rises, so does the crime. It began first within the inner cities, then spread quickly to the suburbs. With no ready money to buy food, stealing increased. With no jobs to be had, many more reverted to the world's oldest profession in desperation. By the third week the streets of the nations greatest cities were starting to resemble third-world slums.

I walked one neighborhood to see three homes in the process of foreclosure, another with a family already being evicted. I saw sections of the inner city become a war zone, little of local businesses left to be robbed. Then I traveled to the richer neighborhoods, places like Beverly Hills to see how well they fared.

I came upon the walled estate of a major Hollywood star; the sort of place worth tens of millions of dollars. Its gate had been broken into and its manicured grounds now littered with an increasing number of homeless encampments. As to the owner of the place, I could see no sign of him. Or perhaps he was one of the dispossessed now camping out with the rest of the unwashed in his own living room.

I had seen enough. The Illuminati-13 had done their job quite thoroughly, and yet I knew this was but the beginning.

Chapter Three:

Famine

Jesus stood back from the line of Seals, looking now to his side as Ashtar reappeared with a grin beside him.

"The First Seal is soon to be broken, which means you will be free to unseal the rest. Be warned, though; each Seal you unleash will bring greater judgement against you when we meet in the realm of Earth."

"And when that happens, I shall see to it that there is no one left of Humanity to fight by your side. No one for you to save. The people of the Earth will fail you."

"I have faith in Humanity. I will never abandon them."

"Then you are a fool! Now stand back while I channel a measure of my Lords Satan's power to bring about the first calamity."

It was with reluctance that Jesus stood back, and with eager intent that Ashtar stepped up to the great gate, laying one hand to its surface and the other stretching up overhead. From beyond the singular metal-bound door the first trickle of Satan's power came, filling up Ashtar's body with a dark radiance which then shot out through his outstretched hand and up through the void to the world above as he called out.

"Let the world feel such hunger as he has never felt before. A great Blight to empty his belly and weaken his resolve. Feel the power of your new Lord Satan!"

Thunder cracked out from Ashtar's hand as in the prison behind the Gate a first rumble of laughter was heard.

I watched through the eyes of a farmer in the Midwest as he stood beside his wife watching his two teenage sons examine another row of corn. The power of Satan as channeled through Ashtar had quickly manifested into something that had the farmer giving a sigh as one of his sons reported back with a look and slow shake of his head.

"I don't understand it," the man said. "First it was the peas and now the corn. I've never seen a blight that could take them both out."

"And so quickly," his wife agreed. "I heard Hank's having the same trouble, and he farms *wheat.*"

"Twarnt bad enough what with the economy, now we got this. Maybe there's something on the radio. Get it, would you Martha?"

His wife replied by turning away for a quick walk over to the jeep that had brought them out to the middle of his farmlands, then started fiddling with the car radio. Meanwhile the two sons brought over a couple broken shafts of corn, the stalks flecked through with dark grey spots.

"I ain't seen nothin' like this, Pa," the older of the two boys remarked.

"Neither have I, Thomas, but maybe the government radio will have something. Some new plague they got a special spray for."

The static hiss of the radio tuning in came from the jeep, then as it resolved into a steady voice Martha called out.

"Bill, I got somethin'."

The farmer hurried over to join his wife by the jeep, his two sons fast behind him. It was the voice of the local farm report.

"...across all counties with no explanation. The blight has so far been recorded as affecting corn, wheat, peas, and beans, while in Idaho there are stories of potato

plants suddenly withering away. As of yet, the CDC and Department of Agriculture have no explanation as to what manner of disease can affect such a wide range of crops. Work is underway to develop a pesticide, but so far nothing tried has even slowed this thing down."

"Turn that thing off," Bill sighed.

Martha clicked off the radio then cast a worried look to her husband.

"Bill, what are we going to do? If this keeps up–"

"I know," he replied. "We've already tried hitting it with every spray I can think of. If this keeps up, the only thing we'll have left will be what's stored in the silos from last–"

He froze, a sudden very disturbing thought hitting him.

"The silos," he realized with shocked revelation. "This blight might not be limited to– We've got to check the silos! Come on."

The four jumped into the jeep and raced down the dirt road in the direction of the distant silos. A race against futility, for when they cracked open the door into the first silo, they saw little more than dust stacked high above their heads.

While Bill and Martha were worrying over their livelihood, across the State similar concerns were being voiced, though this time of a much larger scale. A massive factory complex devoted to the production of various food products. The complex was like a small city, with facilities for the production of everything from bread to cereal. A company that ships to markets all over the country and beyond.

A sign read "Embassy Foods", beneath it a cluster of logos for its various subdivisions. A proud corporate concern, now teetering on the edge of panic.

Riding on a cart through the food factory city came two men. I'll tell you now that they are Michael Struther, CEO and inheritor of the company from his father, and his main executive underling David Daniels. I came to land on a nearby roof to observe just as they were driving away from one of the many warehouse-sized buildings.

"It's like that all over, Mike. Crops are failing left and right from *all* our suppliers."

"What's the percentage?" Mike asked.

"About seventy-five percent. I've never even *heard* of anything like this. Sure, the regular stuff we can supplement with the usual round of chemical additives, but this will absolutely *kill* our organics division."

"Then start adding the additives to the organic products as well, at least until we can find another solution."

"But by law, anything organic has to be–"

"David, it's not like anyone really *checks* that stuff. We have an emergency here. We're already teetering on the edge of bankruptcy with the economic crash, we need to do whatever it takes to save ourselves!"

"Okay, so the organic stuff's not going to be so organic anymore."

"Now, we need to arrange some other suppliers. As desperate as this sounds, what about China?"

The cart turned a corner, headed in a line for a particularly large manufacturing building.

"Already checked," David answered, "and China's closed up tight. Officially they're not saying a thing, but from what some associates on the inside are telling me, the blight's hit their rice fields pretty bad."

"Mexico?"

"Still trying to find out. Ever since that political bomb was dropped on Washington, all trade deals have been suspended until the Attorney General can get a better look at which one of the two hundred jailed congressmen was involved in what capacity. Then I hear that the

President of Mexico is up on corruption charges and too busy to worry about his own skin to–"

"I get the picture. Mexico's out... Australia?"

"Wild fires set by some Muslim radical group. Mike, there's not a place on this planet where we can grab some fresh crops from. Ireland's suffering a potato famine worse than the one of about a century or so back, France's wine crop just–"

"Then grind up some fish scales and call it grain!" Mike shouted. "But just get *something* moving that people can eat."

He stopped the cart as he said this, anger flushing through his face for a moment before letting out with a sigh and shake of his head.

"Sorry about that, Dave, but the stress–"

"Yeah, I know. Everyone's getting stressed out, or have you seen the news lately?"

"I try to avoid it. Okay, get a line out to the Department of Agriculture, see if they got anything. In the meantime–"

"Fish scales and heavy on the additives. Will do."

The CEO of Embassy Foods let out a sigh then started up the cart once again and drove off. It was at that point that I took wing and flew away. I'd seen enough.

From there I performed a random sampling of similar manufacturers across the world, but the result was the same. Of course, neither the corporate manufacturers nor farmers like Bill and Martha could see what I saw: the ghostly specter of Famine riding across the land, spreading his blight far and wide. It came in the form of a plant disease that no one had any ready explanation for, but the result was the same.

The world was about to starve to death and it didn't know why.

Chapter Four:

The Rumbling Of The Land

Ashtar's ghostly countenance once again appeared before the Thirteen, Number One speaking for them all as the expected question was.

"My Lord Ashtar, what would you have of us this time? We have ruined the world's economy, as well as lent an assist in seeing to the starvation of the masses."

"Nice work, my minions," Ashtar grinned, "but there is more. I need quakes and bad weather now. Increasing quakes are supposed to be another sign of the coming of the end; simply a series of earthquakes of mild but quickly increasing intensity. Something to wake up the populace and gain their attention."

"And you want us to make them worse," Number One presumed.

"I will be shooting out a measure of Lord Satan's power, but there is a limit to that as prescribed by God. So, I need you to extend that limit."

"A small bomb placed at a key fault line or two should work wonders," Number One replied. "We also have some operatives in government research that have been working on a few toys that should be able to amplify these quakes, and no one will be the wiser."

"Excellent! Now, what do you have to stir up the weather?"

Number One glanced over to Number Ten who replied with a nod, then Number One turned back to Ashtar's image.

"There is a government military program that was tested in the mid nineties that was shut down because it was too successful. It was supposed to be dismantled but we saw to it that it remains, just in case. Officially it's off the books now. It is called HAARP, with two 'A's. Basically it's a weather control system with which we can create vast storm systems; something like an El Niño. We can have increase hurricanes and tornadoes and the world will blame it on the latest disaster buzzword: climate change."

"That sounds perfect," Ashtar beamed. "Do it. Deadly quakes and storms should soften up the world."

Ashtar's image once again faded away as the Thirteen worked to fulfill his latest commands.

———————————

It began as a series of relatively tame quakes, originating first in the Middle East and Turkey, then spreading across the world. A curiosity for seismologists at first, but then they became more than mere warning signs and increased to that which the people of the world had never before experienced. It was like the Earth was shaking to its very core. I stood upon the winds to watch and record and what I saw was devastating.

You can insert your favorite disaster movie here and still fall short. In California the San Andreas Fault finally unleashed in full. Everyone watched their televisions in horrid fascination as San Francisco basically fell into the Bay, and Mexico City became a hole in the ground. But that was only the beginning, for it triggered something far worse that I wonder if even the Illuminati-13 had calculated for… not that they would have cared one way or the other.

Geologists have long known about the "super-volcano" centered beneath Yellowstone Park. I watched as the popular geyser "Old Faithful" became ground-zero of a volcanic eruption that turned the bulk of Wyoming into a lava pit. Not that the rest of the world was much better off. The quake in California echoed around the fabled Pacific "Ring of Fire", causing quakes from Japan to Australia. Then came Turkey, always a popular place for troublesome quakes, but this one left a couple of its major cities in ruins. Similar stories came from other parts of the globe.

Along with the quakes came the storms. One hurricane after another pounding Atlantic shorelines, tornadoes sweeping in lock step up the Great Plains. Monsoons in India that persisted for far longer than usual. The North Sea became a nearly nonstop rendition of lighting and tossing waves.

Crossing the Pacific came a large oil tanker making its usual run. It had bumped into storms before but nothing like what hit it now. The only sign they later found of it when radio contact was lost, was a broken hull and a hundred-mile oil slick being tossed to even wider ranges by the next storm.

The oil rigs in the North Sea were built to withstand many violent storms, but when one was hit by both such a storm *and* a quake of unusual intensity at the same time, it was finally brought beneath the waves in pieces. And not the last such would it be.

The Mediterranean was choked with storms and what some climatologists would almost swear resembled El Niño-like conditions were it not for the location. Much of Europe seemed to oscillate between disastrous storms and pelting heat waves. Together with the blight still affecting many crops, conditions for famine and starvation only got worse.

And through it all the hand of the Illuminati-13 went completely unseen. News and political commentators quickly blamed climate change, even through a cadre of scientists insisted the science did not support it. In fact, that same group of scientists said that they had evidence that at least the weather conditions were being artificially manipulated and left on a plane for Washington D.C. to present their case.

The plane went down in another freak storm, with no survivors.

Conditions quickly got bad enough that, climate change or not, a sort of war council was formed by the Military at a base in New Mexico. They would have used the one further north in the Rockies, but it was buried by the volcanic eruption.

General John Willmington was in charge of the base, making of it an emergency center of national operations while the President dealt with the chaos washing over Washington D.C.. I came in unseen by mortal eyes just as the General was in his office on a video conference call with the President. Both were looking rather haggard.

"John, I need something. There's quakes all over the planet, the bulk of California's almost a write-off, we haven't heard anything out of Wyoming in days, word's finally coming out of China that they just had a couple of nine-point quakes, and satellites just recorded some major upheavals deep in the heart of Russia. And then we have these bloody storms making hash of any rescue and recovery efforts. We just lost another tanker in the Gulf of Mexico to the third Category Five hurricane in a row; in fact, it was so bad that some scientists want to label it as the world's first Category Seven! Now tell me someone over there knows what's going on, because I'm having enough trouble up here."

"Nothing yet, Mister President," the General responded. "Our best seismologists are on it, but so far the best we've got is a theory that a shift in the Moon's orbit might be causing these quakes. They should subside, but the damage is already done. As far as the storms, I'm looking into the possibility that someone's reactivated HAARP but I've been getting some flack trying to get answers."

*"Harp? Now who would be idiotic enough to turn **that** thing on? Well, you can just tell anyone trying to*

stonewall you that you have direct Presidential authority to get some answers and shut that thing down!"

"Yes, sir. I'm also coordinating with a few other countries on handling all the quake and storm damage, but we could certainly use some disaster relief, sir."

"And I'd love to give it. Unfortunately, Congress is virtually nonfunctional at the moment. We have more Congressmen in jail than in office right now. The taxpayers are certainly grateful for the unveiling of all the corruption we'd long suspected, but it couldn't have come at a worse time. John, the European Union just completely collapsed as a functional entity."

"Sounds bad, sir."

"Bad? Four more countries just left the E.U., Greece is plagued with food riots, France's wine production just bottomed out because of that blight, no one knows who's in charge of Spain anymore, and no one can seem to get through to Belgium."

"It does indeed sound bad, sir, but my immediate concern is this country and how to handle the fallout of those quakes."

"I'm afraid that you're going to have to handle a lot more than that, John. If the worst should happen– and

that's looking pretty probable– then I want you to take charge."

"Take charge of what, sir?"

"Everything. There's so much corruption around here that it's like a bunch of demented children in a sandlot each trying to grab the ball for themselves instead of playing the game. We have millions of people starving, and between the economy and those earthquakes, public services are breaking down completely. It's very possible that I'll have to declare martial law, but it's also very possible that the second I do so my time as President will be at an end."

"Sir? I'm not sure I understand."

*"I'm preparing for the worst, John, including my own assassination by any one of a number of forces that would rather see me fail. Listen, the minute you get word of me declaring martial law, you **act** on it. As of that moment you will have full authority to do whatever it takes to keep this country secure and protect it from itself... I'll even put the Football in your charge if it comes to it. Do I make myself clear?"*

General Willmington sat in silence for a moment or two, then replied with a nod.

"Good. Now I've got a mess to get back to. My only blessing is that three of our most corrupt politicians were killed in that quake in California. Now if I can just keep half of Florida from sinking into the Gulf of Mexico."

The call clicked off, leaving General Willmington alone in the solitude of his office. He sat there thinking, then reached out to call up an image on his monitor. It was a world map, several areas colored red and accompanied by glowing numbers.

"Whoever heard of an earthquake lasting five minutes? Something's not right. First the crops fail and people begin starving, then the quakes. Perfect conditions for diseases to start spreading around before long."

He thought about that for a moment, then pressed another button. Another face filled the monitor, one in a military uniform with officer's bars on his shoulders.

"General?"

"Captain, alert the CDC. Tell them to start ramping up production of every type of antibiotic known to mankind."

"They'll want to know why, sir."

"That's simple enough. Between famine, devastating quakes, and economic collapse, it doesn't take too much to figure out that disease is going to start being a problem and I want to be ready for it."

"Yes, sir. I will contact them immediately."

The image winked out, leaving the General once again alone, thinking.

"Hmm… That mess in Europe is going to erupt into wars before long. Better be ready for that as well… What a mess. Famine, death, disease…"

Then it hit him; an impossible thought that had him shaking his head.

"Nah, couldn't be."

He thought about it for a minute, then shrugged.

"But then again, at the rate things are going, I'll take any straw I can grasp onto."

He hit the button again.

"And Captain. Get me the best biblical scholar you can find."

"Sir?"

"Just *do* it. I need to cover all the bases."

"Yes, sir."

I slipped away to think. It appears that at least one person of significance was beginning to catch onto the course of events, but would that be enough? I'm only supposed to record events, not manipulate them, but maybe... Maybe I can sort of nudge things along a little. Give Humanity a chance to save itself.

If I can find others like General Willmington here and arrange for them to be in contact with one another, then maybe they might be able to come up with something to save the world before it's too late. It'll have to be the right sort of people, but... I can start with that biblical scholar the General just asked for. Find the right one then put his name under the Captain's nose. After that, it's up to them.

But who? I don't have much time to figure that out.

Chapter Five:

Disease

Ashtar unleashed the next measure of Satan's power without anyone the wiser, following as it did in the wake of what preceded it. He didn't even need to use Satan's power for the next sign, simply made a visit once again to that center of power in London and spoke in his ghostly form to another meeting of the Illuminati-13.

"I want you to unleash a plague such as the world has never seen," Ashtar told them.

"Where would you like us to release it, Lord Ashtar?" Number One asked.

The answer was simple.

"Everywhere! Something tricky that cannot be traced, its true design hard to fathom."

"We have just the thing," Number One grinned. "No one will suspect it for it will hide under the guise of a series of different plagues."

"Perfect! Between the famine, economic collapse, overburdened public and social services, that will be the only formula needed to bring forth one of the worst plagues to hit the world. And no one will suspect it as being anything more than a natural consequence of everything else."

Ashtar's laughter lingered for a few moments after his image faded away.

And thus the plague would manifest just as General Willmington had foreseen. Several plagues, in fact.

In my search throughout the world, I happened across a young doctor in a hospital in what remained of the city of Los Angeles. With San Francisco gone, and most of the rest of northern California a wasteland because of the quakes and economic collapse, including the capitol Sacramento, Los Angeles had become overrun with refugees. The sick, the dying, the poor, all of them pouring into hospitals that had little medicine, shelters that had no more bedding space, and food banks that could only nourish them with products of questionable nutritional value.

Yet there was the one doctor there that, no matter how bad things got, would not give up. As outside another storm pounded away at the broken cityscape, I watched as he hurried from one person to another, doing what he could to heal the sick and comfort the dying. A place meant for caring now being robbed of its humanity.

"Nurse, just do it," the young doctor shot back. "Better to give more people a chance with half a dose then lose so many."

"But Doctor," the nurse protested, "that will not be enough to confer the full benefit, especially on the very sick."

The doctor paused for a second in his frantic chasing around, nodded once, then amended his orders.

"Then do this. For the healthier ones half a dose of the antibiotic; that might be enough for them to pull through. Then save the full doses for the very sick."

He was about to pull away when the nurse caught at his sleeve.

"And the terminal, doctor?"

"A prayer."

Leaving the nurse to be about her orders, he made his way down the hospital corridor. It seemed walled with people, decorated with the murals of the dead and dying. A hundred people pleading, only half of which he could give comfort to as he made his way to the double doors at the end.

"If I could turn water into more antibiotic the way Jesus did with water and wine, I might have a chance," he muttered to himself.

Nearly to the doors when through the din of the dying he heard a voice calling out to him.

"Excuse me, Doctor Janson? Doctor Steven Janson?"

The young doctor paused, turning quickly around to see what new disaster greets. It was an older man, black hair balding, dressed in an overcoat and boots recently wet from the storms outside, but his priestly collar was clearly visible.

"Father, I'm sorry, but I really have no time. I have several patients that I have to get to and little in the way of medical supplies left. Not to mention nobody that can pay for any of it anyway; half of the people here have been on the streets starving since before the quakes. We're pretty desperate here, so if you don't mind–"

"That's what I'm here for."

The priest put out his hand and gave the doctor's a quick shake. He seemed to have a youthful energy that not even the disasters of the day could long quell.

"I'm Father Henry Mason. Oh, how I prayed I'd find you. You were supposed to be in Denver at a conference but then–"

"Then the quake hit before my plane could take off. I'm lucky to be alive. I heard about the riots in Denver and the terrorist bombs that took out the main runway at the Denver airport."

"You were saved because God blessed you. He knew that you were needed."

"Well, as it turns out I am. Now if you don't mind, there's a *lot* of people that need me right now."

On a side note, it may not have been entirely accidental that the good doctor's plane didn't take off in time. It seems as the plane's chief pilot had discovered a 'Dear John' letter from his wife a few hours earlier than he was supposed to. Just enough of a delay to steer things in a different direction. As for the priest, after General Willmington's assistant came across a video online of Father Mason speaking as a biblical expert and thence forwarded the information to a certain General, I then made sure that Father Mason stepped on a discarded pamphlet of the upcoming conference that Doctor Janson was going to miss. He did the rest by researching the ones on that pamphlet on his own. He went through six names before he realized that Doctor Janson was by far the best man.

And at no point did I ever interfere with that most sacred of holies, freedom of choice. I may have nudged a few objects into their awareness, but nothing more. The rest was entirely a matter of human choice... A fine distinction, I'll admit, but I would like this story I'm writing to have at least a couple hopeful notes.

"Doctor Janson, please. I'm working with General Willmington to resolve certain aspects of this crisis and right now it appears that you are the most qualified to help our little project."

"A priest working with a General? On what?"

"That's a little hard to explain. I'm a biblical scholar, you see. The General's trying to gather select experts together for– Well, I can't really explain it all here. But you're one of the foremost experts on disease in the world, working with the CDC, discovering a cure for–"

"I am well aware of my record, Father, but if you don't mind I have a lot of patients to deal with. If you need someone for something, contact the CDC; I've got lives to save."

Even as he said this, he spied a sickly looking child in the arms of his sleeping mother and stepped over to see why the child cried so. Soothing words into his ears, gently pulling the child away with one arm, while the other raised an eyelid on the mother he clung to so.

"But that's just it," Father Mason continued. "CDC headquarters in Atlanta was hit with a virulent outbreak that's already taken out half the staff, the rest are under quarantine. And now what's left of Congress just voted to cut all funding for the CDC in favor of sending relief money to Mexico."

The doctor motioned to an attending nurse, then at her approach passed the child onto her and quietly whispered in her ear.

"The mother's dead, but don't remove the body until the child is well out of sight. Put him in the children's ward and give him what can be spared of some antibiotic. And see if we have anything left to feed him."

"Yes, Doctor."

The priest heard this and took pause, making a sign of the cross over the fallen mother as the doctor rose up to his feet to face him.

"Now, you were saying something about the CDC closing down? But that's *insane.*"

"Which would be why the President just declared martial law. Doctor Janson, General Willmington authorized me to follow my nose, as he put it. To seek out wherever God may lead me to find the ones we need to save the world."

"The *world?*"

Before the priest could continue, he had to pause as the ground shook beneath their feet. Not a major quake this time, just another reminder of the world's rapidly changing conditions. After a few seconds the tremor subsided and the priest continued.

"Doctor, you have no idea how bad it's gotten out there. As bad as you have it here in this hospital, it's a thousand times worse elsewhere. We need people that can solve much bigger problems, people with skills. Researchers."

"And biblical scholars?"

"Like I said, it's a long story. But one that ends with you having the chance to save millions. Are you interested?"

Doctor Janson looked out over the hallway of the dead and dying, knowing how many more were lined up throughout the hospital. Ever since the quake had trapped him here, he'd heard little of what else was going on throughout the world. To imagine it could be so many times worse… then that he could have a hand in fixing it.

"Very well, but you'll have to give me a few minutes. There are some patients–"

"You have other doctors and nurses to take your place in something like this, but of everyone serving at this hospital, *you* are the only one that can do what we need you to do."

"Very well," the doctor said with a tired sigh, "but how are we getting out? No planes running, half the freeways collapsed from the quake, and that's nearly a hurricane out there."

"I have a military helicopter waiting that's designed to weather such storms. Now we've got to hurry."

Doctor Janson cast a last look around, bit his lip, then grabbed the priest by the shoulder and hurried through the double doors.

Chapter Six:

The Specter Of War

Ashtar once again placed a hand to the door behind which Satan stirred, this time from his outstretched hand spinning a cone of screaming voices echoing up into the world above. Whispers of dissatisfaction, the echo of displeasures to find their way as seeds into the backs of human consciousness.

"That should get things stirred up a bit," Ashtar said, his eyes gleaming with pleasure. "Then maybe a personal visitation to some of my Muslim friends just to make sure. And no one will ever be the wiser for my hand."

"Some will see the signs," Jesus quietly replied. "Your hand will be known."

"But in the end, will it matter? Remember the story of Princess Cassandra of Troy? She could see the future well enough but was cursed that no one would ever believe her prophecies. That is the fate of the few that will see the hand of me and my father. They may see clearly, but no one will ever believe them."

"And here I thought that I was the one with the parables."

His soft smile even when faced with such a dire truth, Ashtar found to be infuriating. In a spate of anger he spit at Jesus' feet then faced back to the great door. Its edges were starting to glow brightly and through the door could be heard a sound like building thunder.

"Hear that? That's my father laughing. You've already lost, so you can take your sanctimonious cross and shove it up your–"

"Crude insults now? Why Ashtar, I thought you were beneath such things."

Ashtar paused into a scowl, then eased slowly back into a grin.

"You shall not bait me, Son of God. I have the final play of the hand. Soon the First Seal will be fully erased, followed by each of the others in turn. Then my father is unleashed upon the world and we *really* get to see some sport."

"Perhaps."

To see Jesus so calm, Ashtar grumbled sourly, then cast his gaze up towards the world…

From the helicopter Doctor Jenson and Father Mason were taken to a military base, where the storm had finally abated enough to risk the flight. They were hustled onto a heavy-duty military cargo transport with only the most basic of accommodations, but it would get them to where they needed to go without incident. The plane had some viewports, and once it was in flight, the doctor was able to get to his feet for a look out through the small round windows. What he saw as they flew over the countryside, caught him short.

"That looks all grey down there," he stated. "I thought there were some farms out in this direction. Aren't we flying over Bakersfield or something?"

"You are exactly right," Father Mason sighed, joining him by the windows. "That's what's left of the farms after the blight was finished with it. I'm told the smell down there is quite bad, between all that dead plant matter and the bodies."

"Bodies?"

"Cows need grain and hay to live, Doctor. And people need– Well, I hear that many still live, but not in a manner that either of us would be comfortable with."

"I… can well imagine," Doctor Janson sighed. "I've heard stories. Mostly coming from the inner city areas, but… The gangs have set up their own districts like miniature countries. The shipping routes are all down, and in the inner city there are no farms, so in the areas too far away from the coast to try fishing…"

He let the conclusion linger, afraid to give voice to the inevitable. I had seen it for myself, though, and like the priest knew of what he spoke. I have seen where the gangs have killed any intruders, or even gone out on hunting expeditions. The supply of available pets was nearly exhausted, which left only one possible food source remaining.

People.

Doctor Janson turned away from the view, while Father Mason tried offering what ray of hope that could be gleaned.

"There are some places that remain mostly unchanged."

"Like where?"

"I hear the Amazon still looks good," the priest shrugged. "Then there's select parts of the Outback of Australia, and also Mongolia."

"And the heart of Africa, I suppose. All the places where no one wants to be."

"Actually, I'm not too sure about Africa. From what I've heard, some Muslims started raiding many non-Islamic nations there. Apparently their need for slaves has grown quite large."

"Sounds bad."

The doctor sat back down with a tired plop, while the priest remained standing to regard him. He could tell how dejected the doctor was getting even from this little bit of news.

"I'll let the General tell you the rest."

"You mean there's *more?* What hope does anyone have of saving us from any of this?"

"Have faith, Doctor Janson. All this is designed to make the world lose its faith."

"Faith is one thing, but specifics would be very much welcome. Does the General have a plan?"

The priest stepped over, dropping himself down to a seat next to the doctor before replying.

"He has been gathering as many experts in various fields as he can before the President's martial law announcement."

"Yeah, you mentioned that before. Martial law. What does it mean?"

"Well, I'm not a military expert, just a biblical one, but I imagine it means that California's about to get some troops in there to help settle the unrest."

"They could use something more like an army of doctors and construction engineers. Does the General plan for any of that?"

"Again, I'll let the General fill you in. My job was to just fill in some of the spaces he's got on his little war council."

"War? I didn't hear anything about that. Who are we at war with?"

Father Mason paused, took in a breath, then gave his reply.

"The Devil, Doctor Janson. We are at war with no less than Satan himself."

Doctor Janson and Father Mason were escorted through the secure facility to the deeply buried War Room, now repurposed as a sort of backup Command Center for Presidential authority. Large screens littered the walls, each a view of one international disaster or another, fifty computer stations with men and women hard at work keeping everything updated, and at the center of it all the General and his immediate staff atop a raised circular platform with its own smaller ring of six terminals.

"General," Father Mason called out through the hubbub, "I have your medical expert."

General Willmington broke off conversation with those around him to greet the pair as they stepped up to the dais, offering out a quick shake of his hand as the priest made the introductions.

"Doctor Steven Janson, this is General John Willmington."

"Doctor, good to meet you," the General said with a quick shake of his hand. "Welcome to the team. Time is short so I'll keep the introductions brief."

He let go of the doctor's hand and motioned to the others around him.

"Doctor Janson, this is Bob Hardwright, professor of foreign affairs and international relations from Yale."

Doctor Janson reached out to briefly shake hands with a portly gentleman just entering his early fifties before the General moved onto the next one in line. A younger man in his early forties sporting a full head of trimmed blond hair.

"Alexander Dupree, psychologist."

"Specialist in group psychology," Alexander beamed.

"Amanda Stilton," the General continued, this one a woman with shortly trimmed black hair and a suggestion of African ancestry somewhere in her background, "physicist."

"Also a doctorate in chemistry," the woman said as she took Doctor Janson's hand.

"And finally, our financial expert, Mister Milton Six of the Bank of England."

"Just call me Mister Six," the thirtyish man beamed.

"Six?" Doctor Janson asked as he briefly took the hand. "That sounds like the name of a Bond villain or something."

"I get that all the time," the man grinned, "but in the end aren't we all simply numbers?"

"Well, uh… no."

"So much for introductions," the General stated. "Now if I may direct your attentions up to Screen Four off to the right."

The General gestured to one of the people manning the small circle of terminals on the dais, who punched a few keys and brought up a display on the indicated monitor across the chamber. It was a series of news clips, first one with a well-known skyline involving the Eifel Tower, then after a few moments switching to London, then Rome, and ending with New York. In each case the scene was one of rioting, violence, and buildings burning.

"What's with all the fighting?" Doctor Janson asked.

"I'm afraid you'll have to catch up on the fly, Doctor," the General stated. "The economic chaos wasn't bad enough, then came the famine spreading as a result of the crop blights, followed by the quakes, storms, and resultant aftermaths, and now this. What you're seeing is the result of a few mad Muslim clerics and an announcement that came out as you were on the plane over here. All Christians in and about Arabia, Syria, and Iran have been ordered unceremoniously executed."

"Why, that's awful," Father Mason exclaimed. "I would not think that even *they* would dare to–"

"Something about a vision from Allah himself," Alexander Dupree put in. "Considering the already powder keg nature of that region of the world and their beliefs, that was all it took. About a million Christians throughout the Middle East are being executed as we speak."

"A million–" Doctor Jansen began. "Then what are these–"

"Anywhere there was a large enough Muslim population, it seems as they all went crazy," the General continued. "They're killing every Christian they can get their hands on before getting shot down."

"The persecution," the priest gasped. "General, another sign of coming end-times. Soon the First Seal will be broken then the Anti-Christ himself will appear."

"Seal?" Doctor Janson asked. "What seal?"

"Oh, you'll love this one," Mister Six grinned. "Not that I necessarily believe in it myself, but the evidence does seem rather overwhelming."

"The Seven Seals of the Book of Revelations," Father Mason explained. "There are certain signs that will warn of the pending breaking of the First Seal. Quakes, blight, disease, economic collapse; such signs as we have been experiencing, made far worse, I suspect, by the hand of Satan himself. Soon I believe the First Seal will be broken, then after that each of the other six in turn."

"Then the Devil comes," Doctor Stilton blandly stated. "I'll stick with scientific observables, if you don't mind."

"Biblical seals or not," Professor Hardwright observed, "this murderous nonsense will have messy repercussions. I have no doubt that war will soon break out, it's just a matter of where."

"War is another sign," Father Mason said with a knowing nod. "Very soon the First Seal will break."

Doctor Janson shifted his attention to the monitors, each showing a different view of a world falling apart. In one was what looked like a Mosque in front of which a hundred or more captives were lined up facing masked Muslims with guns. Men, women, and children alike were shot dead on the spot. Another showed a scene of miles of dead farmland somewhere in the Great Plains, while yet a third showed what at first looked like a simple ocean view... until he caught sight of a windmill sticking up out of the water in the background.

"General," he said, pointing, "if I may ask?"

"Northern Europe was struck with some pretty severe earthquakes that the seismologists are at a loss to explain," General Willmington explained. "One of them took out the dykes. Then with the increased storm activity over there... Holland no longer exists."

Doctor Janson swallowed a lump at the thought, but General Willmington had no time to let him mull anything over.

"Doctor Janson, you're a part of this team because we have a worldwide plague running loose and we need a cure. The CDC has been taken out, and while the declaration of martial law has stopped Congress' attempts at bringing down this country in its tracks, the damage they did may still be irreparable. As of right now you are the country's leading expert in diseases and we need you to puzzle out a cure for whatever this plague is that's going around. There's a lab all set up, a medical staff, and some affected bodies under the highest degree of quarantine, but the rest is up to you."

"From what others have described," Doctor Stilton put in, "it sounds more like a variety of diseases, but the virulence with which they have all struck has our medics at a loss."

"It was much like that at the hospital where Father Mason found me," Doctor Janson replied, "but I thought it was simply a result of the great quake and everything else."

"We aren't so sure," General Willmington told him. "We have reason to believe there may be a commonality, which is why we need you to look into it."

"One of those Seven Seals?"

He eyed the priest as he asked this, to which he received a single nod.

"At this point," the General stated, "I can't afford to rule anything out."

"Then, I'll get right on it," Doctor Janson began. "Just let me change and then–"

"General!"

The cry came from one of the people on the floor at the terminals. Immediately the General snapped out a command.

"Front and center."

A press of a button, and what the computer tech was seeing was now echoed on the main screen in the center of the great chamber before them. It was a press conference, in the background what looked like Buckingham Palace, at the central microphone a man that the captioning labeled as "Prime Minister of Great Britain", beside him another man labeled as "President of France." It was already in the middle of the speech, but the meaning was abundantly clear.

"...and so because of these barbaric uncivilized actions, it is with great regret that our two countries announce the following resolutions. First, all foreign nationals of Islamic lineage shall be rounded up for immediate deportation. If you resist then you will be shot as readily as you have slaughtered our own countrymen.

Second, against the country of Iran, we hereby declare war. But this will be a war with no holding back. We further invite all other civilized countries to join in on teaching these godless minions a lesson. If you cannot learn to live in a civilized fashion, then you shall not live. Period."

As the session broke off into a storm of shouted questions, the General dispensed it with a wave of his hand, to which the technician switched off the view.

"General," another called out, "response from Russia. They're threatening to go to war against England and France if they escalate this thing."

"Sir," came a third voice, "response from North Korea."

"This one's not too hard to predict," Professor Hardwright said with a sigh. "The Korean Doughboy has found a way to connect England's announcement up with a vendetta against the States."

"He's threatening war, sir," the same tech called back.

"This will bring in China, though not necessarily on North Korea's side," Professor Hardwright predicted. "And whichever side China's on, Russia will find a way to the opposite extreme. General, you may expect an announcement from the President shortly."

"And I have a hunch what that announcement is going to be," the General sighed, then raised his voice for all in the chamber to hear. "Very well, all personnel: prepare to be on a war footing. I want readiness messages sent to all our forces so that when the President makes his announcement, we can strike wherever he points within a moment's notice."

"General, you cannot do this," the priest exclaimed. "I beg of you, this will not make things any better."

"He's got no choice." Mister Six had been quiet for a while but now he spoke up in a discreet tone that nevertheless rankled on Doctor Janson's nerves. "We are all forced into this as surely as night follows day. There will be war and it will swallow the globe."

"I'm afraid he's right," General Willmington replied. "My duty is to protect the citizenry of this country and this may be the only way left."

To the images of death, famine, and pending destruction surrounding the chamber, Doctor Janson could only gasp and exclaim.

"My God! What have we come to?"

"We have come," Father Mason quietly stated, "to the breaking of the First Seal and the nearing end of the world, but Satan is going to make the world suffer before that happens."

In that, I am afraid that the priest shall be proven to be quite right.

Chapter Seven:

The United Nations

The General Assembly was in as much chaos and contention as the rest of the world, only here their petty little arguments had world-spanning consequences. I floated down unseen to the reporter's gallery to see for myself what I'd been hearing from their Internet and television news programs.

The Secretary General was hammering away with his gavel trying to get some order but there were nearly too many people speaking to make anything out. Finally, after much shouting from the Secretary General, things quieted enough for the representative from Spain to stand up and be recognized.

"Mister Secretary, my country is undergoing widespread famine. The European Union either can't or won't help us, so now it falls to me to ask the United Nations for assistance. We need *food,* and I understand that the UN food banks are quite full."

"The representative from Spain's request is heard and acknowledged," the Secretary General replied, "but while the reserves are full, we have requests from many other nations besides your own and must prioritize. In your case, Spain's dues to the UN have been in default the last three years so I am afraid that I will be unable to–"

"Our *dues?!* We have millions of people starving and you're worrying about some ridiculous point of order such as *that?* I should–"

"Mister Secretary," this time it was the representative from Saudi Arabia that stood up, "my country is *not* in default on our dues and hereby requests access to that food bank."

"What?! His country doesn't even *need* it, mine does," Spain screamed. "We have people eating their pets, and reports of some quite possibly eating one another!"

A hard rap of the gavel from the Secretary General and the rising din quieted once again as next a man representing Italy stood up.

"My country had a trade deal with Canada but now their representative tells me they're reneging, and furthermore she says that we–"

"Excuse me," a very offended woman whose placard said 'Canada' stood up, "but you failed to ask as to my preferred pronoun!"

"What?! This is ridiculous," Italy replied. "We are here to discuss important matters of state and you–"

"I demand that Italy be censored," Canada said with a huff. "He has violated my personal mind-space and enacted several micro-aggressions upon me."

"We have a vote for censoring Italy before us then," the Secretary General stated with a pound of his gavel. "All in favor of–"

"Hold on," Italy shouted, "what about my trade deal?!"

Into the resultant confusion another now stood up to scream out his objections, this one from France.

"Mister Secretary, I must lodge a complaint against Iran, Syria, and Arabia for their treatment of many of France's citizens. They have slaughtered many Christians, not only from France but several other countries, but this esteemed body has failed to do anything about it."

"As I recall," the Secretary General replied, "that matter was in a subcommittee. Does anyone remember which–"

"The Committee on Human Rights, Mister Secretary," the representative from Saudi Arabia replied into his microphone. "We are currently reviewing the complaint in light of the human rights records of France, England–"

"Our human rights records," France called back. "Iran is the one doing the killing. As is *your* country. What level of madness–"

Once again the chamber exploded into a storm of verbal confrontation, punctuated by the thunderous exclamations of the Secretary General's gavel. Nearby to where I hovered I could see reporters quickly typing notes into their electronic tablets. I would think that their headlines might involve the irrational behavior of Saudi Arabia or Iran, but for the most part these reporters seemed more intent on twisting things against France and England and somehow blaming the United States. All I could do was shake my head sadly and continue with my own scribbling on my scroll.

Now as the storm began to abate once again, another stood up to be heard, this time a man from Israel.

"Mister Secretary," he began.

"Objection," Saudi Arabia immediately called out. "We would like to officially lodge a human rights complaint against Israel."

"For *what?* I just started speaking," Israel countered. "Okay, that's it. I was going to keep this nice and diplomatic, but time to be blunt. Israel is leaving the United Nations! Effective immediately all Israeli troops are hereby withdrawn, all funds we have contributed or are scheduled to contribute canceled."

Another pounding of the gavel as a new storm of contention arises.

"I will have order!" the Secretary General calls out. "Order! Israel, you do not have the authority to make such a request until the matter of your nation's dues–"

"You're more concerned with your *salary* than what this once-esteemed body was formed for?" France gasped. "France hereby joins Israel in leaving the United Nations!"

"As does Spain!"

Immediately the verbal storm seemed to hit its peak, with a dozen voices all calling out at once. I recorded as many snippets of it as I could, but it seemed as insanity had taken a firm hold on the entire body. First it was the representative from Belgium.

"On behalf of the European Union, I would like to offer my apologies for what France and Spain have said this day. I am sure that once cooler heads–"

"And France hereby withdraws from the E.U. as well. You'll be getting the paperwork in the morning."

"What?! But I–"

"Austria also withdraws from the U.N.; you have done nothing in the past to stop any fighting amongst our southern neighbors, and I doubt that record is going to improve."

"Since we have so many leaving the U.N.," Greece called out, "there should be a lot more food left in the United Nations Food Bank. Greece would hereby like to apply for some of that food to feed its people."

"Now wait a second," Spain stood up and shouted, "we had dibs on that first!"

"But you just quit, so more for the rest of us," Greece called back.

"Mister Secretary!"

The representative from Japan then stood up, looking very angry and frustrated.

"Mister Secretary, I have been trying to get your attention for half an hour now. I was going to complain against a litany of things, including the Muslim radicals from Iran that tried planting a bomb on one of our trains. And while our food situation is not as severe as that of other nations due to our greater reliance on fish over crops for sustenance, the plagues have hit us very hard, wiping out nearly a quarter of our population."

"Mister Secretary, China hereby offers to send a contingent of peace-keeping troops to Japan to help them out."

"Peace keepers?!" Japan screamed. "You mean invaders! You seek to take advantage of–"

"Order," the Secretary General demanded with a pound of his gavel. "It is obvious that Japan is on the edge of wide-spread rioting and–"

"Japan is *not* suffering from riots! We have some problems with the Muslims and disease propagation–"

"So China's request to send in a peacekeeping force to Japan is hereby approved."

The expression on the face of the man from Japan can be described as no less than apoplectic. I could tell that he was trying to maintain his Japanese civility and manners, but one can be pressed only so far.

"If a single Chinese soldier steps foot on Japanese soil, it will be an act of war. Japan hereby withdraws from the United Nations!"

"As does Canada!"

"And Brazil."

"Argentina withdraws."

"South Africa has no more need for membership in this body. We have enough problems with our immediate neighbors."

It went on like that, one nation after another entering their withdrawals as the Secretary General kept up his pounding with the gavel like a roiling storm front ready to break against the shores of disharmony. These metaphorical shores being defined as when Saudi Arabia again stood up to speak.

"Mister Secretary. We would like to enter a proposal for an amendment to the United Nations charter."

"And what is the context of that proposal?" the Secretary General asked.

"That the name 'United Nations' be amended to read, 'The United Islamic Nations', seeing as how so many non-Islamic member nations have seen fit to abandon the cause for peace."

"Peace?" France screamed out. "Your backwards cult is behind more misery in the history of this planet than—"

More gavel pounding, this time accompanied by several security guards spilling out around the perimeter of the room. By degrees the delegates quieted, and once they had the Secretary General looked about to say something, no doubt a belated request for some calmer heads, but then someone stood up that had remained quiet during the entire mess of a proceeding.

"The United States would like to say something."

"The representative from the United States is given the floor," the Secretary General stated with some obvious relief.

The Secretary General plopped back down into his chair, clearly exhausted, and perhaps hoping the heavyweight in the room might be able to reestablish some order and calm. The man from the U.S. was a little portly, a stylish large Stetson hat on his head which he tipped back so that others more clearly see his face. He slowly panned his gaze around the chamber, offering out a smile which as many people took as threatening as others took as hopeful. He waited until he had their attentions, then spoke in a Texas drawl that sounded like a friend talking to a neighbor, though its intent would quickly be seen as otherwise.

"I'll make this as clear as I can... Y'all can get the hell off U.S. soil. The United States hereby withdraws both membership and all support from the United Nations. Have a nice day."

Into the suddenly stunned crowd he tipped his hat then turned to leave, his staff quickly packing up papers into briefcases in his wake. From around the edges of the chamber the soldiers that had entered stepped closer into the light, but now it could be seen that they were all U.S. Marines. A stunned Secretary General raised his gavel once more, only to see one of the nearest Marines step up with a rifle pointed directly at him.

"Put the gavel down, Mister Secretary," the marine said in a level voice.

"B-But this is... preposterous," the Secretary General said in a flustered voice. "You have no authority to–"

The representative from the United States was midway up the aisle when he called out without looking back.

"We'll do this like back in Texas. Anyone not on our friends list that's still around by sundown will be arrested for espionage and crimes against this great country."

"This means *war!*"

The man from Saudi Arabia, arrayed in his white-robed finery, tried to look as indignant as he could as he spoke, but seemed unable to get anything but a smirk from the Texan.

"Do that if you must, but which one of us has the nukes?"

"Why that–"

The Arab glanced up to the Secretary for help, only to see him being escorted down from his podium by a pair of well-armed Marines, looked over to China only to see the man from China make an effort at not noticing, then landed his gaze on the one bastion left. Russia.

The Russian ambassador's assistants were already gathering up their briefcases and laptops as he stood to reply.

"We talked the U.S. out of landing their first missile on Mecca," the Russian shrugged, "though I don't guarantee that we'll likewise hold back if you do not reign in your terrorist friends from Russia's borders."

He picked up his briefcase, stepped away from his seat, then paused to address Saudi Arabia specifically and the General Assembly as a whole.

"And needless to say, Russia does not need the United Nations either and hereby withdraws. Have a nice time meeting in whichever third-world country will have you."

I continued to watch as one ambassadorial group after another left, while scattered pockets remained to continue arguing; at least until they saw that the Marines were serious about escorting everyone out of the building within the hour. The army of reporters were in a frenzy trying to figure out how to spin events to their particular views, when a contingent of marines came up into the gallery with guns pointed to escort them out as well.

It seems as they'd forgotten that the country was under martial law and this building was once again U.S. soil.

Chapter Eight:

Making The Rounds

Doctor Janson was hard at work in the base lab. The best facilities to be had anywhere on the planet, with a staff of the most brilliant medical researchers that remained to humanity. Day and night the young doctor had worked, examining every detail of what was brought to him. Samples from a dozen different plague victims, each sickly victim secured within the most air-tight cleanroom possible, tended to by men and women in sealed white encounter suits with clear plastic faceplates.

The doctor was hard at work at his station when the General walked in. Three monitor screens around him with various displays of one test or another running, medical equipment to either side of his station as he typed into his keyboard. He acknowledged the General with a brief glance then finished what he was doing before swiveling around on his stool to face him.

"I've made some progress, General."

"Then you have a cure?" General Willmington asked. "Because we could really use one."

"Not exactly." He spun around to indicate some graphs on his screen, to which the General immediately waved him off.

"Before you go into what any of that medical gibberish means, just keep in mind that I'm only a military man. Give me the 'Dummy's' version."

"As you wish," the Doctor replied. "First, we have confirmed that there are indeed any one of several diseases that have reached plague levels."

"*I* could have told you that, Doc. What do you have that's new?"

"Well, the odd part of these diseases is that many of them are caused by fairly common bacteria and viruses. The kind that have lain dormant in human biology for eons without causing any problems. At best the worst some of these should be causing is the common cold."

"Then what got them so stirred up?"

The General's interest peaked, he stepped closer to the doctor for a peek at what was displayed on his monitors to see if he could really make sense out of any of it. Graphs of DNA sequences, color-coded charts, a database listing of bacterial names and suspected symptoms; it was enough to make the General's head spin, but somewhere in there lay an answer and the doctor had apparently discovered it.

"That is *exactly* what I asked myself," the doctor replied. "I began to suspect that it was not these diseases themselves but some underlying commonality that has been causing such virulence."

He tapped a few keys and one of the displays was replaced by something else. It looked like an animation of some sort of complex molecule, alongside some cellular diagrams.

"Doc, like I said, this might as well be crayon drawings for all they mean to me. What am I looking at?"

"Oh, well I decided to analyze the base mechanisms underlying disease control in the human body. Basically the immune system, and see what exactly has been going on. What I found was a virus unlike anything else I've ever seen before."

"And it's been causing all these diseases?"

"In itself, no. But what it does– Well, to bypass a lot of technical talk, it basically shuts the bulk of the human immune system down, making people susceptible to any *other* diseases that may be passing through."

"So, it's our immune systems going haywire, is that it?"

"Exactly," Doctor Janson beamed. "The part of the immune system that keeps track of– Well, it'd be like a computer database. The records are all still there, but access to them has been broken. So that measles shot you had as a kid? There's still some part deep within your metabolism that remembers the immunological procedures to keep measles away, but the body's mechanism for accessing that immunological record has been disabled. Just as it has been for *any* disease the body would normally be able to ward against. The capability is still there, but blocked by this new virus."

"So, let me get this straight," General Willmington stated. "All those shots I had as a kid are no longer any good and I could get measles, mumps, and whatever else now?"

"General, as it stands right now, the common cold could turn into a death sentence for many people. That's the problem we've been having with these plagues. The bulk of human medicine focuses on assisting the body's native immune system, but if that immune system is nonfunctional, then the bulk of our medicines will be ineffective. If we don't find a way to treat this one underlying virus, then we could be wiped out by a head cold."

"But if you *can* get this new bug licked, then we can beat the rest?"

"Treat this virus and turn the immune system back on and the body can take care of everything else."

For a moment the General just stood there pursing a lip, then finally gave a quick nod to Doctor Janson.

"Good work, Doctor. That's the closest thing to positive news I've heard all year."

"But General, there's one more thing… This virus, there is no way it can be natural. Someone engineered it."

"You mean this thing is manmade? But how? Why?"

"I don't know," Doctor Janson replied. "I only know that it would have taken quite a bit of money and resources to accomplish it. Maybe some germ warfare experiment that escaped, or from one of the CDC's own labs, I can't be sure. I just know that this bug did not evolve but was made."

"Hmm… I can see that I'll be making a few inquiries in the near future," the General stated. "How soon can you affect a cure against this thing?"

"That's exactly what I'm working on now," Doctor Janson replied, as he returned attention to his monitors and keyboard. "I'm going to have to develop a whole new way of dealing with disease to lick this thing."

"I have faith in you, Doc."

A friendly slap to the doctor's back and the General turned away and started heading back for the door through which he had entered.

"Just try and get it done while we still have some population left."

The doctor gave no response, nor any sign that he had heard the General's quip, for he was already deep into his work, trying to puzzle out the most difficult problem of his career.

⸻

The next stop the General made on his tour of the base personnel was the office that had been put aside for Dr. Alexander Dupree. He knocked once then entered, finding the psychologist hard at work at his desk studying some videos on his monitor.

"I hope you're catching up on current events, and not watching porn, Alex."

"What?" So focused had he been, that Alex only now noticed who had entered, and then what he had said and gave a flicker of a grin. "Oh. No. I was just getting caught up on current events."

"Oh really," General Willmington blandly replied. "I wish I would have thought of that. What have you got for me?"

"Well, I was just watching the breakdown of the U.N., and I can tell you it's going to be even messier than anything else so far. I've already been observing many of the signs of classic societal collapse: wide-spread unrest of the citizenry, political upheaval, disruption of public services, increased sexual perversions, famine, unsustainable public debt; all the sorts of things that brought down the likes of the Roman Empire. Now with the nations all at one another's throats... I take it all military matters are now officially in your hands?"

"In regards to what our ambassador told that illustrious body of nitwits who can shove what where, yes. If the President wants a country erased, or if in my own judgment there is a clear and present danger from some foreign power, then I have the authority to proceed immediately without immediate Presidential say-so."

"Sounds like that makes you a dictator."

"No, just the guy History gets to blame if anyone outside of this base finds out who I am," the General quipped. "So who do you think's going to act first?"

Alexander pressed a key to pause the latest video then sat back in his seat to think. He was well aware that whatever he told the General would have worldwide impact.

"I was consulting with Bob, and would have to say Russia. Certain powers in the Middle East have long been stretching their friendships with Russia and now that everyone's out in the open about their feelings, Russia won't have anymore reason to hold back. They'll attack Iran first and call it a service to Humanity, and grab a few oil fields for themselves in the process. Then when Arabia opens up their mouths they'll launch a few missiles at Arabian military targets, at which point Arabia will call on us to hold up our end of being an official ally."

"That ain't gonna happen anymore," the General replied. "The President and I both agree that we're not going to help anyone whose interests are directly against that of this country. So if Russia wants to attack Arabia, just hope they miss the oil fields. What else… What about China? It's looking like they want to make a move against Japan."

"Probably to grab their technology," Alexander replied. "Though China may have other problems on their hands."

"Muslim terrorists?"

"No, I've seen the report on how they've been slaughtering both Muslims *and* Christians in their country. No, the problem is going to come from Tibet."

"Tibet?! How'd *they* get into things?"

The psychologist leaned forward, tapped a couple of keys, they turned the monitor around for the General to see. It was a web site emblazoned with the caption 'Free Tibet'.

"Professor Hardwright's filled me in on the history of Tibet and how they've been campaigning to free themselves from Tibet for decades. With that in mind I think that now they'll use the current international chaos to their advantage. China will have an internal uprising on their hands that they'll have to deal with. Professor Hardwright suspects that North Korea will also use the opportunity to move against South Korea, which China will have to respond to as well. No, China will have its hands too full to worry about Japan."

"Well, that's something, at least," the General sighed. "Now if you can just tell me how to handle the mess in Africa."

"Simple; stay out of it."

The answer came not from Alexander Dupree, but from the portly form of Professor Bob Hardwright just entering the room. The General gave him a nod as he took a seat before Alexander's desk.

"Everyone's fighting everyone else over there," the Professor continued. "It's a death trap. What *I* would worry about is Europe. I suspect the first match is going to be lit in Paris."

"Why Paris? All the Muslims there?"

"That," Alexander picked up, "and the fact that now that they've been there for longer than a single generation they seem to be claiming it as their 'ancestral homeland'. Silly, I know, but nobody claimed that Mohamed's world-cult had any sanity to it. Someone will do something to grab a whole lot of attention and claim a major victory, to which France will respond."

"Given their history," General Willmington said, "I can't see France as responding with anything but weak words. This war they and England are supposed to be having against Iran has so far just been a lot of posturing and maneuvering of military assets. Not a single shot fired so far."

"It will happen soon, General," Professor Hardwright assured him.

"Of that I have no doubt."

General Willmington then turned away and started for the door, but not before a last request.

"See if you two can dream up some scheme to quell the panic in the streets. Between the famine, quakes, and plagues, we could use something."

"Oh that's simple," the psychologist shrugged. "Declare war on someone that everyone absolutely hates and let patriotism do the rest."

"With hyper special interest groups going off on any number of penny ante things, even that's no good anymore," the General sighed. "The last solid enemy we had that everyone could get behind hating were the Nazis."

That said, he left, leaving the two other men behind him to ponder other possible events.

General Willmington's next stop was in the assigned office of Mr. Milton Six. He found the financial expert busy with a small team conjuring up graphs and reports of worldwide financial activity, the man himself buzzing like a bee from one computerized station to the next. When he saw the General enter he quickly hurried over to his side.

"The Euro officially no longer exists, which has the Exchange Market exploding with activity, seven European countries have been found in default of various loans, it's looking like all of South America is headed for three-digit inflation, China's government has taken control of all banks within its borders, Chinese and otherwise, and Belgium has just completely collapsed financially due to their direct responsibility for all debts incurred by the now-former European Union."

"And a good day to you too, Mister Six," the General said by way of greeting.

"Oh, sorry about the lack of pleasantries, General, but things have been moving at a blur in the financial world."

"Don't you mean what's *left* of it?"

"On the contrary, General, speaking from a high-finance point of view, this is a perfect opportunity for certain people to make billions of dollars."

Between the eager look on the man's face and everything else the General had been briefed on, he finally snapped.

"And spend it *where?*" He grabbed the man by his collar as he said this, his breath blasting angrily into the other man's face. "The world is in ruins and about to get worse. So tell me what insensitive idiot could even *think* of making a buck in the current environment!"

He held there for a moment, Mister Six swallowing a lump then slowly raising a hand to gently tease at the grip on his collar. A moment later the General released him and backed away.

"Sorry, Milton. I've had an immeasurable amount of stress."

"I quite understand, and I apologize for letting my enthusiasm for my chosen field get the better of me. The truth is, there are some very large banking concerns with designs on gaining control of entire countries."

"Sounds positively terrifying, except for one thing," the General pointed out. "How do you foreclose on a country, even a small one? You'd need an army."

"Simple, under current conditions," Mr. Six shrugged. "You just offer to pay people in food reserves you've stockpiled safely away from any blight. You'll have a mercenary army literally overnight."

"That would have to be some pretty big food reserves."

"You'd be surprised," Mister Six said with a trace of a grin. "Ever hear of Embassy Foods?"

"Should I?"

"Largest food conglomerate in the country, and also put into a financially unstable position by recent events. They've just been bought out by one of the Rothschild's banks. I don't think it'll be too long before someone has their own private army to add into the mix."

"Great," the General grumbled. "Like I don't have enough problems."

"In fact, the way governments are collapsing left and right, I don't think it'll be too long before large private armies become more the norm than national ones."

"Not on my watch," the General said after a moment's pause.

He took a glance around at the busy activity of the room, spotting graphics being displayed on large wall monitors of countries and their current economic values, saw a constantly updating list of which companies were being bought out by whom, and made a decision.

"This, at least, I can do something about."

The General began to turn around, but Mr. Six was fast to his side with an urgent word.

"General, I assure you that these events are well beyond–"

"This nation is under martial law, remember," the General growled. "Embassy Foods just became nationalized, and whichever bank that thinks they just bought them out can go stick it."

"General, you can't do this! The repercussions on the market–"

"Bite me!"

General Willmington slammed the door behind himself.

———————

There was one last visit that the General would pay in his rounds: the far quieter and more basic office of Father Mason. His office held little more than a simple desk and the required terminal, and a large cross pinned to the wall behind him. He was praying when the General entered and said not a word but walked over to a small end table where was resting a clear pitcher and some glasses. Taking up the pitcher, he poured two glasses, then came over and handed one to General Willmington.

"Wine, Father?"

"Water," the priest corrected. "You have the look of someone who could use something simple."

"You're reading me like a book, Father."

A quick clink of glasses, then the General downed the contents of his own in a single swig, while Father Mason took a more leisurely approach to his drink.

"I'm having to make some very hard decisions in an impossible situation, Father."

"Just Henry, if you don't mind. I think the collar tells everyone all they need to know about me."

"Okay… Henry."

He walked over to pour himself another glassful, emptied that, then placed the glass down on the end table and faced the priest.

"If you have anything for me at all, I can certainly use it."

"Well," Father Mason strolled over to place his own glass back on the small table, then paced back towards his desk as he spoke, "I can tell you that none of the Seals has yet been broken, because if they had then the world would now be at an end."

"You mean, this isn't it?"

"Not by far, I'm afraid. The world must suffer a whole lot more before the end. The first sign will be when the Antichrist himself makes his public appearance. He will come as a savior to our world's problems, but will be the final nail in our collective coffin. After that each of the other Seals will break in turn and make of the world Hell on Earth."

"My job is to make sure that coffin never gets built in the first place. I don't believe in the inevitable, Henry, just in whatever it takes to get the job done. What I need from you is something to help me in my job. I'll take anything you got. Signs, omens, an angel or two."

"In that, at least, I may be able to offer one small thing. The only thing, perhaps, that *can* save us."

"Anything."

The priest said nothing, only stepped over to before the cross on the wall, then bent down to his knees, brought his hands together, and looked up to the figure on the cross. General Willmington said nothing, but gave a sigh, and stepped over to kneel down beside the priest and join him in prayer.

Chapter Nine:

The Fuse

The General watched it from his main center of operations spread across a dozen different screens, the world saw it on television and internet outlets, heard about it on radio and every other news outlet, and I saw it in person from afar. The advantage of being an angel; I get to instantly appear at the site of every human misdeed and be the first to weep over what I see.

It began as an obvious bid for attention. Another group of radical Islamists taking a group of tourists prisoner and shouting out incoherent demands, responded to by the local militia and some officious looking person trying to talk them down. Just like any other day.

Except that this time the site was the top of the Eifel Tower, and the French official sent to do the talking quickly discovered that you can't talk down a radical.

As another unseasonal thunderstorm raged around the famed tower, the world saw the news reports as it unfolded. It was obvious the Muslim in question was playing for time to be sure he had as much of the world's attention as possible. One reporter's voice came out through the command center's speakers as the General watched along with everyone else. The room was fully staffed, Father Mason and the others that had been gathered all assembled to helplessly watch.

"...They're trying to get a translator up there to see just what the terrorists want, but so far... Yes, we have reports that someone got a microphone close enough to pick up a few phrases. From what some experts are telling us, it appears that the lead terrorist is shouting out prayers from the Koran. To what purpose we can only guess..."

"Come on," the General said under his breath, "take the kill shot."

"General?" Amanda asked.

"Even the French must have at least a dozen sharpshooters trained on this," General Willmington replied. "It's obvious what those terrorists are going to do, not even they would let political correctness get in the way of stopping it."

"Never underestimate human stupidity, General," Professor Hardwright stated. "The French haven't had the nerve to take bold action since Charlemagne."

"...We have word now that the French negotiator in charge of this operation is on the elevator on the way up to speak to the terrorists direct. It won't be long now until we know what it is that they want..."

"No it won't," General Willmington decided. "Is the Sixth Fleet in position?"

"Yes, sir," one of the men at the inner ring of terminals atop the central dais replied.

"Then tell their commander that he can start picking targets of interest at his pleasure but to await my order before launching anything off."

"Yes, sir."

"General," Doctor Janson exclaimed, "what are you doing? It sounds like you're about ready to start a war!"

"No, Doc, those terrorists are going to start it, I'm just going to make sure it's as short as possible. Captain," he addressed another one there in his inner circle, "get word out to the fleet we have around the Sea of Japan. They can start picking targets in North Korea. The second Doughboy opens up his mouth, he gets a missile in it."

"Yes sir."

The Captain addressed bent to his own terminal and headset to begin relaying the command. Meanwhile, Father

Mason was joining Amanda in being shocked at the General's preemptive actions.

"General," Father Mason began. "John, do you realize what you're about to do?"

"I realize what *they're* about to do," the General snapped back, "and since with martial law I don't have to worry about Congress holding things up, I'm going to be ready the instant that terrorist does what I think he's going to do."

"And what would that be, General?"

This time it was the psychologist, Alexander, who more calmly voiced that question, and for him the General had an equally calmly-voiced answer.

"They're going to light that match we were discussing earlier."

Professor Hardwright nodded, Alexander dropping his head with a sad sigh, while the others puzzled through the words as the newsman's voice continued to drone on.

"...The French negotiator has reached the top. We are told that he is accompanied by a translator, as well as a cameraman. We have a direct link to their cameraman and now switch you to the feed coming live from the top of the Eifel Tower."

The view switched, the voices now those in the midst of the actual crisis itself. The chief negotiator was speaking in French to the translator who was in turn relaying his words to the terrorist in charge. One of a dozen Muslim men there, each well armed, a couple keeping their weapons aimed at the six tourists shivering with fear at the back end of the landing, while the rest stood in a shoulder-to-shoulder line behind their leader.

A voice-over did its best to keep up with the various languages as the exchange went back and forth. First the terrorist leader would say something loud and emphatically, which the translator would relay in French into the negotiator's ear, then the reply would be relayed back through the translator.

"...He's invoking the name of the Prophet, something about just rewards... Most of it's rambling... The negotiator is asking for his demands now... The terrorist responds with something about the bright hand of Allah crushing the unbelievers..."

"If they're smart," the General remarked, "that cameraman is a bodyguard or military agent and there's a gun hidden inside that camera."

"These are the French," Professor Hardwright reminded him. "Somebody probably objected to such an obvious necessity."

"...The French negotiator is now offering them safe passage out of the country but the terrorist is continuing to rant."

"Take the kill-shot already," the General prayed.

More ranting words were heard from the lead terrorist then the line of men behind him parted away to either side, revealing what they had been hiding behind them. It was a large metal box four feet long, topped by a couple of dials, an electronic readout, and a feeling of extreme dread.

"Send out the ready command to all fleets," the General ordered. "Doctor Stilton, what can you tell me about it?"

Amanda Stilton was the first to gasp at what came into view, and now she gave it a more studied examination on the terminal closest to her on the central dais.

"Crudely built," she quickly reported, "probably half the yield of Hiroshima at the best, but it'll do the job."

"General," a fearful Dr. Janson asked, "what is she talking about?"

The view spread across half the monitors there now showed the lead terrorists spouting vehemently in his native tongue while raising his left hand to display in full view of the camera and the world watching, what he had been holding. It was some sort of switch and his thumb was pressed onto the button. Immediately the French negotiator tried to run back into the elevator with the translator while the sudden falling view of feed suggested the cameraman had dropped his camera and was now leaping at the terrorist.

The scene immediately switched back to the long distance view and an urgent voiceover by the original reporter.

"We're now being told there is a very high probability that what we saw is a bomb, though we're not sure what type or if–"

Suddenly the image of the Eifel Tower was replaced by a bright flash and an overlay of static, punctuated by the far more urgent tone of the reporter covering the story.

"Oh my God! They set it off. A bomb right on the Eifel Tower, and it looks like–"

The concussion slammed into the news rig, sending the image spinning, the sound of heavy equipment sent spilling over like toys, and people screaming for their lives.

Quick flashes of windows shattering, the front facings of nearby buildings crumbling as the shock wave slammed into them, then visual static before it cut to a station logo.

Everyone in the command center was stunned, Amanda and Dr. Janson with jaws agape, the men speechless, though Mr. Six had seemed to retain his calm detachment. All were in complete shock except for the General.

"Orders to Sixth Fleet," he snapped out in as authoritative a voice as he could manage, "launch at will. Orders to the Sea of Japan: wait on first word of North Korea taking any action. All other forces around the world, prepare to engage."

Seeing a lack of movement from the shocking event they had all just witnessed, the General raised his voice.

"Did I *stutter?* Move it!"

"Yes sir," came a chorus of replies.

The news snapped back on, this time in the confines of a news studio tucked safely away in England, if to judge by the accents. A single male reporter, on the wall behind him an aerial view of Paris and the small cloud that now covered a favored portion of Paris, France.

"We have…" A sniff, quick throat clearing on the part of the reporter, then he quickly continued. *"Excuse*

me. We have confirmation that the terrorists set off a small nuclear bomb right from the top of the Eifel Tower, taking out the historic landmark as well as an estimated half a square mile. We are told that the device was very primitive and crudely made, and so unable to much affect some of the more hardened structures, but it was also what would be termed a 'dirty' bomb. That is, the resultant radiation will be causing more harm than– I can't do this anymore."

The reporter lost his barely-held composure, swept the laptop that he had been reading from off the counter, and faced the camera not like a news reporter, but like a man in shock.

*"Some Muslim scum just **nuked** the Eifel Tower! I hope that our leaders can see that appeasement has not only failed but done so spectacularly. Our leaders should start lining every single one of them up against–"*

He paused, a hand to his ear and the miniature earpiece therein.

"We have a report just in from North Korea..."

"Ready with the Sea of Japan," the General ordered.

"Their leader is issuing a statement saying that the greedy capitalistic scum have gotten what they deserve and that it is hoped that now the world will–"

"Sea of Japan, erase Pyongyang from the map," General Willmington ordered.

"Relaying command, sir," someone acknowledged.

"General," Father Mason asked, his face filled with desperation, "what are you going to do? Surely we can't be so desperate as to–"

"Sir," someone called out from one of the fifty terminals in the room below, "report from central Russia. Missile launch. Looks like it's headed for the Middle East."

"Then it's racing against the launch just recorded from the south of France," another reported. "Straight for the Middle East. Tracking it now."

"*...Switching now to a live newsfeed from Tehran where the Ayatollah is ready to make a statement...*"

"Any bets as to which missile makes it there first?" Mr. Six smirked.

"Milton," Dr. Janson snapped, "not even in jest is that in any way amusing."

"Just making an observation," Mr. Six shrugged. "We got two missiles headed for the Middle East at the same time. I'm just wondering who starts World War Three first."

"It was that terrorist on the Eifel Tower," the General snapped. "As for which missile makes it to the Middle East first, I have my own bets."

The news switched to a view of a bearded old man dressed in black robes speaking before an outdoor assembly of the cheering Islamic faithful. He stood atop a balcony looking down at them as he addressed them, while across the bottom of the screen scrolled a rough translation of his words. Mostly proclamations of victory at how such a great blow had been struck against the enemies of Allah.

The focus of attention, though, began to shift to slightly *above* the Ayatollah, as high in the sky was now seen a bright speck of light, rapidly growing closer. A small star that seemed fixed on the very building in which the Ayatollah was standing.

"Regards that bet, gentlemen," the General said in a humorless tone. "No one beats the U.S. in *anything.*"

The star quickly grew until it filled the entire view, then it was static and back to the station logo once again.

Silence filled the room for only a moment before frantic activity took control.

"Gentlemen," the General addressed the priest and others around him, "I suggest that you adjourn to the observer's gallery and give me room to operate. Dr.

Janson, you have a medical cure to finish, the rest of you I'll need on call in whichever capacity that you can supply. Dismissed."

With much reluctance, and more than a trace of shock, Dr. Janson and the others made their way off the central dais and out of the chamber; Hardwright and Dupree to the observers gallery behind the bay window at the back wall, Amanda to her office where she would keep track of things on her own computer while desperately trying to think of other solutions, Dr. Janson to his lab, and Mr. Six to parts unknown. As for Father Mason, he stayed with the General, though moved himself to a silent corner of the dais.

"This is it," Father Mason said almost to himself. "The start of the Gog-Magog war of Biblical prophecy."

General Mason apparently heard that quiet remark, for he glanced once at the priest before returning his full attention to events as they rapidly unfolded.

"That missile from France," the General snapped, "who launched it? The French government is still going to be in chaos, assuming enough of them are even alive."

"From what we can tell," reported one captain from the smaller circle on the dais, "it looks like a local base commander took it upon himself after watching their source of national pride get bombed."

"The French may be slow to act, but they're a patriotic bunch," the General remarked. "Do we have a trajectory on either missile?"

"Yes sir," came another voice from below.

One of the wall monitors switched to an image of an area map, with two dashed lines etching their way across it. The one from Russia stretched all the way to the middle of Saudi Arabia, while the one from southern France looked to have a similar course in mind. A single red dot labeled "Mecca".

"I see," the General stated. "ETA?"

"The French missile should arrive in... seventeen minutes," one man reported, "the Russian missile in twelve. No wait! Trajectory change on the Russian missile. Rocket velocity is slowing a bit and trajectory... Same destination with a slightly different course, but now it won't be there until eighteen minutes. Sir, why would the Russians–"

"They're giving first blow to France," the General said with a knowing nod. "I guess they feel it only right after the Eifel Tower."

He remained silent for a few seconds, then snapped out another command.

"How are we on North Korea? Get me the map on the main screen."

Immediately the central wall screen lit up with a satellite view of the Korean Peninsula. A nighttime view, with rivers of light where strips of brightly-lit cities lay. Most of the nighttime lighting lay in South Korea, with only a few bright dots here and there scattered throughout North Korea.

Then suddenly one of the lights in North Korea became very bright indeed. Quickly rising flare, hovering in place for a few moments, then dimming back down.

"Direct hit on Pyongyang," someone reported.

"That should keep North Korea out of the picture," General Willmington stated.

That's when Father Mason realized something with a gasp and rushed over to the General's side.

"John, how are you– I thought nukes needed direct Presidential authority. There's a key he has to activate or something."

"It's called the Football," the General replied, "and he activated it about an hour ago when the terrorists first took control of the Eifel Tower. All nuclear codes have been rerouted through this command center ever since."

"But you can't just–"

"Father... Henry. I said that this command post is meant to be the emergency command post of *all* Presidential authority in case of extreme emergency... That includes nuclear weapons. I'm sorry, but if there's going to be a war then I need to make sure that this country comes out on top. Now if you don't mind."

"John, surely there must be–"

"If you want to be of some use," the General told him, "then pray for my soul. Because I do what my country needs me to do but no one else *should* do. For what is come, I take the blame for it all that no one else will have to. Am I understood?"

The priest gave it a moment's thought then a slow nod as he replied.

"You die on your own cross for the world's sins that no one else will be tormented by the guilt... Yes, I do understand."

A last look back at the priest then General Willmington returned his attention to the speed of current events.

"Do we have any action from China yet? What's going on with Tibet? I've been advised that might be the place to focus our attentions…"

I remained there watching for a while longer. For the record I must make, there could be no better point of view to record from. Through angelic will I held back tears and focused on my job as scribe, recording every moment of the start of the slaughter until I decided to move onto something else.

Chapter Ten:

Satan At The Door

The door stood, still in its world between dimensions, the First Seal gleaming brighter than before ready to be unleashed. The Seven Seals were the only things holding Satan back from fully unleashing himself upon the world and the first was ready to give. As it was, the door was straining at the seams as the one on the other side struggled to be free. A deep rumbling could be heard coming through it as Ashtar hovered before it grinning from ear to ear, while somewhere behind him Jesus stood, still silently regarding the other as the First Seal neared its end.

"Do you feel it, father?" Ashtar beamed. "The final phase has begun. Humanity is eating itself. Soon they will be ready to accept you into their hearts and minds."

Another rumbling came to echo through the door, but this time it formed words. Words the tone of which sounded like a cold hand clutching onto your heart, a long needle lancing slowly through your brain. The words of Satan himself.

"I can feel the souls darkening to my command, hear the suffering of His creation and draw great joy from it. You have done well, my son. Soon I will be free to bring about Earth's final destruction. When that day comes, then the real battle between Heaven and Hell will commence."

"Your armies will be vast," Ashtar promised, "their ranks filled by Man's suffering. There will not be a single man, woman, or child left in the world willing to pray for their holy savior to come to their side. They will all pray to *you* as their one true god."

Suddenly the deep well of void rumbled as a voice shot out to nearly shake Ashtar from his feet.

"Enough!"

Ashtar spun around to see Jesus standing a step above him looking down. There was not anger in his eyes, only a sternness that Ashtar found difficult to return in kind. So he resorted to mocking.

"What's the matter, did I finally get to you? Has God's perfect Son finally cracked his ever-calm façade?"

Jesus said nothing at first, simply returning the other's look until Ashtar was forced to flinch away. Only then did Jesus speak.

"Insult and mock me all you want and I will not flinch. Scream obscenities about me into one ear and I will offer you the other. But speak not blasphemy of my Father lest I not wait until our appointed time. Only my Father is the one and true God, and certainly not Satan will stand before him."

Ashtar was surprised at first then composed himself; enough to finally return the other's angry glare with a mocking smile. A step up he took, then another, until he was nearly eye to eye with Jesus. His smile evolved into a smug look, the feel of his words like spoken slime as he uttered them.

"For... now."

Just two words, the temerity of which knew no end. If Jesus would respond with a slap or punch to his face, then Ashtar would have counted it a victory. Even a growl of anger would have had Ashtar crowing in jubilation. But Jesus displayed none of this, simply schooled his features back to their previous calm.

"Do not test divine will, Ashtar. I will not fight you a second before our anointed time in the mortal world. I know your game. You seek to force me into a situation where my Father will have to pass judgment on myself. But that will never happen. I have had my tests long ago and sit at His right hand. This test is for *you.* We will have our final confrontation soon enough."

To which Ashtar simply shrugged.

"You can't blame a demon for trying."

He stepped away, skipping back down to the side of the door, remarking under his breath as he went.

"Though that's about the biggest load of sanctimonious drivel that I've ever heard in my life."

"Ashtar, watch your words," Jesus cautioned, "lest I repay you for them in the final battle."

"Oh, excuse me," Ashtar said, spinning around, *"divine* sanctimonious drivel. Better?"

Jesus said nothing, so Ashtar faced back to the door before him and the Seven Seals.

"Father," he called to the door and the one beyond it, "the time draws near. The Gog-Magog War begun."

The voice of darkness came once again from beyond the door, a chill to the soul.

"Do not let His son get to you. Know thy patience and the time will soon come when we will face him on the final field of battle. Me and the legions you have gathered in my name, against Jesus alone. It will not be long before we will bring down the Gates of Heaven together."

"And that day cannot come soon enough," Ashtar grinned. "I will make for you a robe of screaming souls and a crown of darkness and force Jesus to his knees before you."

To that the rumble of laughter came once again from beyond the door, yet still Jesus said nothing. He remained in silence, regarding Ashtar with a level look that not even the son of Satan could read. It was enough to make Ashtar shiver once before looking away.

Ashtar was soon giggling once again as he looked up towards the Earth and what new mayhem was being wrought there.

Chapter Eleven:

The Third World War Begins

The meeting was held in that same high-vaulted chamber overlooking London like the chief jewel on a crown. All were present, except of course the one seat held empty by tradition, and a vacancy of one of their own. The white haired old man that held the post of Number One glared out at the rest, his gaze focusing on the one empty chair.

"Where is Number Six?"

"He sees to his mission in person," replied the brown-haired Number Seven. "He has secured himself deep within the U.S. President's own command circle. In a deeply laid military base."

"Excellent," Number One carefully nodded. "But how are we to contact him then to know what goes on? That place will be very carefully guarded and monitored."

The reply came from one whose placard was labeled as Number Nine; a blond-haired gentleman with a Swedish or Norwegian look to himself.

"Then it is fortunate that one of the companies that was contracted to make and install their computer and communications equipment is owned by one of our subsidiaries," the man grinned. "He has a device on him that will neutralize any nearby security electronics and open all communications equipment to his use without logging the attempt. All he needs is time alone and unobserved."

"Very good," Number One stated. "Then we know everything going on in their bunker?"

"We have a tap into all of their communications," Number Nine replied, "including some they might wish to be a lot more secure than they really are."

"This part sounds like it's going to be interesting," Number Two, the elderly woman, remarked. "Pray tell us more."

"It's simple," Number Nine shrugged. "We were able to listen in on a certain communication from their President. The one where he was transferring nuclear launch authority direct to that bunker. We now have copies of all the nuclear launch codes."

Everyone at the table broke out into a slow malicious shared grin, particularly Number One.

"That would be the one piece that we have been missing all these years," Number One then stated. "And now we have it. Okay then, let's start with a quick update on the significant events and see what we can twist around. Number Three, how looks India?"

"Enjoying an unexpected economic bloom since the wages of their workers quadrupled practically over night," the middle-aged Hindu man reported. "But soon to come crashing back down to lower levels than before since their economy can't handle it. They're also scheduled for another unseasonal and very destructive monsoon. Oh, and a quake in New Delhi. Within a month they should be *very* dissatisfied."

"Then in six weeks stage liberal levels of civil unrest. Get some paid protestors into the action," Number One ordered. "Now Number Four, how goes the war?"

The one who attention was now directed at was a somewhat portly Texan with a large Stetson hat currently on the table beside him.

"Well now, without the questionable efforts of the U.N. to slow things down you might expect it to be going gloriously, but it seems as a certain General was a bit too quick on the trigger for our purposes, and Russia is looking a bit too genial towards the States. North Korea was quieted down before they even had a chance to really get going, Saudi Arabia is in chaos after Mecca became a glowing hole in the ground, and Tehran's absence means that Iran just got a new government that's a lot more compatible with the rest of the civilized world. China's even staying quiet, a bit too busy with Tibet and not eager to start a real shootin' war."

"Oh, this will never do at all," Number One said with a shake of his head. "We must get China involved. Any unrest anyplace we can use?"

"All the major powers have their war fleets active and on high alert," Number Two answered. "France's governing body was missed by the terrorist attack, so they've just sent a fleet over to the Middle East along with England. Their destination is Iran but it looks like they're going by way of the Suez Canal to get to the Persian Gulf, which will put them within shooting range of Arabia and a few other Islamic powers. Syria and Jordan are ready to march on Israel but the United States has a fleet out there to keep things calm."

"Hmm," Number One mused, "there must be something..."

"What about the nukes?" Number Seven, a brown-haired man, suggested. "A few accidental launches could stir things up."

"Excellent idea," Number One beamed. "Number Nine, see to it that the United States accidentally launches a range of its nuclear missiles direct into the heart of China. Make it some military targets just to be convincing. Oh, but one civilian target just to get everyone's emotions stirred up. Nothing that will take out the governing body of China, just get them angry enough to start launching stuff themselves."

"That will bring Russia into it," Number Four put in. "As stirred up as them folk can get, they'll just blindly side against the U.S. and with China for a while."

"At which point let's see if we can't arrange for a missile launch from China into the heart of Russia," Number One grinned. "That should get everyone fighting against everyone else."

"It sounds like we have a plan," Number Two stated. "All we have to do is sit back and watch."

"And see to it that nothing hits London," Number Three pointed out, "or we'll be getting pretty hot under the collar."

"Have faith, Number Three," Number One told him. "Lord Ashtar will protect us… Not to mention that there isn't a single portion of these affairs that we do not control. Now, launch those nukes…"

Away in the deeply buried Command Bunker, General Willmington was keeping an eagle eye on things when Mister Six came up to his dais demanding his attention. A trivial matter in the General's eyes, something about economic repercussions, but it took his eyes away from his command duties. Twice he tried to get past the man, only for him to block his way once again to continue his financial tirade. Finally on the third try he put his hands to Mr. Six' shoulders and bodily moved him into the grip of a nearby soldier.

"See that he stays *out* of this room until I call for him! The War Room is no place for a banker."

"Yes, sir."

"But General," Mr. Six called out as he was being led away, "we must discuss these matters before things get much further along."

"Bankers," the General snorted to himself, "you can dump them in that same ocean trench as all the lawyers."

His attention once again on his work, he stopped short when he saw something on one of the monitors ringed round the dais. Reaching over he tapped a couple of keys to bring up a detailed report.

"I didn't authorize this," he gasped, then louder to the room in general, "Why am I seeing a missile launch? I didn't authorize anything."

"I– I d-don't know, sir," a flustered technician reported from one of the outer terminals.

"Track that thing!"

To the General's command, the technician called the display up on the central screen, followed quickly by the tracking data. A world map showing a launch from somewhere at sea.

"Three missiles from a couple of our subs in the Sea of Japan," another tech called out. "Destinations were encrypted so the subs would have had no idea as to–"

"But what do *we* know?" the General demanded to know. "Where are they headed?"

"In a moment… There."

Three locations lit up as the map zoomed in on China, the one speaking then continuing with his explanation.

"All headed to China. Two military bases and one headed for... Sir, it's going straight for Shanghai!"

The news hit him like a freight train, as did the implications. For a moment the General could only stare at the map and the three glowing red dots, then he quickly shook himself out of it and called out another command.

"Transmit abort codes *immediately.* Self destruct those things."

One man's fingers raced across his keyboard but to no satisfactory result.

"I'm trying sir, but we've been locked out.

"Sir," another called out, "I've traced the origin of the command and it came direct from this base. Your own authority, in fact."

"Well, *I* didn't send that command which means we got a mole. Lock down everything and start fine-tuning that trace, coordinating it with all security footage of who in this base touched what when. I want to know who to fillet for starting World War Three. And get those missiles aborted!"

In the end all would be helpless to watch as three missiles stabbed deep into the heart of China, one hitting what was very much a civilian target. Minutes later China would respond and an hour after that Russia would get into it. The Third World War had begun in full.

Chapter Twelve:

One Angel's Perspective

I decided at this point to start hopping around the world; sort of spot-check various sections of the global conflagration and record the highlights. I started by following China's response to the three missiles that the U.S. supposedly landed in the middle of their country. I even eavesdropped on their internal strategy meeting a little.

The gist of their discussion was that the States were too far off for any sort of direct battle by anything save missile attack, and for that they had no idea of the capability of whatever antimissile program the U.S. may have. So they decided to start local and work their way out. They used what happened to Pyongyang as an excuse to hit South Korea and Japan at the same time.

Exactly three missiles were launched out from China, the same number as they had been hit with. The first landed in Seoul, the second in Osaka, and the third in Kyoto. Nothing small like for Hiroshima at the end of

World War Two, just enough to leave nothing but glowing dust where once had been a city.

I watched as the great shining towers of South Korea's jewel suddenly turned to vapor, the most modern and magnificent city on the Korean Peninsula made into a million-degree kiln to melt down glass, steel, and flesh into a runny puddle and forge it into a clarion call for war. I heard the millions of cries as their lives suddenly ended.

If there be a ray of sunshine in this then it would be that a measure of suffering came to an end. I'd seen the streets of downtown Seoul, transformed by plague and famine into refugee camps; where there existed apartment complexes that no one would go near because of the stench of the dying, and partially toppled skyscrapers from the great quake that had ripped through the center of the city.

I saw one mother squatting down by the roadside as rain pounded down on her, huddling her three children close to her praying for a miracle then looking up and seeing the expanding point of light land in the middle of the business district, and in that brief moment send up a quick prayer of thanks before being turned to ash.

The two cities in Japan were much the same, except over there before the two bombs dropped, life had become far worse than their representative at the United Nations had described. Osaka was a glittering metropolis of brightly colored neon lights alongside thousand year old traditional Japanese architecture, canals with ferry boats, and rows of cherry trees with their white blossoms. But with Japan's lack of space and high population, by necessity it had also evolved into a city of layers. Triple-decker golfing ranges, a train station that had one berth stacked atop another, by necessity the Japanese had to build upwards.

But now such a design became a prison for many of them. I saw many such high-rise constructions where no one dared to go to the upper levels anymore; the few up there that had survived plague and famine without easy street access did so by preying on others who came too near. Bullet train cars were each accompanied now by armed guards– something the Japanese never would have seen the necessity of before. Most of the country's dead lay in those uppermost realms, and in many cases I saw that those living in the lower levels had sealed off all access to the upper floors, trapping any survivors above them.

Those triple-decker golf courses had become camps for the homeless, as had the beautiful parks strewn about the city. To escape the famine and plagues of the countryside, many had flocked to the inner city in hopes of salvation, only to discover that such a crowded city is never a good place to go in times of plague. Then came the great quakes that toppled many of the large towers and trapped the citizenry within Osaka's borders.

The city had become their prison.

When the bomb came, I heard as many thanks for being freed from this nightmare as cries of horror.

Kyoto was more the quaint suburban village that happened to roll on for several miles. With few structures in its outer sections taller than three stories that were less than three hundred years old, and streets paved in cobbled stones and steps carved into city hillsides, it was a city where the character of the old met against the bright lights of the modern age. A place more relaxed than Osaka and very popular with tourists.

The great quake had split the city in two, separating off the more modern inner city from the rest with a wide rift. In a way that was viewed as a mixed blessing, since that cut the plague-ridden inner city off from the rest of Kyoto, and some locals seemed determined to keep it that way. The city had developed a split personality, with gangs acting as border patrols ready to toss back anyone trying to cross the rift into the more suburban sections and add to their own problems.

I saw entire bamboo forests withered by blight, cherry trees blackened and lifeless, and dead forests where not even the desperate homeless dared to go, then turned into a dead swamp by the unceasing storms. The one positive note I will give them is that when the economy collapsed and the banks tried to move in to collect on everyone's debts, the locals of Kyoto formed a line to keep them out, then blocked the roads and essentially formed their own miniature city-state.

Yet all of that too came to an end when China's third missile impacted, reducing a city of dreams and character to a charcoaled lump.

From there I watched as China's fleet formed a noose around South Korea, and sailed into Tokyo Bay with guns blazing. It was a messy contest, and one not easily won by either side.

When the uprising in Tibet became too much of a distraction, China simply sent in an army with orders to shoot anyone they came against.

After seeing so much misery, I had need of a change of pace, and headed down for India... where I met an old friend.

"Gabriel, Father sends me to see how it goes with your scribing."

"Michael?"

Yes, it was archangel Michael, with his golden wings and blond hair flowing to his shoulders. He joined me by my side as I walked the filthy streets, neither of us seen by mortal eyes. I greeted him with a welcome clasp of arms then continued my walk, now at least with some company.

"Your presence is very much welcome, Michael. The record I must make is most disheartening."

"I can well imagine," he said with a slow glance around.

The streets of New Delhi have never been the bright point of human endeavor under the best of circumstances, with streets paved in grime and air scented with poverty, parts of it were already barely a step away from being sewers. Now, though, the scent of death lingered heavily in the air, with swarms of flies buzzing around the walking dead and making for some the only meal they've had in days.

In the distance we could hear the call of military authority trying to clear the streets and restore some order to life. Not that there were any big riots; the people were too weak from starvation and disease for that.

"It's even worse in Calcutta," I told him. "The dead pile high in the streets."

"Any cannibalism?" Michael asked.

"Not so far, though I've seen it in many other countries," I told him. "You have a lot of people here that won't eat meat, they certainly aren't going to start eating one another. They just... die."

We walked a bit more down the street, trying to ignore the ever-present smell of decay, the sight of children and adults with their lower ribs and backbones showing through their thin bellies, as clouds of feces-laced dust waft through the air. Finally I asked him.

"Why are you really here, Michael? I know it's not just because Father wants to see how I'm doing."

"I just thought you could use the company. You have a lonely and unenviable job, Gabriel."

"Lonely and disheartening," I admitted. "To be the one to record the end of humanity... I would like to take them all and hug them until their misery would all disappear."

"I can sympathize with you, Gabriel... But you're wrong in one thing."

"Oh? And what is that?"

We turned a corner where we saw the source of the soldier's cries. It seems as a truck was slowly passing through the street collecting the dead, but one young mother refused to release her dead child. From the look of the puss-filled sores on her body, though, it will not be long before she joins her offspring.

"This is not an ending, Gabriel, but a transformation. One that even Satan has a roll to play in, though he perhaps thinks to take advantage of it."

"A transformation? How? What is Mankind transforming into?"

To that he only smiles, then reaches out to give a light tap to my scroll upon which I have been recording everything.

"They'll need to know where they came from and how difficult was their journey, so make sure that you keep an accurate record."

I look at him uncertainly, wanting to inquire further into what he means, but then I catch a fresh scent of death upon the winds.

"Something new?" Michael asked, apparently catching my expression.

"India just dropped a nuclear bomb on Pakistan; Islamabad, from the feel of it."

"Pakistan will respond, but with their capitol taken out, who will be left to give the order?"

"There's a group of extremists I've been keeping track of," I told him. "And they'll discover that Pakistan has its own nuclear bomb program. Not many missiles on either side of this, but the winds will carry the radiation across half of India, most of Pakistan, and even parts of Afghanistan. A hundred million people will be exposed to radiation sickness."

"What about neighboring areas? Bangladesh, Bhutan, and Nepal?"

"Nepal is too high up in the mountains to worry about anything... They just get to watch everyone below them die."

"A comforting thought," he said with a sad sigh. "Well, I will leave you to your work. Right now I have my own duties to get to."

"Readying the armies of Heaven?"

He said nothing, just gave me a look, then spread his wings and took off.

I took up a position high in the atmosphere, the better to get a wider look at the complex unfolding of events. Even from here my angelic eye can pick out details as small as a single child wandering a war-torn street wondering where his family went to.

I watched and recorded as the Middle East became a flashpoint. The combined fleets of England and France had made it through the Red Sea but not before having to eradicate a Somalian pirate fleet. Now they marched on Iran's southern coast, while within its borders Persians of one sect or another struggle to make of themselves the new government. In the end Iran will fracture and the Europeans will not be sure who they invade.

The U.S. fleet had no trouble helping defend Israel against Syria, Jordan, and Lebanon, but then the Russian fleet came out through the Black Sea to challenge them on more equal footing, while another Russian army invaded Ukraine... again.

The war in Europe was more of one in the streets, as Europeans of one nation or another fight off the refugees-turned-invaders, and the refugees unveil every trick of terrorist sabotage that they can dream up. From Spain to Greece, Italy to Germany, the war in the streets brought life to a standstill. London seemed to be the one unassailed capitol remaining to Europe, but I know well the reason for that.

When you are wondering where the lair of your real enemy lies, simply look for the one place still intact.

I saw Russia advancing into Iran from the north, no doubt to take advantage of the situation and grab a chunk of land for themselves, and I saw them sail a force across the Bearing Straits to Alaska. For that latter I knew it had to be a desperate grab for oil... the same as for their intrusion into Iran, now that I think about it. Russia must be running short on fuel for their machines.

Then just when it looked like Russia and China would be teaming up against the United States, three more missiles were launched. This time it was from China, shooting through the sky into the middle of Russia. One of them was shot down but the remaining two erased some industrial cities from existence. China plead ignorance as to the reason behind their launch, but China has lied too many times to be believed.

After that, alliances began to switch on a daily basis and the world started to shake from the impact of war.

Chapter Thirteen:

Nuclear Greetings

General Willmington was on his central dais to the command center, looking at one disastrous report after another festooning the screens hung around the walls of the large circular chamber like draperies. One screen showed a list of trajectories and estimated destinations, others satellite views of different sections of the Earth, each centered around an expanding glow of heat. When one trajectory in the updating list would be replaced with the designation 'Target Achieved', a new satellite image would appear on one of the monitors showing a freshly expanding cloud. On occasion one of the trajectories on the list would disappear, replaced with the words "Missile Destroyed", but that happened all too few times.

The images showed views of Europe, China, and Russia, as well as India, and North and South America. On the main screen at the center was displayed a world map, bedecked with red dots the world over. A line of such dots drew a course down the west coast of the United States, with one around Anchorage Alaska. Europe had several such dots, as did Russia and China, though Australia yet remain untouched… by the bombs, at least.

"General," a voice called out, "fresh launches coming in from over the North Pole. A cluster of them."

"Estimated trajectories?" the General asked.

"Looks like parts of Minnesota and Wisconsin," came the reply.

"They found out we still have some nukes there," the General mused. "Okay, get our antimissile batteries in the North Pole to shooting down as many of those things as we can and launch some aircraft from our nearest Canadian base to intercept what's left."

"Sir," another voice called out from another section of the room, "missile launches from Russia. Course looks to be western Europe."

"Not that there's much left there to be of concern to them," the General stated. "Okay, authorize use of the antimissile batteries we have in Germany and launch interceptors. How's eastern Europe doing?"

The reply came from a Captain at one of the terminals on the inner circle of the central dais, who quickly read off from the list of reports before him.

"Ukraine has fallen to Russia, Poland nearly so, and that new fleet out from the Black Sea looks to be headed straight for Greece."

"Predictable," the General sighed. "Okay, get one of our subs in the area to plant a nuke right in the middle of that fleet headed for Greece, then launch out a series of missiles and see if we can make it through to Moscow this time."

"Yes sir."

"How's the Middle East doing?" the General then asked another Captain.

"In a word," the man replied, "a mess. Sir. The West Bank region is firmly back in Israeli hands, and the Golan Heights is free but probably unlivable for the next thousand years."

"That place was never worth fighting over to begin with," the General grumbled.

"A Muslim group responded by blowing up an ancient building in Jerusalem," the report continued. "A temple, I believe."

"The temple in Jerusalem?" the General said with a cocked eyebrow. "The Padre's not going to like that; I think that's one of his end-times signs. What else? What about our little contest with the Russians?"

"Going in our favor, sir. Though it looks like Turkey just launched a small force to join in and we have no idea whose side they're going to be on."

"Probably picking around for leftovers. Okay, get me a–"

"Sir," came a cry out from the forward section of the room, the soldier there relaying the information as he read it off from his terminal, "Russia just invaded China."

"Central screen!"

To the General's command, the view on the main screen switched to a regional map of China with a series of red lines with arrows drawn to indicate the attack points. One arrow swept down into Korea, another into Manchuria from southeast Russia, and a third in through Kazakhstan into western China. Accompanying them were several more slender expanding lines flying over Mongolia towards the heart of China.

Seeing this, the General gave a shake of his head and looked ready to either scream or give up.

"Coffee?"

"Huh?"

He turned around to see Father Mason standing beside him holding out a steaming hot cup of coffee.

"I even Irished it up for you," the priest added. "Thought under the circumstances that God wouldn't mind."

"Thanks, Henry."

General Willmington took the cup and gave it a long sip, after which he reacted with pursed lips and a quick shake of his head.

"Just how much Irish did you *put* in this thing?"

"Enough to help you deal with this mess. So, what's all the colorful lines crawling across the big screen?"

"You sure you want to know?"

"I had some Irish just before I came in. Give me the worst."

"You're looking at it. Those fat lines are where Russian forces are rolling into China, while the skinny moving ones are missile trajectories."

"Looks like about twenty of them," the priest noted.

"All nukes, and all headed into the most populated sections of China."

"Civilian targets? Wouldn't they just hit military targets?"

"No doubt some are, but when you have a billion people to throw around, and a government that doesn't mind enlisting a few million people straight off the streets when you're desperate, suddenly even civilian targets are looking pretty military. Russia plans on dissecting the country."

"But that's awful! Isn't there something that–"

"Wait for it," the General told him, then to one of the Captains nearby, "Superimpose China's response."

A few seconds later, another series of skinny lines appeared, these launching out from northern China in various directions towards Russia.

"Computing exact trajectories now," that same Captain reported. "Sir! We have a second flight of missiles, but these are headed east towards our west coast."

Now yet another set of lines appeared on the map, these headed from China in the direction of the United States.

"That's an awful lot of missiles," Father Mason said with a nervous swallow. "And they're all headed for us?"

"If they can make it this far," the General stated. "Captain, I want every jet, antimissile system, and base we have between Japan and the west coast targeting those things."

"Yes sir."

"But surely," the priest continued, "they must realize that after all the disasters that there's not much left of the west coast?"

"Which is why they're probably headed more for Texas and places east. A bit far for their missiles, but I'm not taking the chance that they might—"

"Sir, one of the missiles looks to be targeting Hawaii."

One of the lines on the map now stretched out with a dashed line to Hawaii. Now the General's demeanor lost what control he had been maintaining and flecked through with a burst of anger.

"That's my favorite vacation spot. Okay, no more messing around. Activate Thor System!"

"Yes *sir.*"

The grin on the face of the replying Captain had the priest wondering, so he asked the obvious just as Dr. Stilton walked into the room.

"If I may… What is Thor? Besides the obvious mythological connections, of course. A bigger nuke?"

"Thor really exists?" an excited Dr. Stilton exclaimed.

As she hurried over to the dais, looking equal parts nervous and excited, General Willmington quickly explained.

"A little something we've had up in orbit since the late eighties. Nothing nuclear, so no radiation, but bad enough. Amanda, you seem to be up on this, why don't you explain it while I run this war?"

As the General turned his attention to the myriad details of worldwide destruction, Father Mason stepped over to the physicist's side for a quickly whispered conference.

"Thor is essentially a spear," Amanda began.

"Doesn't sound too harmful. A bit primitive for things, I would think."

"Not when the spear is all metal, about the size of a Cadillac, and dropped from space. A common meteor slamming down from above is bad enough, but imagine something shaped like a missile so it won't melt on re-entry, but just pick up speed on the way down. No explosives onboard, just a pointed hunk of metal picking up velocity from several miles above us."

"I see... That would leave quite the hole in the ground, then."

"Like a small nuke, only without the fallout. You can try shooting it down, but it has no guidance system to foul, no explosives on board to prematurely detonate. It's a dead hunk of metal and even if you manage to hit it with a missile, its pieces are still going to land *somewhere* nearby the target zone. On top of that, from what I hear its outer surface is coated with something that protects it from being picked up by radar or other systems."

"Not until it's too late," the priest said with a slow nod. "Primitive but… insidious."

"No telltale radiation signature, no engines or exhaust trail, just a stick dropped from space."

"Like a bolt of thunder… Thor."

He gave a shake of his head then poised another question.

"How many other things like that do we have up there?"

Before Amanda could reply, they heard one of the Captains call out in response to the General's latest order.

"Trajectory laid in. Weapons platform will be in position inside of ten minutes."

"Then as soon as it is, start dropping them," the General commanded. "One every half minute, a dozen in all. With the drift of the platform that should give a good spread across our target."

"And just what *is* the target."

Father Mason came up to the General's side with concern in his voice and written clearly on his face, behind him a nervous looking physicist afraid to hear the answer.

"When the serpent threatens you, you cut off its head," General Willmington replied. "I'm hitting Beijing."

Amanda let out a gasp, Father Mason looked like he'd swallowed a lemon whole, then the priest reached for the cup of coffee still in the General's hand and downed the remains in a single gulp.

———

In the quarters assigned to Milton Six, the financial expert had been left to his own. Not much left of the world to advise on financially, his duties were thought basically done, leaving him trapped in an underground haven while the world outside burned.

But Mr. Six still had other duties to be about. After making sure that he was truly alone and his door locked, he brought out a small electronic device and set it onto his desk. Switching it on, he waited until a green light lit up at the base of it then flipped out the attached screen and sat down before it. A moment later a logo filled the screen; a pyramid topped by a single eye. The voice accompanying the logo was quite familiar to the man.

It was the voice of Number One.

"Number Six, how goes your end of things?"

"The General is frustrated enough that he's close to launching every nuclear missile available to end it all, and he has the Presidential authority with which to do so. With martial law, he has to run a war *and* a country."

"Then his frustration is about to get even worse. He should soon be getting word that the President was just assassinated by a terrorist bomb. Try to look surprised."

"I will, Number One. What about the outside world? How much longer do we have to keep this farce up?"

"About another billion or so deaths should do it. Then we can contact the Jesuits to be on the lookout for the arrival of Ashtar's fleet."

"I can't believe our time is so close. Just imagine, soon our lord and master will arrive and we'll be there right by his side. The Princes of the world... But what about my extraction? How much longer do I have to stay down here?"

"I would imagine until the radiation clears when the nearest of those missiles from China hits. Or was it the

ones from Russia? Either way, you will be alerted when the time comes. Until then, make sure that General Willmington's anxiety level stays high."

"After what I've been sneaking into his coffee pot? Not a problem. Number Six out."

He pressed a button and the logo vanished, then folded down the screen, turned the device off, and pocketed it. From there he got to his feet, grabbing up the first stack of papers he saw on his desk, then headed for the door.

"About time I bugged the General again about some useless detail of finance. That's always good for distracting him."

I still find myself amazed at humanity's capacity for preying upon itself.

Chapter Fourteen:

The Fall Of Humanity

The war continued until people forgot the reasons why.

The Arab world sank beneath a combined assault involving all the major powers as alliances came and went. Then the winners started grabbing pieces of the precious oil fields for themselves, after which it became a matter of actually holding onto them. That got the world fighting anew.

Between the previous disasters, continued terrorist activities by the remaining extremists still willing to die for Allah, and assaults from Russia followed by counter-offences, the bulk of Europe had become a wasteland. London held out, as did Rome, but precious little else.

China finally fractured, with Tibet gaining its freedom but only after suffering greatly at the hands of the Chinese army. In the end, it was the invasion from Russia that had the effect of saving Tibet, too distracted were the Chinese now in defending their own grounds.

As far as Russia, between the Chinese and American missiles, Russia was left to fight its harsh winters with little in the way of centralized authority. Armies marched, invasions came and went, and national borders shifted several times. It was in the face of such changes that necessitated a regular meeting with General Willmington and his advisors, still buried deep beneath the sands of New Mexico.

At least during such times when the pause of marching armies and flying missiles allowed them the opportunity.

General Willmington sat in the briefing room with the others. The General looked like he'd aged twenty years in the last two, though the others didn't look much better off. Father Mason's youthful energy had been depleted as much as his remaining hair had, while Amanda Stilton's trim black locks had begun sporting a few grey strands. Bob Hardwright's portly frame had lost a few inches, not from dieting but purely from stress and the lower quality of food they were forced to deal with, while Alexander Dupree's blond hair had started into a touch of premature greying. Only Milton Six still seemed fit and energetic enough despite the passage of events.

"Where's the Doc?" General Willmington asked in a tired tone.

"Said something about his lab," Amanda replied in an equally fatigued voice.

They sat around a long table, the General at the one end, behind him a projection wall ready to display whatever he called up via the terminal before him. Before each seat a similar terminal rested, with only one seat yet remaining empty, and that would soon be filled by the unusually exuberant entry a moment after the physicist's reply.

Doctor Steven Janson still looked young, though extremely haggard. As if he hadn't combed his hair for a week nor bathed in a month. Not that anyone cared anymore. But now as he entered he was filled with an energy that he had not known in too long a time. He rushed in bearing a hypodermic needle and a handful of finger-sized ampules.

"Sorry I'm late, but I had to finish something up."

He rushed around the outside of the table, passing up his empty chair and pausing with his needle jabbing into Dr. Stilton's shoulder.

"Hey! What the heck?!"

Pulling out the needle, he loaded a fresh ampule into it as he stepped quickly over to Dr. Dupree. Before the psychologist could object to the coming needle, Dr. Janson continued to explain.

"It took a little bit of effort to track it down, but–"

He was cut off by both Dr. Dupree's brief cry from the injection and the General's suddenly hopeful statement.

"The cure! You finished the cure?"

"A bit late, I know," Dr. Janson said as he now moved onto the General's willingly bared arm, "but I finally have it licked. I still have no idea who engineered this bug, but this injection will stop that virus in its tracks and allow the body to once again have access to its own ability to fight disease."

Next was Professor Hardwright, a quick injection while Mr. Six asked the obvious question.

"And how difficult is this cure to make? A cure does no good if it's too expensive or difficult to create."

Professor Hardwright done, Dr. Janson moved onto Mr. Six next as he replied.

"Surprisingly easy, once you know the trick. Let's just call it a secret ingredient and leave it at that. I've tested it in petri dishes against the virus, I've tested it against our sample patients– who are back on the road to wellness, I might add– and I've tested it on myself. In all cases it remains flawless."

He was injecting Father Mason now, who while willingly submitting to the injection, was casting a suspicious look up to the doctor.

"The past few months," the priest finally spoke after his injection was finished, "you've been asking me to bless a lot of holy water… Steven, what did you do?"

"Water?" Amanda said. "Did you just give us a placebo?"

Dr. Janson paused before finally sitting down, securing his hypodermic then explaining.

"I've had the necessary ingredients that should have been able to deal with the virus once they met up, the problem was getting that formulation to the virus itself without running afoul of one of its chemical countermeasures. I needed a good carrier substance. I tried everything, then in desperation… Yes, I tried Father Mason's blessed water. Now before you say what I know you're going to say, I did a double blind test against ordinary water. In both cases the water was distilled and came from the exact same source, just one sample was blessed by the Father and the other was not."

"Holy water?" Dr. Dupree said with head cocked to one side.

"Hey, it worked," Dr. Janson shot back. "The serum gets past the chemical blockade that the virus is able to put out, then my concoction gets to work knocking it out. After that, the body's immune system is back and ready to roll."

"This smacks more of something a witchdoctor would come up with than actual medical science," Mr. Six began. "I think we need to hold off until we can be sure that–"

"I don't care if this stuff is made with unicorn piss," the General cut in, "it works and that's all I care about. Doc, how soon can you copy out the procedure to make this stuff?"

"Already loaded into the system," Dr. Janson replied.

"Then let's start up by getting enough made for everyone in this base. After that just keep producing this stuff so we can start distribution."

"We'll never be able to manufacture enough for what's needed," Professor Hardwright pointed out. "For millions of people we'd need some very hefty manufacturing facilities."

"And we'll have them," the General replied. "Doctor Janson, get ready to transmit the procedure to everyone we can. I've already nationalized the likes of Embassy Foods and every pharmaceutical company left in operation; we'll use *them.*"

"And for the holy water?" Father Mason asked. "What about that?"

"We'll send away to Rome for more priests, if we have to," the General snapped, "just make the arrangements and get this stuff moving."

"Right," Dr. Janson replied. "But General… we need to give this discovery to everyone. Enemies too."

General Willmington thought for a moment then answered with a single nod, to which Mr. Six immediately voiced his objection.

"General, you can't be serious?! At least sell it to them for something."

"Milton," Father Mason put in, "we may be at war, but we're all still of the same people. This disease affects us all. We may not survive as a species unless we share this."

"Sooner or later this war will end," General Willmington stated, "and when it does we'll all have to get along. When that time comes, I'd rather people remember which side they got their medical salvation from. Now, Doc Janson, after this meeting you will start immediately making arrangements. I'll assign you a Captain to help with the details.

"Yes sir, General."

"And Milton, anymore objections to something that will take away at least *one* of our problems– even if this late in the game– and I'll belt you myself, understood?"

"Yes, General."

"Now, to the main briefing at hand. Bob, why don't you start us off. Who's friends with who this week?"

Bob Hardwright reached forward to tap a few keys at his terminal, then began listing things off. A world map appeared on the big wall screen, and in each case as Professor Hardwright mentioned a country, its outline would flash, or if he talked of allies then the allied countries mentioned would flash together in green, while mutually opposing ones flashed red.

"Well, to start everything west of the Rockies is effectively dead. We still hold Alaska but the Russians set some of the oil fields on fire with a small tactical nuke before leaving. Enough of Canada got caught in the fallout from Russia's attempted missile incursion over their lands that they finally agreed to be annexed by the United States. Except for Quebec; they've been talking about independence for so long it's been a running joke for the last thirty years. They'll still work with us, they just want to remain on their own.

"We'll give Quebec this one," the General agreed. "Continue."

"We finally got some people into Mexico. The winds have carried the bulk of our radiation fallout across their northern territories, effectively turning them into wastelands."

"No more border crossing problems," Mr. Six shrugged.

"Milton, shut it," the General snapped. "Continue, Bob."

"As I was about to say, the rest of Mexico is ruled completely by gangs. No more government, the army disbanded, and no sign of their President or the rest of his staff. Central America's in even worse shape, what with the blight turning their jungles into a garbage pit."

"Dr. Janson, that's your next task," the General cut in, "to find a solution to the crop blight."

"I'm not a botanist, but I'll see what I can do," Dr. Janson replied.

"That's all I can ask. Continue, Bob."

A tap to his keyboard and Professor Hardwright shifted attention over to Europe.

"Ignoring South America, which hasn't had a government lasting longer than three months or a single active productive resource in the last full year at the least, and Africa where everyone has devolved into animals, Europe appears to have a new leader. Germany has reached out to unite with France, northern Italy, and Spain to form a new Union to stand against the Russian forces at Poland's border."

"What about the rest of Italy?" Dr. Dupree asked.

"Central and Southern Italy has been brought under the dominion of the Vatican as the New Papal States, while Sicily claims it never really ever *was* a part of Italy anywhere in its history."

"But that's preposterous," Dr. Stilton remarked.

"Not if you know Sicily," Professor Hardwright said with a tired grin. "But to continue… Everywhere between Hungary and Greece is a mess of everyone fighting everyone else, punctuated by the occasional nuke from Russia. And Turkey has now declared war on Russia."

"I'm afraid to ask," the General sighed, "but why?"

"Sabotage attempt by some Ukrainian nationalists against some Russian assets," the Professor explained. "It brought done one of their missiles right in the middle of the

Black Sea. Wiped out some Russian ships, but the radioactivity spread through the water and is now washing up all along Turkey's northern coast. Dead fish everywhere, not to mention a few fishermen."

"So Russia's going to start nuking Turkey next," the General summed up, "what else is new. And the rest of the Middle East?"

"Borders have effectively ceased to exist," Professor Hardwright reported. "Syria, Jordan, Lebanon, Iraq, Iran, even Saudi Arabia; the whole area is run by hundreds of regional tribes and warlords. Though in Arabia there *is* someone claiming to be one of the last surviving Saudi princes who's been trying to get something together."

"I wish him luck," the General quipped.

"He has sent a communiqué to the effect that he wants to open up military relations with the United States."

"Not *that* much luck. We got little enough left for ourselves as it is to be sending anything out into a dead desert."

"The Prince makes an offer of oil and states that he will even open up friendly relations with Israel."

"Ask Israel what they think of the offer. Any other highlights?"

"That's it except that, save for a few scattered terrorist actions, Australia has escaped largely unscathed."

"That's because no one cares about a million square miles of Outback that makes the Sahara Desert look like a summer house," Dr. Stilton remarked. "Especially with the extreme temperatures and drought that have been hitting it lately."

"They're trying their best to not become a target," Professor Hardwright told her. "Which is why they have now sent us notice that they want all U.S. military presence removed from their soil. They say we can go to New Zealand."

"And New Zealand?" the General asked.

"They declared war on Australia in response," Professor Hardwright replied. "Though in this case 'war' might be little more than a long range drinking contest, with the Kiwis doing that native war dance of theirs."

The General had listened to every single word, and now he sat back in thought. Professor Hardwright canceled the wall display with a swipe of his hand across his keyboard then waited with everyone else until the General decided to speak.

"A very solid report, Bob. But what it amounts to is this: there is no one left to fight with, and yet everyone is still fighting everyone else. We had another earthquake that sank the lower half of Florida and split Cuba in two, and probably the only thing that saved us from a direct hit from Russia's latest round of missiles coming across the Atlantic was the latest freak hurricane that planted itself in the middle of the ocean for a couple of weeks. Sank some of our own ships as well. I would like to declare peace with someone, only I'm not sure we can get a communication through to anyone to even do *that*. The world has gone to hell in a hand-basket, and the hand-basket's on fire. If anyone has any ideas of what to do I'm all ears, because right now I'm tapped out."

He glanced from one face to another hoping to see some glimmer of a suggestion. But in each case all he got back was a blank stare. The cure that Dr. Janson had finally developed had been a beacon of hope, but a beacon lost in the darkness. For the greater problems at hand, there was nothing the General could see that might bring sanity to the world.

———

Once again Mr. Six activated his device in the privacy of his quarters, waited for the green light to come on before flipping out the screen and awaiting the logo.

"Your report, Number Six?"

Mr. Six's reply contained only two words.

"They're ready."

Chapter Fifteen:

The Jesuit Connection

Buried deep within the bowels of the Vatican, now at the heart of the New Papal States, was a humble little sanctuary carved from the niche in the side of an ancient corridor. An entrance into the lower catacombs to one side, and the bottommost level of the Vatican Archives to the other. A room made to be simple quarters for a man living only with the basic needs of life.

A bedroll across the stone floor, small wooden desk and basic writing supplies, and a single old fashioned phone with a rotary dial sat atop the desk, physically wired into the wall. A phone that had rung little in the last twenty years the man had called this place home.

The small cell of a room had a single adornment fixed up onto one wall. A large sunburst design, inside of which were the letters "IHS", topped by a cross, with three nails drawn just beneath the letters. The symbol of the Jesuit order.

He was on his knees on the bare floor saying his daily prayers when the phone rang for one of the very few times in the last twenty years. His head jerked up, ears alert to be sure he was not mistaken. Then the phone rang a second time.

Immediately he was up on his feet and leaping over to the desk. He picked up the phone from its cradle, then calmed himself before speaking.

"This is Father Mulhare."

"Still at your post, I see."

"Always," he replied to the elderly female voice. "I help manage the archives for both the Vatican and Jesuits."

"Which keeps you in the perfect position, the same as your predecessors. This is Number Two."

Upon hearing that, Father Mulhare immediately brought himself to attention.

"You're standing at attention, aren't you? This isn't the military, now just relax and listen. You have been keeping track of world events, I take it?"

"As part of my duties."

"Buried down there like a gopher, you just never know. Okay then, know this. The time has come, the arrival is at hand. So as it has been written, is it now to come."

"And coming, will it be written," the priest replied. "Yes, I understand."

"I'll bet you've been waiting half your life to use that pass phrase. Okay, stop smirking and listen. You are to pass word to alert your order and activate the Lucifer Project. Repeat, the Lucifer Project."

"The Lucifer Project, yes Number Two. Do we have an exact arrival date?"

"Just keep your eyes peeled. Your people will know what to do."

"Yes, Number Two."

"I hope so. After coming this far and all we've done... Number Two, out."

The line went dead a second later; no dial tone, just like the ancient phone had never been connected. He carefully hung up the phone, smoothed out his robes, then faced the one door into his small chamber.

"My time is finally here. I have the honor of starting things off. I will not fail my mission... Ave Satanas."

He reached for his door and left in a brisk walk.

———————————

Father Mulhare met later with a younger priest outside the Vatican in a small roadside shop serving coffee and sandwiches. They spoke not in English or Italian, but Latin and even then a dialect not known to most Catholic priests. For benefit of this record, I will of course translate what was said.

"Father Mulhare, it is not often that I see you outside your cell."

"It is not often that something brings me out, Father Darcy. But now the most magnificent of news calls me into the daylight."

"Then you had better hurry up and relay it to me before another terrorist comes by with a bomb."

Father Darcy said that with a teasing grin, but as he took a sip of his cappuccino, he saw the serious regard in the other priest's face and paused with his shot glass to his lips. He caught the other's eye, Father Mulhare replying with a slow nod, then as Father Darcy brought the glass carefully back down to the table, the other spoke.

"I have been contacted by Number Two. We are to begin the next phase and contact the Lucifer Project."

"The Lucifer Project… Are you sure?"

"Code phrases confirmed, our orders are clear. Our contacts in the observatory in Arizona are to begin their project, while the media contacts play along. Soon our

Lord Ashtar will come, and before he does we must make the world ready to accept his coming."

"Then it will be done," the other smiled. "A toast to his coming."

They raised up their cappuccino shot glasses and clinked them together.

———————————

Deep in the heart of Arizona, where the city lights cannot cloud the nighttime view, a large observatory sits that scans the sky through its array of telescopes. The project a division of SETI, the goal to find new worlds and any sign of life from other stars. As of yet nothing definite, but the people who worked here had their hopes.

One man sat the night watch, keeping one eye on the zoo of equipment and readouts that surrounded him, and his other eye on his bagel. He was leaning back in his swivel chair, legs up on a counter, when something buzzed. He took a bite out of his bagel and glanced over to the security camera. It was a face he knew, so a press of a button and he buzzed him in. By the time he had swallowed his bite, the other was turning the corner in the maze of equipment and coming over to his station.

"Ted," the man with the bagel said by way of greeting, "what brings you all the way out here in the middle of nowhere?"

Ted said nothing, just pulled something out of his pocket as he walked over, then tossed it on the counter before the other. It was a coin the size of a silver dollar, but stamped with the symbol of the Jesuits. The man immediately put down his bagel and straightened up.

"We're safe," he reported to his visitor. "No one else around. What's up?"

"Direct from Rome. The Lucifer Project is to be activated."

"You sure?"

"Absolutely. The word comes down from Number Two."

"Then it looks like this is it. Time to get to work."

As the man leaned forward into his console to work, Ted now had his own questions.

"Ray, are you certain you have all the details worked out?"

"Been fine-tuning this thing for ages now," Ted replied as he started typing. "Nothing else to do on the night shift. When I run the program, a false image will be recorded by our telescopic array. I don't even have to be here to be the one to pick it up. When someone moves the dishes to confirm it, they will see the same thing. Additionally, the program is designed to update the image so it will be seen to grow, as if something rapidly getting closer."

"But won't they just think it's a meteor or something?'

"At first, but then meteors don't make course corrections."

"They'll ask other observatories to confirm the sighting."

"Ready for that one too," Darcy grinned. "All observatories share data, either though direct links or something like the Internet. By the time someone spots it on this end, my little program will have been uploaded to every observatory on the planet. They'll be watching a nice and gradual approach; far faster than anything natural or manmade, but still slow enough to have time to gather worldwide attention."

"Sounds good. Now what happens when it's supposed to be close enough for your average backyard telescope to pick up?"

"That would be about lunar orbit, and by *that* time Lord Ashtar's fleet of fake UFOs will be ready to come out from behind the Moon and make their grand entrance."

He worked a bit more, then relaxed when a "Loading" progress bar appeared on his screen.

"What about the press?" Darcy then asked.

"The press is about ready to handle itself," Ted reported with a grin. "Something as big as this after everything the world's gone through? They'll eat this up."

"Good thing I never believe anything I see in the press," Darcy grinned.

The loading finished and the progress bar vanished, replaced by nothing more than a standard "Operations Control" display.

"I don't see anything changed," Ted remarked with some concern.

"You won't, that's the whole idea. It's working in the background now. Most of the pictures are recorded electronically now, so those will be easy to rig, and the radio pics are taken from the combined input of the array outside, so that's *all* electronic. Some of the older all-optical scopes won't be able to pick anything up, of course, but then I have yet to see any new stellar phenomena that was able to be picked up by every single telescopic array on the planet. Don't worry, this will sell itself."

"It had better. What about audio?"

"Transmissions will start about the time it appears to get within Mars orbit."

"And how are you handling *that* one?"

"Bounce a signal around a few satellites until it looks like someone out there is using our own satellites to direct a broadcast from about Mars orbit down to the Earth," Darcy shrugged. "Like I keep telling you, I'm an underappreciated genius. If anything needs some fine-tuning, I can log into any terminal of an affected system and take care of it."

"My boy, it sounds like you just might make this project fly! I'll tell my superiors the good news then they can get everything else rolling."

"Great. Now you'd better get going. My relief is due to arrive in about half an hour. I figure I'll feign being half asleep and let him make the discovery. The first man to detect an alien presence moving into our system."

Ted slapped Darcy on the back then left. Soon after that Darcy's relief arrived to find the man fast asleep in his chair... and something on the local star map that the computer confirmed had not been there before.

Chapter Sixteen:
First Sighting

News of the sighting came first through General Willmington's bunker where he conferred with his staff in the conference room before he would decide on whether to clear it for general public release.

"Word's already leaking out through the foreign observatories," the General was saying, "so we've got to act fast. What exactly are we looking at?"

Dr. Stilton took charge of the briefing at this point, from her terminal causing a slide to project onto the wall screen. It was an image of a field of stars, with one point of light in particular circled for attention.

"It was first picked up out by Saturn orbit. At first someone thought it was another new moon."

"I take it there is some doubt regards that designation," Dr. Dupree remarked, "else we wouldn't be here."

"Twenty minutes later it was here."

The slide switched to another view, this one showing Jupiter in the background. Dr. Janson was the first to catch on.

"Wait, it went from Saturn orbit to *Jupiter* in fifteen *minutes?* Why, it'd have to be going–"

"About half the speed of light," Dr. Stilton supplied.

"That's *some* speeding comet," Dr. Dupree remarked. "Are we sure it's the same object?"

"First thing we checked," Dr. Stilton confirmed. "Then an hour later this picture was taken."

A flicker but the slide didn't seem to change.

"That's the same picture," Professor Hardwright pointed out.

"No it's not," she told them. "That object came to a *dead stop.* It actually paused for a look around then began moving again."

"That can't be natural," Mr. Six said with a shake of his head. "And I refuse to believe the implications."

"Believe it, Milton," the General stated. "We have a bona fide alien craft of some sort. On top of everything else, we got aliens."

"Are you suggesting alien invaders, General?" Mr. Six asked with a sneer. "It has *got* to be a hoax."

"No hoax, Milton," Dr. Stilton told him. "And soon it will be near enough for the whole world to see, because this thing is coming on a direct course for *Earth*. Gentlemen, we are about to have a first contact situation."

"Great," Mr. Six said in obvious jest, "then maybe they can help end our wars for us. Nothing else seems to be working."

To those words, Dr. Dupree started to look thoughtful. Meanwhile the General took back the reigns of the conversation.

"Amanda, where is it now?"

"Mars orbit. It seems to be taking the scenic tour, so if I had to guess it's obviously to get our attention. Not spook the natives before they make their final arrival."

"Consider me spooked," Professor Hardwright remarked. "Are they coming to help, or coming in for the kill? Against something like this we'd be hard put to defend ourselves under the best of circumstances, but these are certainly *not* the best of circumstances."

"There's also something else," Dr. Stilton stated. "About ten minutes ago we received this. It's a bit garbled, but we can still make enough of it out."

She pressed another key and now the room filled with what sounded at first like static, then a garbled voice punctuated now and then by actual words.

"...intergalactic... million worlds that wish to... Ashtar leader of... greetings to people of Earth..."

"That's about the best we can make out. It should get a lot clearer as it gets closer, but I'm guessing that their speed is what's disrupting the signal. Or at least our ability to receive it. Still, its intent is pretty clear."

She blanked out the screen with a touch to her keyboard, then stood up to address them with her body trembling.

"Gentlemen, they are transmitting their greetings to us. They are coming to help."

For a long moment, the room was struck with silence. The weight of the world was already on the General's shoulders, now it seemed as there would be a lot more than that. But it was Dr. Dupree that finally broke the silence.

"We can use this," he began. "Whether they come as saviors or conquers doesn't matter. People will unite in the face of a common unknown or enemy. I recommend that you release this information, but only *after* other countries have confirmed it with their own equipment."

"So we don't look like fools if this really *is* a hoax?" the General asked.

"On the contrary," the psychiatrist corrected. "If we are the first to confirm it, the other major powers will think that *we're* the ones faking it. But if we later only reluctantly admit that we had seen it, then they will assume that it's authentic just because there was a conspiracy to cover it up. People are strange like that, General; they'll believe in a conspiracy before they do the simple truth."

"Sad, but true," the General reluctantly agreed. "Okay, we'll play it that way. Then the second someone calls for a pause to hostilities to unite against this unknown, we fall in with the rest. The fighting ends, hopefully these aliens mean well, then our death toll stops– What *is* the death toll now, anyway?"

"Worldwide," Professor Hardwright reported, "about two and a half billion people."

"Unimaginable," the General sighed. "Okay everyone, hop to it. I want constant updates on this thing's progress in addition to everything else. Meeting adjourned."

It was not long before Mr. Six was back in his office speaking into his secretive little device with Number One.

"Yes, just keep it coming in gradually and by the time Ashtar arrives the world will be waiting to receive him."

"The entire program is automatic, thanks to our operative, Number Six."

"Good, then what about my extraction?"

"When the leaders of the world call for a cease fire in light of this pending arrival, you will be called to England to serve as advisor direct to the Queen. From there you will join us to be by Ashtar's side when he picks out his representatives from the gawking crowd. The son of Satan will be invited in and we his chief disciples will be his lieutenants. A plan a long time in the making will bear fruit at last."

"Plan? Son of Satan?"

Mr. Six's head snapped up at the new voice to see Professor Hardwright standing in the doorway holding onto a bottle of champagne. Immediately Mr. Six whipped a gun out from the top drawer of his desk and leveled it at his unexpected visitor; a gun with a needle-thin tip.

"Number Six, who was that? What's going on?"

"Milton... a mole? For who?

"Nothing serious, Number One. But I'm afraid that Professor Hardwright here was just about to have a heart attack. Pity that."

"Milton, who are you–"

Before the Professor could finish his sentence, Mr. Six pulled the trigger. No bullet came out, but rather a very tiny dart no longer than a couple of millimeters. It hit into the Professor's neck where it started melting into his skin. The numbness began immediately around his throat, paralyzing his speech, but it was swift to spread from there. Within seconds the Professor was unable to move.

"Chemical dart, melts completely into you," Mr. Six explained with an almost cheerful smile. "Simulates a heart attack, which with your frame is very much possible."

He quickly put away his weapon, all the while the Professor struggling to talk, scream, or move something.

"I won't bother with the expected villain's soliloquy– big waste of time, that– but go straight into my act. Your body should be about ready to go limp, so if I time this just right..."

Mr. Six quickly switched off his communication device, and as he was putting it away changed his tone, assuming now that of a man being greeted by an unexpected visitor, pitching his voice so it might barely be overheard by anyone standing outside or possible overzealous security devices.

"Bob, what brings you– Champagne? Yes, I guess we *do* have reason to celebrate. Wait a second I just might have some glasses around... Bob, is something wrong? You're starting to look a little pale."

The Professor's complexion was indeed getting paler, but more from the shock of betrayal than a legitimate heart attack. The champagne bottle was slipping from his grip, and as it headed for the ground, Mr. Six bolted up from his chair.

"Bob! What's wrong?"

He ran around from behind his desk, tapping a communication button on the edge of the desk as he did so, while Professor Hardwright sank slowly to his knees.

"Medical emergency, my quarters. Something's wrong with the Professor!"

Dr. Janson and two of his staff would find Professor Hardwright on the floor with Mr. Six trying to give him CPR. But as Dr. Janson would confirm, the Professor was already dead and not a thing the shocked financial consultant could have done to save him.

Chapter Seventeen:

Contact

I watched as a world hung suspended, a thread of hope unwinding before them. Other observatories quickly picked up the strange light in their distant sky and over the days tracked it. At first the United States, under the voice and direction of General Willmington, denied knowing about it, but then as evidence mounted that there was definitely something out there, he finally sent out a press release stating that they had known about it for several days.

It then happened exactly as the psychologist Dr. Dupree said it would. People believed in it the more because it had at first been denied. The next question then on everyone's lips was, did their presence bode good intent or ill?

Internet and radio carried opinions from all factions. From those believing them to be invaders, to some scattered cults that proclaimed they had been waiting decades for just such an arrival to take them to the stars.

Over the days the lights came closer, little more than blips on the cosmic radar of Man, pausing on occasion, making course corrections, then resuming speed. With such erratic behavior, there was no doubt in anyone's mind that these were craft under intelligent guidance.

An international conference was quickly held in the old United Nations building, abandoned since its dissolution but now quickly repurposed to deal with this most unique event in the history of the world.

General Willmington had the U.N. feed displayed on one of the wall monitors in his War Room, while a couple others displayed tracking data on the UFO. The sudden death of Professor Hardwright had hit everyone hard, but even that event had been overshadowed by the alien coming as everyone pressed hard into their work. Amanda found herself hard at work at one of the stations on the central dais, trying to glean another drop of information out of the observable data, while Dr. Janson was kept very busy trying to get information on the making of his cure widely enough distributed, and Dr. Dupree was on nearly constant call by the General to offer estimates on the effects of approaching aliens on the mass psychology of Man.

Father Mason found himself simply watching and staying to himself.

Mr. Six walked into the War Room, calling out as he approached the dais.

"You sent for me, General?"

"Yes," the General replied, turning away from a view of the U.N. meeting, "you've been recalled to England. Apparently they need your advice on the financial implications of what's happening."

"Well... I can't say as that's entirely unexpected. But are you sure you won't be needing me here?"

"My place in things ceased involving anything financial a long time ago," the General replied. "See what you can do out there now that the bombs have stopped dropping. There's a helicopter waiting on the upper level to take you where you need to go."

The General stepped over to the edge of the dais, reaching out to hand Mr. Six a sealed envelope which the other then took.

"Your orders, Milton."

"I'll pack up and leave immediately."

He gave a nod to the General, then to the rest a quick look around with a flicker of a smile.

"It's been... interesting."

"Devastating would be more accurate," Amanda corrected. "And a few other choice words. Enjoy life out in the daylight."

"You have not been the most agreeable person to live with," Dr. Dupree said from behind the General, "but then this has not been the most agreeable of situations. Good luck."

"I just wish that Professor Hardwright could have been with us today," Mr. Six replied.

"As do we all," the General stated. "Now get going."

Mr. Six gave a nod, then turned on heel and left the room, all eyes following until the door closed behind him. Then attention was back on events in the U.N. building.

Dr. Dupree went back to the terminal he had been working from, sticking an earpiece in his right ear to listen to the feed. Meanwhile Dr. Stilton returned her attention to the latest shots of the approaching UFOs.

"They're getting close to lunar orbit," she reported. "Approaching from the dark side of the Moon."

"Updated ETA?" the General asked.

"If they don't change their velocity anymore... they be coming out from behind the Moon within the hour. At that point even a good backyard telescope should be able to make them out if the glare's not too bright."

That's when the General caught the distinction in Amanda's words and shot her a question.

"You said *they* and not *it.*"

"Not an accident, General," she said as she looked up from her examination of the images with a tired grin. "They're close enough to distinguish now. What we thought was one single blob of light is actually several. I've been running an image processing program, and it looks like it's a clump of as many as fifteen to twenty objects."

"Any estimates as to size or configuration?"

"Not yet, I'm afraid. Once they're past the Moon I should be able to get a lot more information."

"Captain," the General said, turning to one of his aides about the dais, "get the word out. I want every telescope on this planet aimed at the Moon. All observatories are to channel their feeds through this Command Center. They can share data if they want, but I want to see every angle of those things up on my screens."

"I'll get right on it, General."

As the Captain turned away to be about his work, General Willmington turned his attention back to the U.N.

feed, taking up an earpiece to better hear the exchanges. Behind him Dr. Dupree was paying more careful attention to the faces of the men and women in the General Assembly room.

"They're all extremely nervous," the psychologist reported. "I'd say many of them don't know if to be more afraid of each other or what's approaching. That representative from Russia looks equally ready to start aiming his nukes towards the UFO as to anyone else, while the one from the new European Union just might be willing to prostrate himself before the aliens the second their craft land. What's the chatter?"

"Much like what you've just said," the General reported as he listened. "Motions on how to greet them, others to maintain a defense screen with what's left of our weapons platforms... Greece just asked if the aliens have any food to give."

"Sounds typical," Dupree shrugged. "Not that I blame them."

"General," one of the soldiers at the central dais computer stations suddenly spoke up, "message coming in for your eyes only."

"I'll take it here."

The General pressed a few keys at the terminal he was looking down at and the view switched from that of the U.N. to a text message. At the same time the wall monitor with the main U.N. feed showed someone at the podium pounding a gavel.

"Looks like they just passed some sort of resolution," Dr. Dupree noted.

"And I'm reading the results of it right here," the General reported. "Pending full approval of the Assembly– which they just got– they want the brain behind the plague cure to come to New York immediately and supervise its worldwide production and distribution."

"Looks like Dr. Janson gets to see the light of day as well," Dr. Dupree quipped. "But any reason why he can't simply continue to do it down here?"

"Looks like the Suits want to bring greater public attention to the new program as well as show the aliens that we *can* present a united front for something. I can see their point."

He took the earpiece out and looked up from the display he was bent over.

"But I'm leaving the choice up to Dr. Janson. If he thinks that he can do the most good out there, then more power to him. Captain," he said turning to another, "get the good Doc up here immediately."

"Yes, sir."

As the Captain turned to his console to relay the request to the doctor's office, Amanda glanced up from her station with a sigh.

"Looks like our happy little group is breaking up… and I may be next."

"Amanda?" the General asked.

"General… John. Those ships are going to land somewhere, and when they do I want to be there. I can tell a lot more about their design and capability from direct observation than I'll ever be able to from some video images. For one thing, no cameraman is going to know where to aim his rig that would be of best use for my observations."

"Amanda, these creatures could still be very dangerous, and I can't afford to lose you if the worst should happen. I need my team—"

"Where they'll be most effective," she finished. "And I will be most effective for this out in the field. I'll keep a link on me at all times, go out with whatever security as you see fit, and New York has so far escaped the radiation winds. But I *need* to be out there when they land, *wherever* they land. Can you understand that?"

"Yeah," he said after a pause, "you want to be our field spotter. And I'll admit, we could really use one for this… Unfortunately, I'm short on qualified personnel and you may be it… Very well, but you only leave when and if we have a confirmed landing zone."

"Thank-you, John. This may almost make up for everything else."

For the first time since they had all secured themselves deep within this bunker, the General saw a smile on her face, sweaty relief coursing down her face. But the General, I could tell, still had his doubts. But then again, that was his job.

As for Father Mason, I looked around to see him still at the back of the room, either praying or pondering.

———

It was just under an hour later when the War Room exploded in renewed activity. Dr. Janson was already on a fast jet to New York and the need for his cure when the alien ships had appeared out from behind the Moon and now in full view of every decent telescope in the world. A dozen different views littered the War Room's large screens, with one reserved for the feed from the U.N.

building. Techs called back and forth across the room with updates on the alien approach, while Dr. Dupree continued to study the reactions of the U.N. assembly from one of the stations on the central dais.

"Direct visual coming in now, sir," one tech reported. "Running visual processing."

"Main screen as soon as you get it cleaned up," General Willmington ordered, "then Dr. Stilton is going to see what she can tell us about it."

The central screen filled with a blur of pixilation, then as the image smoothed out by steps, nearly all activity in the chamber quieted until all eyes were fixed on the forthcoming results, most of all Dr. Stilton. She was like a child waiting to see her Christmas present unwrapped. A final update then the image snapped into crystal clarity.

In shape they looked metallic and roughly saucer-shaped. Like something out of an old 50's movie. A brilliant golden glow surrounded each vessel as they zipped along in their tight formation.

"The classic flying saucer," Amanda said with jaw agape. "Looks like all those old Roswell stories were on the money."

She held her gaze for a few moments, then snapped herself out of it to glance back down at her display.

"Velocity increasing a bit now," she reported. "It looks like they're on final approach."

"How many?" the General asked.

"Twenty," she replied.

"Do you have a trajectory yet? Do we know where they're going to land?"

"Working on that."

As Dr. Stilton now worked furiously at her keyboard, another tech called out excitedly from his computer station.

"Sir! We have a communication coming in from the alien fleet. Just a handshake signal right now, but– And sir, it has a *video* component."

"Main screen!"

The central screen switched now to a still image. It was a roughly triangular shape imbedded with a honeycomb background, in the center of it an image of a beehive topped by a single large eye, with what looked like an angry bee drawn front and center. The picture held there for several long moments before fading away to give the world its first view of alien life.

He looked like a young man, handsome of features, with blond hair to his shoulders. He wore a golden suit patterned with a similar honeycomb-like design, and emblazoned on his chest was a pyramid symbol centered with a single eye. He stood at the center of a brightly lit room, behind him a row of other creatures that were definitely unlike anything human.

The others with him stood about the same height as the first, but their suits were blue though with the same pyramid symbol on their chests. Their heads, though, were reptilian, with large flanged ears. Additionally the ones on the ends each held what looked like some sort of futuristic rifle out of a science fiction movie.

"They got weapons," the General noted.

"Wouldn't you?" Dr. Stilton shot back. "They're going into an armed camp, of *course* they'd have bodyguards."

She returned her attention to the video, face beaming with delight.

"Just look at them. Actual alien life!"

Only now did Father Mason walk over to the dais and step up to join the General by his side, though still not a word said. He seemed to be studying the General's face as much as he was the video.

Then the central human-looking one finally began to speak. His tone was deep and rich and commanded authority, something about his visage that seemed to calm the viewer.

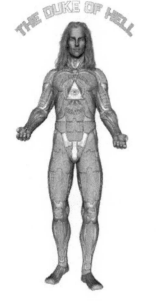

"I am Commander Ashtar, chief representative from an interstellar collective of a hundred million different worlds. Long have you thought yourselves alone in the Universe, but I am here now to say that you are not. We are come as brothers, here to help you in your time of direst need. We have seen your situation and bring with us the means to help you out. We are here to stop your wars, to feed your starving, cure your sick. We are the union of uncountable world working together for the benefit of all. We are... Hive."

He paused for a moment, perhaps to give the world time to absorb what he said. The screen holding the view of the U.N. meeting now showed a rapt audience there as well as the representatives, all held focus to a large four-foot monitor that had been fixed to one wall. Just as people around the globe were now equally fixated. If they were like Professor Stilton, they were reacting as awestruck children.

A world in such soul-wrenching distress now to see their apparent savior before them.

"My relief fleet will be landing in a place you call New York City, to meet with your representatives in your United Nations building. Send us your leaders, your best, your brightest, and we will choose those who will be our intermediaries. Our arrival is scheduled for three of your hours from now, to give you time to make preparations. I am Ashtar of Hive, and we come to save you."

The image of Ashtar's smiling face held for a moment longer before being replaced by the logo once again.

Professor Stilton was the first to speak up, nearly jumping eagerly up to her feet.

"General! I've got to get to New York! You said that when we have a confirmed landing zone that I could–"

"Someone ready a jet for Miss Stilton," the General said with a nod to one of his Captains. "With security on board and escort. I'm not risking the safety of my best physicist no matter how handsome their head alien looks."

"Oh, thank-you thank-you," she beamed.

She hopped over, planted a quick kiss on the General's cheek, then nearly leaped down off the dais on her way out the room.

"I've got so many things to pack. My laptop, some instruments… Oh, what do you wear to a first contact situation?"

She had barely left the room when Dr. Dupree spoke up.

"If you don't mind, General, I'd like to make that trip as well."

"Eager to see our cosmic visitors?" the General asked.

"Eager to see for myself the reactions of all concerned," he corrected. "We've never had a situation like this before, I want to see what it's going to cause. Will people trust them, or fall to their knees in supplication? How will they all react? Considering the people directly involved are our world leaders and representatives, I think this is very crucial to know."

"I'm with you on that," the General replied. "Very well, accompany Amanda. And keep an eye on *her* reactions and maybe prod her now and then if needed. I do not need her blind to different possibilities just because some alien savior walked in the door."

"Understood, General."

A nod from Dr. Dupree, then he too left the room, though in a far more sedate manner. Father Mason, meanwhile, had been keeping a close eye both on the video and General Willmington and had noted something about the General: the man's expression had not changed one bit from his studied look. No joy wrote itself across his face, nothing but cold calculation.

Father Mason waited until the psychiatrist had left before stepping up next to the General for a few quiet words.

"You don't trust them, do you? The aliens."

"It's not my job to trust *anyone* blindly, not even alien benefactors."

"But it's not just that. You caught some details the rest missed in their eagerness."

The General looked at the priest, saw nothing in him that even hinted at the same exuberance as the rest of the world seemed to be enjoying, and replied.

"You don't trust them either."

"I trust in God… not aliens. And I've learned to trust in your judgment… once I know the reason behind it."

"Okay, you want details? First off, this Ashtar guy looks like some idealized human. Not anything alien.

Exactly like the image of Germany's master race back in the second world war. Yes, an alien union with that many worlds would have chosen the closest match to our own race as they have, but for it to happen to be their leader? I don't buy the odds. Then, if they have so many races, why not a delegation with a sampling of some of them? Why have all of them be the same reptilian species? And why do they look more like soldiers than anything else?"

"All quite sound reasoning," Father Mason agreed, "though I would add in that, as much as some will laugh at this, those reptiles bear a closer resemblance to... demons. If you'll pardon me for saying so."

"Like I've been saying these past few years, I'm open to any possibility. But there's one more thing about them that sells me on this being something a bit unsavory."

He paused, looked up at the logo still fixed on the main screen, then reached over to a terminal and typed a couple of keys. The image zoomed in so now it was centered on the angry bee at the center.

"Bees are an *Earth* species," the General pointed out. "Why would a group of a hundred million worlds pick an insect from a nothing world like ours to be their logo? Out of all the infinite possibilities they must have, their main symbol just happens to be a bee, and their very name is an Earth word– an *English* word referring to where bees live. No, Henry, something about this smells rotten and I'm going to stay right here at my command post ready to handle whatever comes up next."

"Then God will be by your side. Or at least, I will."

It seemed out of all the people remaining to this world, there were at least two key individuals with a healthy respect for Greeks bearing gifts.

———————————

I flew back to the chamber of the Illuminati-13 for a last check on them. This time all the seats were filled, save the one they reserved for Ashtar. Mister Six had rejoined them in what was their last planning meeting before the arrival of their lord and master.

"Glad to have you back with us, Number Six," said Number One. "Can you give us any last updates on the view from within?"

"Nearly everyone is sold on it," Number Six replied. "General Willmington will still be suspicious, but that's his job, and I have my doubts about Father Mason. As far as my assassination of Professor Hardwright, the only one that might have detected the tiny pinprick my gun left would have been Doctor Janson. If he'd even had reason to do a complete autopsy, and if he'd had the time before that timely request shipping him out. You're doing, I take it?"

"Number Eight's suggestion. The plague has run its course anyway, and this takes their chief medical researcher away from his lab."

Number One then faced the rest, scanning across every face there, before making the announcement they all had been waiting so very long to hear.

"We must leave immediately for New York. We will be in the crowd with the other leaders when Ashtar arrives. He will make a speech, then select his representatives from amongst those present. He will, of course, choose us. Then we will organize the final subjugation of Mankind and our own reign under Lord Ashtar for eternity."

To the growing looks of eager self-interest, he made one last pronouncement before the meeting was adjourned.

"Glory be to Ashtar, Duke of Hell. "Ordo Ab Chao."

"Glory be to Ashtar," they all echoed. "Ordo Ab Chao!"

After thousands of years of planning, Ashtar's new world order global government is finally at hand.

Chapter Eighteen:

The Arrival

I arrived to witness the event for myself and record it upon my scroll. New York City was packed with the hungry and the desperate, all trying to crowd their way around the United Nations building, some for a look at the supposed aliens others to plea before them. Merchant prince and beggar alike, humanity dispossessed from itself now all gathered to behold their miracle.

Vicious storms had been pounding the city for weeks, along with an occasional quake to stun a citizenry used to far more stable ground. But now with the approach of the alien fleet the quakes stopped and the storm subsided, the clouds above parting to permit a clear view of the sky and the first bright rays of sunlight any there had seen in a month.

A ring of soldiers around the building only allowed the elite through, though very few questioned who exactly controlled these soldiers. The princes and leaders of the world were allowed through, there to gather with some other notables that the world had never known of. I saw Dr. Amanda Stilton in their ranks, too preoccupied with what was coming to notice Mr. Six amongst a group of others, including one very old white-haired man that looked rather like a wrinkled potato, an elderly lady, a slightly portly Texan with a Stetson hat, and a middle-aged Hindu man. They all were allowed to gather in a wide open area before the main building, while everyone else was kept well away.

Amongst the crowds gathered outside the line of troops I saw Alexander Dupree, though he was giving a more careful study of the faces of the ones at the center of attention.

Cameras and video drones of all types were clustered around, carrying their live feeds of this event far and wide. The one thing the wars had left untouched were the satellites, so despite everything else, people could still follow along with their video phones, televisions, and radios while they were busy dying. Somewhere I knew that General Willmington and Father Mason were also watching, the first with his finger hovering above a firing button, the latter with his hand holding onto a cross.

The fleet came first as a distant dot high in the sky, but as the minutes passed and excitement grew, it got larger until they could be seen with the naked eye. Small dot growing quickly, resolving into what might be a large high-flying plane, then more distinctly as several round objects. Down they came and the crowds gawked and whispered, a few cheering, until they could be seen plainly a thousand feet above their heads.

Even from that height they were large. Their width must measure the length of an aircraft carrier. They spread out, taking up positions over the bulk of New York City, while one in particular held in place directly above the U.N. then lowered in slow stately grace.

The golden light still surrounded them, growing as they neared, and in its illumination all observing knew sudden unexplained peace and calm. Many there might even call it a divine calm, but with my angelic sight I could well see the trick behind the façade. For this light was nothing less than a form of brain washing, made possible by the desperate mindset that recent extreme events had instilled into Mankind. It was a falsehood that the bulk of the world was now ready to accept.

All voices ceased, even the quiet whispers of commentators into their microphones. Their collective breath was held as the one craft came down towards the center of the assembly then halted just above the top of the main building.

In basic form it looked just like your classic saucer, golden in color, topped by a pair of some sort of curved shields or antennas that the imagination might view as horns. Visible across the bottom side was that same eye-in-pyramid logo, below it the ship's serial number or registration; the latter easily ignored in the excitement of the event by all save General Willmington in his War Room as he immediately zoomed in on it.

The number was '666'.

The craft held in place for a moment before something started to grow down from the center bottom of the craft. A landing platform, atop which rode Ashtar and his contingent of twelve demonic guards– the Hades-13, as I would refer to them. He came down with a wide smile to cheers and proclamations of thanks as the platform detached and floated down, landing finally before the gathered leaders.

Speeches were then made by both sides; various leaders to give their greetings to the alien visitors, then Ashtar to assure humanity that he was here to bring peace and stop their suffering. I ignored most of it, just kept my gaze fixed on the son of Satan. I knew he could see me, and that the smile he now gave at the end of his speech was not meant for Man but for me alone that I may note the exact point at which Mankind abandoned its humanity to fall into lockstep behind him.

After that came the choosing, and I do not have to record how that went. The princes of the Illuminati each stepped forward in turn, and when Mr. Six was chosen, Dr. Stilton cheered while Dr. Dupree pursed a lip and General Willmington swore under his breath.

It was complete now, the thirteen arrayed alongside Ashtar with the twelve demonic guards behind them, looking down to cheering crowds as the people of the world sigh with tearful relief.

One last visit I must record, and that is of the door at the bottom of the Well Between Worlds, where the first of the Seals has long been flickering. Now the First Seal finally breaks, unleashing in full the first phase of judgment and the Anti-Christ's public appearance upon the world. Satan laughs with dark thunderous peals at the naiveté of Mankind, as when in the nearing future each of the other Seals in turn breaks, a greater measure of his power will thence be allowed to stretch out. What the world has seen has only been the result of the breaking of the First Seal; with each Seal's pending break, Man will only suffer the more until the day of the Seventh Seal and Satan's full release. It is for that day that Satan awaits. Outside Jesus too awaits, looking sadly down upon the Earth biding his time until finally called.

I now stand upon the sky looking down as the people of the world greet their tormentors with open arms and cheering voices. If my next entry into this divine journal be something of more positive note I cannot say. I can only say that you still have time for a choice, a final judgment upon yourself. Choose carefully for it is more than simply your lives at risk.

It is nothing less than your very soul.

Epilogue

And I watch as the leaders of a dispossessed world gladly lead their presumed savior into the halls of power, unknowing of what really hides behind the smile and pleasant exterior, nor what is yet to come. For this is only the beginning and there is much yet to tell...

About The Author

Mr. Terry L. Cook has been a published author since 1994 and has written more than a dozen best selling books since then. He holds AA, AS, BA, BS, and MBA Degrees, plus two college teaching credentials and two college certificates. He is a retired Government Professional, a Military War Veteran, and a former National Guard Officer. He is also an FAA licensed Commercial Jet Airplane Pilot (ATP) with 3000 hours of total flying experience. Additionally, he has appeared as an expert guest on thousands of international radio and TV shows during the past 25 years, including the prestigious

www.DukeOfHell.com

2012 H2-History Channel TV special entitled, "Countdown To Apocalypse", which was re-aired thereafter on Global television for several more years. But of all of his life's experiences, writing is his passion. This book is his first fictional novel and he hopes you enjoy it.

www.DukeOfHell.com

Made in the USA
Middletown, DE
11 May 2020